ARISTOTLE ON POLITICAL REASONING

ARISTOTLE ON POLITICAL REASONING

A COMMENTARY ON THE "RHETORIC"

LARRY ARNHART

NORTHERN ILLINOIS UNIVERSITY PRESS

DeKalb 1981

Publication of this book was made possible in part by a grant from the Earhart Foundation.

Library of Congress Cataloging in Publication Data

Arnhart, Larry, 1949-
  Aristotle on political reasoning.

  Bibliography: p.
  Includes index.
  1. Aristotle. Rhetoric. 2. Rhetoric, Ancient.
3. Rhetoric — Political aspects. I. Title.
PN173.A73A7   808.5   81-11330
ISBN 0-87580-080-7   AACR2

Dedicated to George Anastaplo

CONTENTS

ABBREVIATIONS

An. Post.	*Posterior Analytics*
An. Pr.	*Prior Analytics*
Cat.	*Categories*
De An.	*De Anima*
De Motu An.	*On the Movement of Animals*
Eth. Eud.	*Eudemian Ethics*
Eth. Nic.	*Nicomachean Ethics*
Int.	*On Interpretation*
Mag. Mor.	*Magna Moralia*
Metaph.	*Metaphysics*
Part. An.	*On the Parts of Animals*
Ph.	*Physics*
Poet.	*Poetics*
Pol.	*Politics*
Rh.	*Rhetoric*
Soph. El.	*On Sophistical Refutations*
Top.	*Topics*

ACKNOWLEDGMENTS

Whatever merit this book has is due largely to the influence of four teachers: Leo Paul de Alvarez, George Anastaplo, Joseph Cropsey, and Herbert Storing. I should also acknowledge the useful comments on this work offered by Brian Barry, Morton Frisch, Father William Grimaldi, Jane Mansbridge, Eugene Miller, Henry Veatch, and a couple of anonymous reviewers. Perhaps none of these people would agree with everything I have written here; but it was precisely their instructive criticisms that often helped me most.

Irving Kristol was generous with his support in arranging for publication of this book. The Earhart Foundation provided financial assistance. And the people at Northern Illinois University Press were patient in dealing with a young scholar writing his first book. I should also not forget my parents, whose financial support of my education gave me the leisure to write the first draft of this book.

Finally, I should thank those friends who listened—usually without complaint—to my Saturday evening lectures on Aristotle: Gina Demos, Harvey Lomax, Marianne Mahoney, Gary Schmitt, Debbie Smith, Greg Smith, Henry Sokolski, and Rick Sorenson.

Larry Arnhart
Pocatello, Idaho

ARISTOTLE ON POLITICAL REASONING

1

INTRODUCTION

Science, Rhetoric, Sophistry

Is rhetoric some form of rational discourse about the intelligible reality of politics, or is it merely a means for verbally manipulating people through fallacious arguments and appeals to irrational impulses? To put the question more briefly, can rhetoric be distinguished from sophistry?

Does not the rhetorician—by the use of public speech to interpret, evaluate, and deliberate about political action—maintain somehow the rule of reason in political affairs? Does not rhetoric require political people to *talk* about and thus to *think* about what they have done, are doing, or will do? Does not rhetoric elevate politics by bringing *thought* to bear upon *action?* "We weigh what we undertake and apprehend it perfectly in our minds," Pericles declared in his funeral oration, "not accounting words for a hindrance of action but that it is rather a hindrance to action to come to it without instruction of words before."[1]

Yet rhetoric also has a darker side. Does not the rhetorician sometimes employ emotional appeals and deceptive arguments to move his listeners to whatever position he wishes? Indeed, does not rhetoric consist of techniques that can be used as easily for the *wrong* as for the *right* side of any issue? There surely is some justification for the ancient criticism of rhetoric as a discipline empowering speakers to make the weaker argument appear to be the stronger. As Gorgias observed, "Many are the men who shape a false argument and persuade and have persuaded many men about many things."[2]

Thus the problem is that while rhetoric seems in some respects to be the means by which reason guides political action, it often seems to be an art of deception, inimical to rational deliberation. Furthermore, to the extent that rhetoric is the primary mode of political reasoning, the way in which one decides the question of whether rhetoric is a genuine form of reasoning will also determine how one decides the larger question of the place of reason in political life.

3

The rationality of rhetoric becomes especially dubious if scientific demonstration is taken to be the sole model of valid reasoning; for it is obvious that rhetorical argument cannot attain the exactness and certainty of scientific inquiry. And if — as has been the case in the twentieth century — the canons of scientific demonstration are assumed to coincide with the standards of mathematical logic, the irrationality of rhetoric seems even more manifest.

As a result, rhetoric becomes virtually indistinguishable from sophistry. Since there are no rational standards for political discourse, the power of rhetoric must depend upon manipulation through verbal deception and not upon any persuasive intelligibility of the speech itself.

As a further consequence, the political itself becomes irrational. Since the ordinary discourse of citizens about political things has little to do with knowledge, and since most citizens are incapable of the scientific reasoning through which they could acquire genuine knowledge, the political life of men must be understood to be guided by opinions with little foundation in reason.

But could one perhaps save the rationality of political speech — and of the political as a whole — by viewing rhetoric as occupying some middle ground between science and sophistry? This could be done if one could show that the realm of reason extends beyond the confines of scientific demonstration and, therefore, that rhetorical argument can be in some sense truly rational even though it lacks the certainty and exactness of scientific knowledge. In this way one would restore the meaning of rhetoric as rational discourse.

And in fact this would seem to be the project that Aristotle sets for himself in the *Rhetoric;* for there he criticizes the sophistical rhetoricians, whose common practice is to use purely emotional appeals to distract their listeners from the subject at hand, for failing to see that the true art of rhetoric is essentially a mode of *reasoning* although without the rigor of apodictic proof. He goes on to explain rhetorical reasoning as reasoning through enthymemes, and it is in his conception of the enthymeme that his theory of rhetoric is most fully embodied.

How Aristotle uses his theory of the enthymeme to differentiate rhetoric from both science and sophistry becomes clearer in the light of four tripartite distinctions. 1) *Persuasion,* which is the aim of the enthymeme, differs both from *instruction* and from *compulsion.* 2) *Opinion,* which provides premises for the enthymeme, does not conform to absolute *truth;* but neither is it absolute *falsehood.* 3) The *probability* characteristic of most enthymematic inferences falls somewhere between *necessity* and mere randomness, or *chance.* 4) And finally, the

4

enthymeme itself differs from a strict *demonstration* but without being a sophistical *fallacy*.

Each of these points requires further comments. In what follows, the intention is to state in general the interpretation of Aristotle's theory of rhetoric that will be substantiated in detail through the subsequent commentary on the text of the *Rhetoric*.

Instruction, Persuasion, Compulsion

That human beings are by nature both rational and political is manifest in the natural human capacity for speech. Aristotle says in the *Politics* (1253a5-18) that men are naturally more political than gregarious animals because human community rests upon a union in discourse and thought.[3] Other animals may signify to one another with their voices their sensations of pleasure and pain,

> but speech [*logos*] is for indicating the expedient and the harmful, therefore also the just and the unjust; for this is the peculiarity of men with respect to the other animals—that only men have perception of the good and the bad, of the just and the unjust, and of other things; and it is the community in these things that makes a household and a city. (1253a15-18)

Human beings achieve a more intimate community among themselves than is possible for other creatures, because only human beings can found their association on mutual understanding through speech.[4]

One might conclude from this that rhetoric—the artful practice of public speech—is the fundamental activity of politics, and that, insofar as political activity is founded upon rhetoric, politics expresses the rational nature of mankind. But does rhetoric encompass the whole of politics, or is it perhaps important for only a limited realm of political life?

That Aristotle does not simply identify politics with rhetoric is clear from his remarks at the end of the *Nicomachean Ethics*. Speeches or arguments (*logoi*), he observes, are not sufficient to make men virtuous (1179b4-1180b28). At best they are effective with youths who, because of some natural endowment or good moral training, have a love of the noble. Most men, especially in their youth, live by passion and the pleasures of the body; hence, they can be controlled by force but not by arguments. It is necessary for these people that laws coercively habituate them from their youth to do those virtuous acts that they would never choose to do on their own. Thus the moral training of a community requires that the legislator apply legal compulsion where moral persuasion would be futile.

It is at this point that Aristotle criticizes the sophists for showing their ignorance of politics by making it the same as, or lower than, rhetoric (1181a12-16). This is often taken to indicate that Aristotle considered the sophistical view of politics too cynical, but from the context one might infer something quite different: the sophistical assumption that the art of persuasion can govern all political activity manifests a naive blindness to the true harshness of political life.[5] Rhetorical reasoning displays the nobler side of politics, that area of political activity governed by persuasion through speeches. But most men respond not to persuasion but to force, and therefore the greater part of politics must be concerned with compelling men, and through repetition habituating them, to do without thought what they could never be persuaded to do.

The success of rhetoric, Aristotle implies, presupposes the formation by the laws of an *ethos* in the community that makes people open to persuasion. The taming of the most irrational impulses demands force rather than argument; but once the lowest part of the soul has been subdued, the rhetorician can appeal to that part of the soul that can be persuaded by reason. Rhetoric is therefore subordinate to politics since the multitude of men would never be amenable to rhetorical reasoning unless they were first properly habituated by the laws.[6]

Hence rhetoric introduces the rule of reason into human affairs since it moves men by persuasion rather than force. And yet Aristotle makes it clear that rhetoric fails to attain the highest level of reasoning insofar as rhetorical *persuasion* falls short of scientific *instruction*.[7] The exact knowledge and complex demonstrations necessary for scientific instruction are rarely effective in political speeches. To be persuasive, the rhetorician must draw the premises of his enthymemes not from the first principles of the particular sciences, but from the common opinions of his audience. And he must simplify and abbreviate his line of reasoning so that ordinary citizens can grasp it quickly and easily. Thus the good rhetorician can persuade, but he cannot instruct.

Truth, Opinion, Falsehood

Since the premises of the enthymeme are derived from common opinions, and since opinion surely differs from truth, it might seem that the enthymeme is a false form of reasoning and therefore that all rhetoric is sophistical. But in fact, Aristotle regards the common opi-

6

nions that enter the enthymeme as being for the most part neither completely true nor completely false. Rather, they are at least partially true.
Although reliance on opinions does impose certain limits on enthymematic reasoning, this does not prevent the enthymeme from being
a valid form of reasoning.

The "reputable opinions" (*endoxa*) on any particular subject are
usually confused and even apparently contradictory, but Aristotle
assumes that in most cases they manifest at least a partial grasp of the
truth and, therefore, that any serious inquiry into moral or political
subjects must start from them. Hence, Aristotle treats certain subjects
differently in the *Rhetoric* than in the *Politics* or in his ethical
treatises—since rhetoric involves opinions in their original state without
the refinements of philosophic examination—but his expositions in the
Rhetoric still reflect in some fundamental manner those in his other
works.

Furthermore, in its dependence on common opinions, rhetoric is
distinguished both from science and from sophistry. For each science
begins not with common opinions, but with the primary truths fundamental to the science. And sophistry consists either of arguing from
what *appear* to be common opinions but are not or of making
something *appear* to follow necessarily from common opinions when it
does not. Moreover, the fact that sophistical arguments cannot be truly
derived from common opinions confirms the epistemological solidity of
these opinions.

Necessity, Probability, Chance

One of the limitations of common opinions is that they usually hold for
the most part but not in every case. Therefore, enthymemes have
probable but not necessary validity, since the conclusions are true in
most, but not all, cases. Enthymemes, then, rarely achieve the necessity
of scientific demonstrations. (The one exception noted by Aristotle is
the enthymeme founded on a "necessary sign" [*tekmerion*].)

The fact that enthymematic reasoning usually involves probability
rather than necessity does not make the reasoning invalid, according to
Aristotle; for both those things that happen always or by necessity and
those that happen as a rule or for the most part, can be objects of
knowledge. Probability must be distinguished from chance because,
unlike probable things, those things that happen only rarely or by
chance cannot be known.

Indeed, that rhetoric rests upon probabilities is consistent with the Aristotelian principle that one should demand only that degree of certitude that is appropriate to the subject matter. Like ethics and politics, the subject of rhetoric has as its content human action, and the regularities of human action can be known with probability but not with absolute certainty.

Demonstrations, Enthymemes, Fallacies

Since the enthymeme rests upon opinion rather than absolute truth, since its premises and conclusions are usually probable rather than necessary, and since its final aim is persuasion rather than instruction, enthymematic reasoning lacks the rigor of scientific demonstration. Still, rhetorical argument is a valid form of reasoning that provides an alternative to sophistry. Popular opinions reflect a commonsense grasp of reality that cannot be dismissed as simply false. Probabilities are fit objects of reason because they presuppose regularities in things, and regularities are not random or chance events. And finally, the persuasion for which the rhetorician strives requires an appeal to reason rather than force.

However, to support the claim that Aristotle's *Rhetoric* is a theory of rhetoric as truly *rational* discourse, which is the interpretation advanced up to this point, requires that answers be provided to the serious objections that could be made to this claim. The following four objections deserve particular attention. 1) It could be argued that enthymemes cannot be valid because Aristotle defines them as incomplete or otherwise defective syllogisms. 2) Futhermore, even if the enthymeme is a genuine syllogism, it could still be argued that Aristotle's discussions of persuasion through the character of the speaker and through the passions of the audience show the reliance of rhetoric on irrational appeals. 3) Since Aristotle insists that rhetoric includes *apparent* as well as genuine "proofs," and since he describes it as a neutral instrument that may be used on either side of any issue, it might be inferred that he does not clearly distinguish rhetoric from sophistry. 4) Finally, Aristotle's discussions of the style and arrangement of speeches in Book Three of the *Rhetoric* might seem further evidence that he does not view rational argument as the foundation of rhetoric.

Adequate response to these objections demands detailed examinations of the text of the *Rhetoric*, which will be undertaken in this commentary. At this point it is necessary simply to introduce the arguments that will be elaborated more fully in subsequent chapters.

The Enthymeme as a Syllogism

Aristotle's enthymeme is a true syllogism; therefore it is not, as has been commonly assumed, an incomplete syllogism. To cite only one argument from the text, why, if the enthymeme were an invalid or incomplete syllogism, would Aristotle distinguish between apparent and true enthymemes and declare that apparent enthymemes "are not enthymemes since they are not syllogisms" (2. 22. 1397a3)?

Since the premises and therefore the conclusions of the enthymeme are founded on common opinions and are usually probable but not absolutely certain, the enthymeme differs from the scientific syllogism; and since the enthymeme must be simple enough to be understood by the ordinary man, it differs from the dialectical syllogism. But neither of these points leads to the conclusion that the enthymeme is an invalid syllogism.

Aristotle does recommend that enthymemes be abbreviated whenever the listeners will clearly supply the missing elements themselves. But this is a practical rule and not part of the definition of the enthymeme; even when it is abbreviated, the enthymeme is an intellectually complete syllogism despite its verbally incomplete form.

Aristotle acknowledges, however, that it is difficult in some cases to distinguish genuine enthymemes, which are syllogistically valid, from apparent enthymemes, which are not. This is particularly true of enthymemes derived from "non-necessary signs." Insofar as "non-necessary signs" are "unsyllogistic" (*asullogiston*), they are sources of apparent rather than true enthymemes. But some of the "signs" are syllogistically valid, and even those that are fallacious can often be transformed into valid inferences. Moreover, even fallacious "signs" contain some truth since "truth exists in all signs."[8] Therefore, Aristotle must consider "non-necessary signs" as sources of both true and apparent enthymemes.

The Enthymeme as Combining Reason and Passion

Aristotle begins the *Rhetoric* by condemning those sophistical rhetoricians who rely exclusively on exciting the passions of their listeners, thereby preventing them from making a rational judgment about the issues at hand. These speakers ignore the enthymeme, which is "the body of proof" for rhetoric. But when Aristotle sets out the three "proofs" (*pisteis*) of rhetoric, he includes appeals based on "character" (*ethos*) (that is, the "character" of the speaker) and "passion" (*pathos*) as supplementary to persuasion through the "speech" or "argument" itself (*logos*); and in Book Two he carefully delineates the passions with which the rhetorician must deal. Thus Aristotle seems to throw into doubt the rationality of rhetorical argument by introducing the same techniques for moving audiences through their passions that he initially condemns.

Closer examination will show, however, that Aristotle's emphasis on the enthymeme is consonant with his treatment of the passions, because the enthymeme combines reason and passion. Since it is "the body of proof," the enthymeme is the vehicle not just for one of the three "proofs," *logos,* but for all three — *logos, ethos,* and *pathos.* Enthymemes may be used not only to establish a conclusion as a probable truth but also to alter the emotions of the listeners or to develop their confidence in the character of the speaker.

Aristotle discusses the nature of the passions so that the speaker can know how to employ enthymemes to reason with the passions. The assumption is that the passions are in some sense rational, for a rhetorician can talk an audience into or out of a passion by convincing them that the passion is or is not the appropriate response to the circumstances at hand.

Aristotle denounces the sophistical rhetoricians not because they appeal to the passions of the audience, but because they do this in a defective manner. Their solicitation of the passions would be acceptable if it were an integral part of an enthymematic argument pertinent to the subject under examination. As it is, their exclusive reliance on the passions with no connection to any form of argument only distracts the listeners with things irrelevant to the matter at hand.

That enthymemes are often directed to the emotions of the listeners indicates again the difference between enthymematic and demonstrative reasoning. Emotions are irrelevant to scientific demonstration; but since enthymematic argumentation is a *practical* form of reasoning, its aim is to move men not just to *think,* but also to *act;* and argument cannot move men to action unless it somehow elicits the motivational power of emotion.

Rhetoric in the Service of Truth and Justice

The interpretation of the enthymeme that has been advanced here suggests that Aristotle considered rhetorical argument to be governed by definite epistemological standards. But his treatment of enthymemes includes a study of "apparent enthymemes" — that is, fallacious arguments — and there are other examples of the care with which

Aristotle instructs the rhetorician in the techniques of verbal deception. Indeed, the art of rhetoric is said to consist of the power to be persuasive on the opposite sides of every question. What is to prevent this art from being used to advance falsehood and injustice rather than their opposites? In other words, what is to prevent cynical misuse of the *Rhetoric* by sophists?

First, Aristotle himself recognized the need to provide strong arms for the good-intentioned rhetorician, who must know all the tricks of sophistry so that he can properly defend himself. Moreover, the rhetorician might even have to employ such tricks in that category of cases where otherwise bad means are justified by their advancement of good ends.

It may also be said that, although the rhetorical art in itself is a morally and epistemologically neutral instrument, rhetoric tends to serve the true and the just. Even though the art itself has no intrinsic ends, ends are prescribed by the rhetorical situation—the speaker, the subject matter, and the audience. Since speakers who display good character are more persuasive, the noble rhetorician has an advantage over the sophist, who must attempt to hide his bad character. Also, the sophistical speaker is restrained by the nature of the subject matter and by the opinions of the audience. With respect to the subject matter, it is generally the case that the true and the just are naturally more easily argued and more persuasive; and the opinions of the audience generally reflect this tendency. In most cases, therefore, a speaker with something to hide is more vulnerable than one who can speak freely and in truth. It is difficult to give a good speech for a bad cause.[9]

This is certainly not to deny that the weaker argument can sometimes be made to appear the stronger. But could it be said, in defense of rhetoric, that it is usually easier to make the stronger argument appear to be the stronger, especially when it is skillfully presented? The sophists thought such a belief naive, and their own success with techniques of rhetorical deception was their best evidence. But the popular indignation eventually aroused by the sophists suggests that the rational criteria of rhetoric are not so easily evaded. In any case, I shall consider this issue at various points.

The Style and Arrangement of Speeches

Matters of style and composition may appear to be extraneous to the rational content of rhetoric since they would be apparently unnecessary for the substantive argument of issues. Indeed, when Aristotle takes up these matters in Book Three, he begins by complaining that a concern with such things is only a concession to corrupt audiences.

Yet Aristotle stresses in his treatment of these elements of rhetoric the extent to which they contribute to rational argument. For Aristotle, good style is not merely ornamentation, since the goodness of style is determined by how well it satisfies the natural desire of listeners for learning through reasoning. This is particularly evident in the case of metaphor, which delights listeners by allowing them to understand something unknown through its likeness to something known. And in his comments on the arrangement of speeches, Aristotle criticizes the practice of dividing speeches into many parts—most of which he believes to have little to do with genuine argumentation—and insists that the essence of good arrangement is simply to state the case and then to prove it. Thus, even in discussing style and composition, Aristotle continues to emphasize the rational character of rhetoric.

Conclusion

The purpose of this introductory chapter has been set forth in broad outline the interpretation of the *Rhetoric* that will be advanced in more detail in the commentary. The major thesis of this interpretation is, again, that Aristotle views rhetoric as rational discourse, and that he wishes to show that rhetoric is a genuine form of reasoning to be distinguished from sophistry, even though rhetorical reasoning is less exact and less certain than scientific demonstration.

In recent years, it has been suggested that a revival of the tradition of rhetoric might be necessary in order to recover an understanding of the meaning of ordinary political discourse: the principles of rhetoric might allow a more adequate study of political argumentation than is possible when scientific proof is assumed to be the model for all reasoning. And such a renewal of rhetorical studies might well begin most fruitfully with a reexamination of Aristotle's *Rhetoric*.

A recovery of Aristotle's rhetorical theory might also be an important contribution to modern political science. For as I shall argue in the concluding chapter, Aristotle points to the importance of common political opinions as the starting point for political science, and thus he challenges the modern assumption that to study politics scientifically one must reject the commonsense political awareness of men.

2

RHETORIC, DIALECTIC, AND SOPHISTRY (1. 1-3)

Rhetoric, Dialectic, and Sophistry (1. 1)

The first chapter of the *Rhetoric* is devoted both to showing the importance of the subject under discussion and to clearing away common prejudices that might make the reader unreceptive to the argument.[1] Aristotle wishes to begin by distinguishing true rhetoric from that practiced by the sophistical rhetoricians. In contrast to the base practices of the sophistical speakers, he argues, genuine rhetoric is a truly rational activity, essential for advancing the true and the just in public speech. True rhetoric is a form of argumentation comparable to dialectic.

Rhetoric the Counterpart of Dialectic (1354a1–11)

As these lines demonstrate, Aristotle emphasizes the resemblance of rhetoric to dialectic from the very beginning of the book:

> Rhetoric is a counterpart [*antistrophos*] of dialectic; for both are about such matters as are in some manner common things known to all and of no definite science. Hence all in some manner share in both; for all, up to some point, try to examine or uphold an argument and to defend or accuse. Now, some of the many do these things at random, others through practice from habit. But, since both ways are possible, it is clear that the same things can be done by direction [*hodopoiein*]; for it is possible to examine [*theorein*] the cause through which some succeed through practice and others by chance; and such all would agree to be the function of an art.

In this way Aristotle begins his book with an argument that becomes one of the major elements of his theory of rhetoric, namely, that rhetoric is a rational art that involves a form of reasoning similar to that of dialectic.

By his choice of words, Aristotle draws attention to the fact that this view of rhetoric differs from that attributed to Socrates in Plato's *Gorgias*. Plato's Socrates defines rhetoric as "the counterpart [*an-*

tistrophos] of cookery in the soul, as it is in the body," which makes it a "part of flattery" and a mere "knack" (*empeiria*) rather than a genuine "art" (*techne*) (465d–66a). But Aristotle claims that rhetoric is a "counterpart" or a "part" of dialectic (see 1. 2. 1356a31): it is, therefore, a reasoned activity and thus a true *techne*.[2]

But what does it mean that rhetoric is the *antistrophos* of dialectic? Aristotle uses *antistrophos* in his logical treatises in reference to the "convertibility" of premises or forms of inference. But in this sense, rhetoric and dialectic would be ultimately identical since they could be converted from one to the other without changing the meaning.[3] That Aristotle does not consider rhetoric a convertible equivalent of dialectic is indicated by his description of rhetoric as an "offshoot," a "part," or "likeness" of dialectic (2. 1356a25, 30–31). *Antistrophos,* therefore, must be taken to mean some sort of correspondence that falls short of complete identity or convertibility.

It seems likely that Aristotle intends to compare rhetoric's relation to dialectic to the relation between the *antistrophe* and the *strophe* of a chorus in a Greek play. One commentator argues that Aristotle is borrowing the term *antistrophos* from the movements of a chorus in performing the choral odes:

> *Strophe* denotes its movement in one direction, to which the *antistrophe,* the counter-movement, the wheeling in the opposite direction, exactly corresponds, the same movements being repeated. . . . It is extended to the words sung by the chorus during the latter of these evolutions, and signifies a set of verses precisely parallel or answering in all their details to the verses of the *strophe.*[4]

Rhetoric, then, is the "counterpart" of dialectic in the sense that it reflects dialectic while moving in the opposite direction. In what respect, then, does rhetoric resemble dialectic? And in what other respect does it differ?

According to the opening passage quoted above, rhetoric shares in the universality of dialectic. Rhetoric is not restricted either to a specialized subject matter or to a specialized group of people; it concerns all subjects as discussed by all men. Neither rhetoric nor dialectic is a special science; rather, both are universal arts concerned not so much with particular objects of reasoning as with reasoning as such (*see* 1. 4. 1359b12–17).[5]

Although all men employ rhetoric in some sense, most do not possess it as an *art.* For the many acquire rhetorical techniques either by chance or by habit; but this is insufficient for the *art* of rhetoric, because the function of the art is not the practice of argumentation but the theoretical grasp (*to theorein*) of the cause or reason (*aition*) for the practice being as it is. One possesses rhetoric as an art only when one knows the reasons for the success of some techniques of persuasion and the failure of others.[6]

Aristotle accepts the argument of Plato's Socrates that rhetoric can be an art only if the rhetorician provides a rational account of the nature of persuasion. No matter how successful in practice a rhetorician may be, if he lacks a knowledge of the reasons for his success, he possesses a "knack" but not an "art."[7] Rhetoric becomes a genuine art only insofar as it involves a knowledge of causes. Like every art, rhetoric must combine theoretical and practical components. Success in practice is not enough: rhetorical practice must be guided by rhetorical theory.

But in claiming that rhetorical argumentation is a true art, Aristotle presupposes a particular view of what it is that constitutes an art. It is therefore appropriate to consider briefly his comments in other writings on what is required for the possession of an art.

The Nature of Art

An "art" (*techne*), Aristotle says in the *Nicomachean Ethics* (1140a21), is "a certain habit [*hexis*] concerned with making involving a true course of reasoning." Hence an art has a theoretical side as well as a practical one. A true art results in "making" (*poesis*) but requires a prior "act of thought" (*noesis*) in the soul of the artist.[8]

That which is to be produced exists first as a "form" (*eidos*) in the artist's mind. The artist reasons to a conclusion starting from the "form" that points to what he can do. For instance, a doctor reasons from the "form" of health to conditions productive of health until he discovers some particular thing to do to the patient he is treating. He then reverses the process in *poiesis*, moving from the conclusion back through the chain of connections to create health.[9]

The natural desire of all men to know shows itself at the lowest level in the delight that men take in the senses, especially sight, because of the knowledge they give. But greater knowledge results when sense experience is preserved in memory, and when many memories combine into "experience" (*empeiria*).[10] A still higher level is reached, however, when from experience art and science are born.[11]

The artist is wiser than the man of experience because, while the man of experience knows *that* something is so, the artist knows *why* it is so: "experience" is a knowledge of particulars, but "art" is a knowledge of the general principles that explain particulars. Since action is concerned with particulars, and since the man of experience does know particulars, he may be more successful in practice than the man of art. But without the artistic knowledge of the general principles involved, the man of experience cannot give an account of his activity, cannot explain why he succeeds, and therefore cannot teach his skill.[12]

Since art is both theoretical and practical, it is both like and unlike "science" (*episteme*). Both art and science rest on a knowledge of causes that distinguishes them from mere "experience." Yet art is not scientific, since an art always serves some practical end.[13]

A hierarchy exists among artists. The "hand-artisan" (*cheirotechnes*) is subordinate to the master craftsman or "ruling artisan" (*architekton*), because the former merely performs the labor to carry out the instructions of the latter; the master craftsman is wiser, not because of his practical skill but because of his knowledge of causes. Yet even the master craftsman is defective in knowledge since what he knows is for the sake of "production" or "making." The highest wisdom belongs to the theoretical man who seeks knowledge of the whole, of "being" as such, for its own sake, rather than for the sake of doing or making something.[14] Therefore, "it is necessary not that the wise man receive orders but that he give them, and not that he obey others but that the less wise obey him."[15]

From Aristotle's reflections on the nature of art, it is clear that in presenting rhetoric as a true art, he affirms its rationality as a form of practical knowledge. It is not sufficient that the genuine rhetorician have a "knack" for persuading people; he must understand the reasons for his success.

But what does the hierarchy of artists suggest as to the status of the rhetorical art? Does Aristotle consider the practical wisdom of the political rhetorician subordinate to the theoretical wisdom of the political philosopher? Perhaps the *Rhetoric* itself is Aristotle's own attempt to guide rhetorical practice through a persuasive account of the rhetorical art. But if this is his aim, he will have to demonstrate the superiority of his rhetorical teaching to that of the sophists. And his crucial argument will have to be that the rhetorician can learn more from the study of dialectic than is possible from the study of sophistry. To fully understand the implications of this Aristotelian alliance between rhetoric and dialectic, some knowledge of Aristotle's view of dialectic is necessary.

16

Dialectical Reasoning

It is especially important to have some understanding of Aristotle's theory of dialectic, which is found principally in the *Topics* and *On Sophistical Refutations,* in order to avoid the mistake of assuming that Aristotle's use of the term "dialectic" is the same as Plato's. The reason for this is that it can be argued that Aristotle's bold claim that rhetoric is the "counterpart" not of "cookery," but of dialectic, rests upon a disagreement with Plato, not only about the nature of rhetoric but also about the nature of dialectic.[16]

An extensive discussion of Aristotle's account of dialectic cannot be attempted here, but some points that are especially pertinent to the *Rhetoric* can be briefly sketched in.

Through dialectic, Aristotle says, one can reason from "common opinions" (*endoxa*) in a consistent manner about any problem.[17] This suggests at least two major characteristics of dialectic that deserve special attention: dialectical reasoning is founded on common opinions, and it is applicable to any problem.

Since dialectic begins with *endoxa,* which are probable but not absolutely certain, its conclusions must be of the same character — probable but not certain. Dialectic falls short of the exactness of philosophic or "demonstrative" reasoning for this reason.[18] Its reliance on *endoxa* does not mean, however, that dialectic must always follow the opinions of the majority. A thesis contrary to common opinion can earn the attention of the dialectician if it has been stated by a famous philosopher or if it simply seems rationally defensible.[19] Indeed Aristotle thinks it is necessary for the dialectician to distinguish in argument when one should and when one should not accept the opinions of the many.[20] The dialectician must name things as the many name them, but he must not allow the many to decide what things are of such a sort and what are not. For instance, the popular definition of "healthful" as "that which is productive of health" should be accepted; but one must follow the guide of the doctor rather than that of the many as to whether something under discussion is productive of health.

Since the dialectician draws premises from *endoxa,* and since the scope of *endoxa* is universal, the scope of the dialectician's inquiries is also universal. Unlike demonstrations in a specialized field of knowledge, the premises of which are based on first principles restricted to the particular subject matter, dialectical reasoning is applicable to a great number of different fields because its premises are not restricted to any specific subject.[21] The expansive range of dialectic is evident even

17

when Aristotle attempts to specify its applications, such as when he says that the problems suited to dialectical examination can be *ethical* (for example, whether one should obey parents or the laws), *logical* (whether knowledge of contraries is or is not the same), or *physical* (whether the universe is or is not eternal).[22] The dialectician can argue equally well about ethical, logical, or physical problems since he views them from a commonsense perspective that does not require a specialized knowledge of any of these fields. He reasons on the basis of "common principles" (*koina*) applicable to many realms of knowledge; these are different in kind from "specific principles" known only to the specialists.[23]

Aristotle speaks of the *koina* (also called *koinai doxai, koinai archai,* and *axiomata*) as the fundamental principles of reasoning assumed by all the sciences, in contrast to the principles restricted to particular sciences. His most common examples of *koina* are the principle of non-contradiction and the axiom that when equals are subtracted from equals the results are equal. Since *koina* arise from common opinions, and since they are the fundamental presuppositions of the specialized fields of knowledge, they could be said to constitute the prescientific foundation of the sciences.[24]

But because it relies simply on "common principles," dialectic cannot reach the level of strictly "scientific" or "demonstrative" reasoning.[25] To demonstrate something scientifically, one must reason from those specific principles (*archai*) that are peculiar to some definite art or science. Truly "instructive" reasoning is the syllogistic exposition of an art or science for a student who accepts the *archai* of the art or science in question; the *archai* themselves must be taken on trust. But the dialectician does not reason from the *archai* of a definite art or science; he proceeds instead by interrogation and reasons from whatever premises are granted by the interlocutor. Dialectical argumentation is for the sake of inquiry and experimentation, but scientific demonstration is for the sake of teaching and learning.[26]

Because it cannot produce scientific demonstrations, dialectic, then, is lower than science. But in another sense dialectic is higher than science, for the examination of the first principles of each science is possible only through dialectic. As Aristotle explains it, the *archai* of science cannot be discussed within the bounds of the science itself since all scientific reasoning assumes these as self-evident premises, but in dialectic these *archai* can be discussed through the pertinent *endoxa*. Hence dialectic "has a way to the *archai* of all methods."[27] Through reasoning founded on common opinions, dialectic opens a path to the prescientific foundations of the sciences.[28]

From this one might infer that Aristotle is restating the Platonist view of dialectic, according to which dialectic is the means by which reason climbs to the top of the "divided line" in order to reach "the unhypothetical at the beginning of the whole [*he tou pantos arche*]."[29] But despite the significant resemblance, Aristotle's account of dialectic diverges from Plato's in that Aristotle denies that dialectic coincides with genuine philosophic knowledge in any fundamental manner.[30] According to Aristotle, dialectic is based on "opinion," while philosophy is based on "truth."[31] Dialecticians put on the "mask" (*schema*) of philosophy since they discuss everything and thus seem to investigate the whole. But dialectic is always merely "exploratory" (*peirastike*), whereas philosophy is "knowledgeable" (*gnoristike*).[32] Dialectic serves philosophy by providing exercise in raising difficulties on both sides of any question. Thus it increases the skill of a philosopher in discovering both truth and falsehood on every point.[33]

Even so, the dialectical ability to argue either side of any question seems sometimes hard to distinguish from sophistry. Like rhetoric, dialectic is a neutral instrument. What prevents the dialectician from using his knowledge to defeat opponents by fallacious and unfair argument is unclear.

Aristotle does, however, clearly separate dialectic and sophistry. Dialectical arguments are syllogisms from common opinions, but sophistical arguments are "syllogisms or apparent syllogisms from what appear to be but are not common opinions."[34] Thus the sophist chooses to appear wise without being so. Sophistical fallacies, then, are either formal or material. A formal fallacy consists in falsely assuming that something follows necessarily from prior premises. A material fallacy consists in falsely assuming that the premises are common opinions.

The sophistical use of fallacies confirms indirectly the epistemological, if not the moral, solidity of *endoxa*. To make the weaker argument appear to be the stronger, the sophist cannot rely on reasoning from *endoxa;* instead, he must either reason from premises that appear to be *endoxa* but are not, or he must make something appear to follow from *endoxa* when in fact it does not. In either case the sophist seeks to escape the restraints of common opinion.

Despite the opposition that he sets up between dialectic and sophistry, Aristotle does suggest, cautiously, that some circumstances justify the use of fallacious reasoning by a dialectician. One example appears early in the *Topics* (108a19-37, 110a23-110b15). Stressing the importance of being able to recognize equivocal uses of terms in order to avoid confusion and fallacious reasoning, Aristotle concedes that such

an ability can also be used to reason fallaciously with someone who cannot detect the equivocation. But such deceptive reasoning is not
"suitable" (*oikeios*) for dialectic; therefore, dialecticians "must absolutely beware of such a thing . . . unless it is quite impossible to argue
about the subject any other way" (*Topics* 108a33-37).

Whenever he comes across a technique for winning an argument
through deception, Aristotle warns his reader that great caution is in
order since such legerdemain is "unfitting" for the dialectician. He
repeatedly uses a verb—*eulabeisthai*—that denotes "discretion," "cir-
cumspection," or "fearful watchfulness."[35] The dialectician should
"beware of" using fallacious reasoning, but he should also "beware of"
allowing these same fallacies to be employed against him by sophists to
make him appear to be refuted. Further, he must be prepared in such
cases to defend himself with the same techniques of deception used
against him.[36]

The dialectician wishes to employ the best possible arguments for his
position, but sometimes the best arguments are ineffective because of
the poor quality of the interlocutors. In such cases the dialectician will
sometimes have to use inferior and even false arguments, knowing that
they are the only ones acceptable to those with whom he speaks.[37] It is as
true for dialectic as it is for rhetoric that the character of the argumentation reflects the character of those to whom it is addressed.[38]

Aristotle advises the dialectician to try to avoid discussions with
sophistical polemicists;[39] for such men are so overcome by a passion for
defeating others in argument (*pleonexia*) that they will use whatever
means necessary for appearing to be victorious. The dialectician is,
therefore, compelled to defend himself with arguments that appear to
be true but are not strictly so. Such being the case, it is best not to speak
with such people at all:

> One ought not to discuss with everyone, nor to exercise oneself
> with any random person. For it is necessary with some that the
> arguments become petty. For with one who tries everything to ap-
> pear to escape, it is just to try everything to infer by way of
> syllogism, but it is not becoming. For that reason one should not
> readily come together with random persons; for it is necessary that
> debased argument result; for those who are exercizing are unable
> to avoid discussing contentiously.[40]

The general rule, then, with respect to the dialectical use of deceptive
or fallacious arguments is that the dialectician should always attempt to
speak only with those who can maintain discussion at a high level.
However, when he does find himself debating unscrupulous opponents,

the dialectician must be willing to defend himself with the opponents' own weapons, perhaps even to the point of showing himself more skillful with their weapons than they are.

Even when forced to engage in "debased argument," the dialectician differs from the sophist; for unlike the sophist, Aristotle implies, the dialectician employs deceptive argument to promote justice rather than injustice.[41] Explaining that what is "simply" (*haplos*) just can differ from what is just in particular circumstances or for particular people, Aristotle insists that "nothing prevents the saying of things that are unjust from being just" (*Soph. El.* 180b35). That is, while deceptive speech is, as a rule, unjust, it is just when it is used in a way that is beneficial for a particular audience in particular circumstances.

Thus does Aristotle carefully distinguish dialectic from sophistry. Therefore, when he opens the *Rhetoric* by declaring rhetoric to be a "counterpart" of dialectic, he clearly differentiates his own rhetorical theory from that of the sophists. Further, he explains after this opening statement how his account of rhetoric differs from that in the existing handbooks of rhetorical practice.

The Deficiences of the Rhetorical Handbooks (1354a12–1355a4)

Aristotle has spoken in very general terms of what is required if rhetoric is to be an art. He now becomes more specific and names the enthymeme as the fundamental instrument of the rhetorical art. "Proofs" (*pisteis*) are the sole foundation of the art; everything else is extraneous; and "the body of proof" (*soma tes pisteos*) is the enthymeme (1354a12-16). Furthermore, since the enthymeme is a type of syllogism, this reliance on the enthymeme extends the correspondence of rhetoric and dialectic: the enthymeme is the rhetorical counterpart of the syllogism of dialectic.

Aristotle recognizes that this view of rhetoric is not generally accepted. The current theorists of rhetorical practice have at best succeeded in developing only a "small part" of the art, because they do not understand that the only truly artful means of persuasion are "proofs" and that the enthymeme is the vehicle of "proof."

Those who have compiled the handbooks on rhetoric, Aristotle complains, have devoted their attention solely to techniques for arousing emotions that distract listeners from the issues at hand; they have thus ignored the enthymeme, even though it is the chief instrument for rhetorical reasoning. In addition, these authors have been preoccupied with forensic, rather than deliberative, rhetoric because judges in the courts are more susceptible to emotional appeals than are judges in the political assemblies.

If Aristotle intends to stress the purely rational or logical elements of rhetoric as embodied in the enthymeme, as his criticisms of the current teachers of rhetoric imply, it may be asked why he treats so extensively in the *Rhetoric* the modes of persuasion founded on the character of the speaker and the passions of the audience. Indeed, some readers of the *Rhetoric* have thought it a surprisingly obvious contradiction for Aristotle initially to condemn those rhetoricians who rely on appeals to the passions and then later to provide his own careful study of the passions.[42]

Closer examination, however, reveals that there is no contradiction. Aristotle observes from the beginning that those who have founded rhetoric on passion (*pathos*) have provided at least a "small part" of the rhetorical art (1354a13). Their mistake is in relying *exclusively* on this part of rhetoric rather than treating it as ancillary to the enthymeme (1354b18–22). The result of such a *direct* appeal to the passions, with no connection to enthymematic argument, is to distract listeners with "irrelevancies" or "things outside the subject" (1354a15).

Those concerned solely with moving the judge through his emotions are preoccupied, Aristotle says, with laying down rules for the different parts of the speech, such as the proem and the narrative. But they disregard the "artful proofs" (*entechnoi pisteis*) by which one becomes skilled in the use of enthymemes (1354b16–22). The significance of this point is that whereas the traditional rhetorical theorists separate persuasion by *pathos* from rational proof, Aristotle argues that they should be combined. In the "proem" (*prooimion, principium*), according to the traditional theories, the speaker would win the goodwill of his audience; in the "peroration" (*epilogos, peroratio*), he would arouse the passions of his listeners in favor of his case; and only in the main body of the speech would there be a statement of the facts (*diegesis, narratio*) and proof of the position being advanced (*pisteis, confirmatio*).[43] Aristotle deprecates this method of analysis by insisting first that *pisteis* alone are relevant to the rhetorical art and second, as he soon makes clear, that these *pisteis* include *ethos* and *pathos* as well as *logos;* all three, of course, contribute to enthymematic reasoning. For Aristotle the speaker's winning of the audience's goodwill and his handling of their passions are integral elements of the argumentation supporting his position. The fault of the teachers of sophistry, then, lies not in their use of emotional appeals but in their teaching that such appeals are independent of rational proof.

The kind of rhetoric criticized by Aristotle is exemplified by Gorgias's *Helen*. In this speech, Gorgias describes the control of rhetoric over the emotions of the soul as an irresistible force that works through "witchery" and "sorcery" (10). Such an appeal is said to influence the soul as drugs influence the body (14); thus the emotions appear to be almost purely physiological: psychic motion is reduced to physical motion. From Gorgias's viewpoint, to persuade listeners through emotions is to move them by a type of *persuasion* that is indistinguishable from *compulsion*.[44]

Thus it is that, when *pathos* becomes the sole means of persuasion, rhetoric becomes merely a mode of deceptive manipulation whose purpose is to lead listeners to judgments based on irrational dispositions instead of the genuine arguments about the issues under examination. This is not to say, however, that *pathos* should be excluded from rhetoric; on the contrary, it is essential for rhetorical proof so long as it enters as an integral part of enthymematic reasoning.

Yet one might reasonably wonder whether anything intrinsic to public speech keeps speakers from employing the sort of rhetoric deplored by Aristotle. Indeed, are not sophistical rhetoricians quite successful at what they do? Aristotle sees two sources of restraint. One pertains to deliberative rhetoric and the other to forensic.

In deliberative assemblies, citizens tend to have little patience for speakers who stir up emotions without concern for the question at hand. Political issues are bound up too closely with the interests of the listeners for them to tolerate evasive speeches (1354b22-1355a3). This is why the writers of sophistical handbooks prefer to deal with rhetoric for the law courts, which tend to handle private disputes that do not involve the interests of the jurors. So long as the jurors think that their judgment will have no effect on themselves, they are little interested in the true merits of the opposing cases and prefer speeches that are pleasurably stimulating.[45]

Yet there is some restraint even upon forensic rhetoric. For all men, Aristotle thinks, recognize the evil of forensic speaking that is irrelevant to the facts of the case; this recognition, he believes, is reflected in the laws that require forensic speeches to be pertinent to the particular case under examination. The rule of law is superior to the rule of men since law is free of passion.[46] Therefore, the general rules of justice and expediency should be determined by the legislator, so that jurors decide only those particular issues that could not be anticipated by the legislator. But, in fact, such arrangements are perfectly attained only in regimes with the best laws (1354a17-1354b16).[47] Thus does Aristotle introduce a

23

theme that runs throughout the *Rhetoric* — the dependence of rhetoric upon the laws of the regime under which it is practiced. The character of the laws — and concomitantly the character of the people who shape and are shaped by the laws — determines the character of rhetoric. In corrupt regimes one must expect to find corrupt rhetoric.

Therefore, much of what Aristotle says about the true art of rhetoric does not apply in a corrupt regime. This becomes especially clear in Book Three, where some of the very techniques of the sophistical rhetoricians denounced by Aristotle are said to be sometimes necessary where the corruption of the regime, and thus of the audience, is so great that the better forms of rhetoric are ineffective (3. 1. 1403b15-1404a12, 14. 1415a5-1416a2).

Having distinguished the genuine art of rhetoric from the rhetoric of the sophists, Aristotle is now concerned to show the usefulness of true rhetoric, even to the point of suggesting that rhetoric is essential for creating the kind of political discourse that is most conducive to the discovery of truth and justice.

The Use and Abuse of Rhetoric (1355a5–1355b7)

In contrast to the defective rhetoric of the sophists, the truly artful method of rhetoric, Aristotle reiterates, rests upon "proofs" (*pisteis*). A "proof" is "some sort of demonstration" (*apodeixis tis*). "Rhetorical demonstration" is an enthymeme, and the enthymeme is "some sort of syllogism" (*syllogismos tis*) (1355a5-10). Hence the distinctive feature of Aristotle's theory of rhetoric is his understanding of rhetoric as fundamentally a form of reasoning — reasoning through enthymemes.

Aristotle refers to the enthymeme as "a sort of syllogism" (*syllogismos tis*), and some readers have taken this use of *tis* as implying that the enthymeme is not a true or complete syllogism.[48] But the falsity of this interpretation is made evident by a passage in the *Prior Analytics* (24a10-16, 25b26-31). Here Aristotle explains that his theory of the syllogism in the *Prior Analytics* is more general than his theory of "demonstration" (*apodexis*) in the *Posterior Analytics:* "for demonstration is a kind of syllogism [*syllogismos tis*], but not every syllogism is a demonstration." Since there is no reason to believe that a "demonstration" is anything less than a true syllogism, it is clear that the phrase *syllogismos tis* is intended only to indicate that a "demonstration" is *one kind* of syllogism, to be distinguished from other kinds.[49] Likewise, the enthymeme can be one distinctive type of syllogism without being syllogistically defective; this is borne out by Aristotle's repeated references to the syllogistic character of the enthymeme.[50]

24

What, then, distinguishes the enthymeme from other types of syllogisms? Stating that expertise with enthymemes requires a knowledge of the matter and forms of the syllogism and of the subject matter of enthymemes and their differences from "logical syllogisms," Aristotle explains that to know the truth and to know what is *like* the truth belongs to the same "faculty" or "power" (*dunamis*). He further adds that one who can discover the "reputable opinions" (*endoxa*) will also be able to find the truth (1355a11-17).[51] He implies that, unlike some other types of syllogism, the enthymeme is founded on common opinions, which are not simply true but which bear a resemblance to the truth.

It must be stressed that the derivation of the enthymeme's premises from common opinions does not prevent the enthymeme from being a genuine syllogism. Common opinions can be a valid source of premises for both rhetoric and dialectic, because the generally accepted opinions of men reflect or resemble what is truly so. As Aristotle says, men have a "natural inclination" (*pephykenae pros*) for the truth (1355a15). In other words, whatever has become widely accepted among men is likely to contain some element of truth.[52]

The solidity of rhetorical reasoning thus depends largely upon the solidity of the opinions commonly held by men. But in his comments on the usefulness of rhetoric, Aristotle makes it clear that the reverse is also true: the commonsense wisdom of the multitude cannot become fully efficacious without the assistance of rhetoric. In fact, Aristotle's opening remarks (1354a3-6) would seem to suggest that all the interpersonal persuasion from which common opinions arise is in some sense rhetorical activity.[53]

Aristotle specifies four respects in which rhetoric is useful (1355a20-1355b2).[54] First, it reinforces the natural strength of the true and the just by ensuring that the advocate of truth and justice will not suffer defeat because of his ignorance of rhetorical techniques. Second, it allows one to speak to the multitude of men on the basis of their own opinions, thus avoiding the futile task of attempting to instruct scientifically those incapable of such instruction. Third, rhetoric gives a speaker knowledge of sophistical fallacies so that he can protect himself against them. Fourth, rhetoric permits a man to defend himself through the use of something distinctively human—the capacity for speech.[55]

The second of these four points deserves special notice since it clarifies the distinction between "instruction" (*didaskalia*) through "science" (*episteme*) and "persuasion" through rhetoric, a distinction implicit in the opening passage of the *Rhetoric*. Most people are incapable of scientific instruction, but they are open to rhetorical persuasion; for rhetorical reasoning rests not upon special premises known only to a few, but upon the "common things" known by all—that is, upon common opinions. The importance of rhetoric in this respect is obvious. Through rhetoric the political discourse of ordinary men can become a rational activity, but such discourse could never become rational if scientific instruction were the only form of reasoning.

Yet what keeps the techniques of rhetorical reasoning from being misused? With reference to the first and third points listed above, is there not some conflict between Aristotle's preference for rhetoric used in support of truth and justice and his impartial exposition of all the means of persuasion for all sides of any issue? There seems to be nothing intrinsic to the art of rhetoric to prevent it from being employed for bad ends as well as good. Like dialectic, rhetoric enables one to prove opposites, to be persuasive on either side of any question. Hence, some of the methods of rhetoric that are "most artistic" are also "most unjust" (3. 15. 1416b7).

Aristotle argues, of course, that the misuse of rhetoric should not be grounds for condemning all rhetoric, since even the most beneficial things can be harmful if they are improperly used (1355b2-7).[56] But he goes even farther and suggests that some elements of the rhetorical situation direct rhetoric to the service of truth and justice.

First, Aristotle assumes that students of the *Rhetoric* will be men with good intentions and, therefore, that they will not misuse their knowledge. "The speaker must be able to be persuasive as to opposites, just as in syllogisms; not that we should do both—for one must not be persuasive as to bad things—but that nothing of the case will escape us and that, if another uses unjust arguments, we may be able to refute them" (1355a29-35).

Aristotle seems to think that to set forth careful studies of the various deceptive techniques used by sophistical rhetoricians (such as is done in 2. 24) can help only the speakers with good intentions. It will not help those with bad intentions since they are likely to be already knowledgeable about all the tricks of sophistry. But it is essential for virtuous speakers if they are to be well armed against their sophistical opponents. To be successful in rhetoric, good men must see to it that they are not naive.[57]

Richard Whately, a modern rhetorical theorist in the Aristotelian tradition, explains this point nicely in the preface to his *Elements of Rhetoric:*

With respect to what are commonly called Rhetorical Ar-
tifices—contrivances for "making the worse appear the better
reason,"—it would have savoured of pedantic morality to give
solemn admonitions against employing them, or to enter a formal
disclaimer of dishonest intention; since, after all, the generality
will, according to their respective characters, make what use of a
book they think fit, without waiting for the Author's permission.
But what I have endeavored to do, is *clearly to set forth,* as far as I
could, (as Bacon does in his Essay on Cunning,) these sophistical
tricks of the Art; and as far as I may have succeeded in this, I shall
have been providing the only effectual check to the employment
of them. The adulterators of food or of drugs, and the coiners of
base money, keep their processes a secret, and dread no one so
much as him who detects, describes, and proclaims their contrivances, and thus puts men on their guard.[58]

Aristotle does not have to prescribe the ethical uses of rhetoric if he
intends his *Rhetoric* to be a tool for the virtuous men who would rule in
good regimes—men who could be trusted to employ the various means
of persuasion in whatever way would best promote the true and the
good.[59]

But he does not have to rely solely on the good intentions of the
speaker as a source of moral and epistemological ends for rhetoric:
while the art of rhetoric is impartial with respect to truth and falsity,
justice and injustice, the subject matter of rhetoric is not. Although
rhetoric provides a capacity for proving opposites, the subject matter of
rhetoric is such that the true and the just in most cases are by nature
"stronger," "easier to prove" (*eusyllogistotera*), and "more persuasive"
than their opposites (1355a20-23, 35-38).

What does Aristotle have in mind here? Perhaps the thought is that
truth is generally easier to support than falsehood because lying requires
contrivances that allow the liar not to betray himself and that also hide
the truth. But by saying that the true is more persuasive than the false *in
most cases,* Aristotle leaves open the possibility that in some situations
the truth might be less plausible than a lie that is carefully contrived to
be credible (but see 2. 23. 1400a5-13).

The ultimate justification for the claim that truth and justice are
stronger in speech than their opposites surely lies in the character of the
common opinions of men. Aristotle insists throughout the *Rhetoric* that
men are naturally inclined to prefer the true and the just and that this is
manifested in their common opinions. Popular opinions reflect the
presence in men of a desire to know and of a sense of justice.[60] Insofar as

the rhetorician must ground his arguments in these opinions, he must therefore respect the moral and epistemological standards that they embody. The rhetorician is thus constrained to argue truly and justly lest he violate the opinions of his audience.

However, Aristotle observes elsewhere in the *Rhetoric* that "in most cases men do injustice whenever they can" (2. 5. 1382b9). In public, men praise what is just and noble, but in private they wish for what is expedient. The opinions affirmed in public speech favor justice and nobility, but the private and secret wishes of men favor ignoble self-interest.[61]

Men show a better grasp of the true and the just in what they say in public than in what they do and wish for in private. As a community, men are better than they are as private and separate individuals. While the multitude of men may be quite defective in their individual judgments, their *collective* judgments can still manifest a commonsense wisdom and a sense of justice.[62] Since public speech, therefore, is governed by the collective wisdom of men as expressed in common opinions, true and just arguments tend to be rhetorically stronger than their opposites. It is hard to speak well for a bad cause.

This is evident in the unpopularity of the sophists, who try to escape the popular standards of the community by dismissing them as "conventional" and appealing to the private desires of men as "natural."[63] Sometimes they succeed. But Aristotle observes: "Customarily even if the multitude is utterly deceived, subsequently it hates those who have led it to do something ignoble."[64]

It should be obvious by now that in showing the dependence of rhetoric on "common opinions" (*endoxa*), Aristotle does not intend to depreciate the solidity of rhetorical reasoning. But what, then, is the epistemological status of common opinions? To pursue this question, one must consider the fundamental importance of *endoxa* for Aristotelian logic.

Reasoning from Common Opinions

Since Aristotle thinks men naturally seek the truth and, in most cases, attain it to some extent, he considers common opinions to bear a likeness to the truth (1. 1. 1355a13-17). The things that men commonly find credible are "either things that are [*ta onta*] or things that are probable [*ta eikota*]" (2. 23. 1400a5-13). So the necessity for rhetoric to be founded on common opinions usually insures that rhetorical argument is governed by a commonsense grasp of reality.

Thus, Aristotle denies the complete malleability of common

28

opinions, and in doing so he denies the foundation of sophistical rhetoric. Gorgias argues, for example, that the manipulative power of rhetoric depends upon the plasticity of the opinions through which men view reality; only because he believes common opinions have no clear and solid connections with objective reality, can he be confident that the speaker is free to shape the opinions of his listeners as he pleases.[65] But from Aristotle's viewpoint, common opinions impose definite standards upon the speaker, standards both epistemological and moral.[66]

Opinion is, however, a somewhat defective form of knowledge. "We opine things that we do not entirely know."[67] Truth is attained in *nous, episteme,* or *doxa,* Aristotle explains.[68] But while the truths of *nous* and *episteme* are necessary, those of *doxa* are contingent. Necessary truths are of those things that are and cannot be otherwise; contingent truths of those that are but can be otherwise. Scientific (or demonstrative) knowledge—*episteme*—can have the same object as opinion, but the object is viewed differently. Through demonstration a predicate is shown to belong essentially, and thus necessarily, to a subject, while through opinion a predicate appears to belong to a subject though such is not necessarily the case. For example, by demonstration "animal" is apprehended to be a *necessary* attribute of "man," because it belongs to the *essence* of "man"; but by opinion "man" is apprehended to be "animal" without this being seen as an essential—and therefore necessary—predication.[69]

Nevertheless, although common opinions do not always convey the whole truth, they are not merely nonsensical. Opinion simultaneously reveals and conceals the reality of things. Because of what it conceals, it falls short of the simple truth. But because of what it reveals, it can be the basis of reasoning that leads to conclusions which in some manner approximate the truth.

Aristotle does sometimes use "opinion" (*doxa*) in a pejorative sense, particularly when it is employed in contrast to "science" or "knowledge." But he also uses "opinion" to refer to some conviction derived from the common experience of men and sanctioned by wise men, which therefore deserves the respect of anyone seriously investigating the subject to which it pertains.[70] In this stronger sense "opinion" is often indicated by the use of *endoxa* rather than *doxa;* for while the opposite of *doxa* is *episteme,* the opposite of *endoxa* is *adoxa* or *paradoxa.*[71]

Aristotle defines *endoxa* as "what are thought to be so by all or most or the wise (and as to these [the wise], all or most or those most known and reputed [*endoxoi*])."[72] That *endoxa* cannot be simply dismissed by

29

any thoughtful man is obvious from the fact that some *endoxa* are accepted by *all* men. Presumably these are those fundamental principles of thought and action known by all men based on their common experience of what the world is like.

By defining *endoxa* as the opinions held by all, by most, or by a wise few, Aristotle excludes the opinions of a few unwise men.[73] The opinions held by a few men are respectable only if the men are wise. The opinions of ordinary men or of small groups of ordinary men are unreliable. But when *most* ordinary men agree on certain opinions, these opinions must be assumed to be rather solid. In other words, the multitude of men can possess *collectively* an excellence in judgment that they do not possess *individually*.[74]

The Philosophic Uses of Common Opinions

Every form of demonstration proceeds from common opinions, Aristotle says.[75] Hence common opinions are the foundation of even the most rigorous types of knowledge. Scientific or philosophic knowledge must emerge out of the prescientific, prephilosophic knowledge embodied in opinions.[76]

Even in the *Metaphysics* and the *Physics,* Aristotle shows a respect for the opinions of his predecessors. He likes to argue that his doctrines are a refinement of what others have thought on the subject. In explaining his doctrine of the four causes, for instance, he claims to have set out clearly what earlier investigators conceived only vaguely.[77]

But the importance of common opinions is most obvious in Aristotle's ethical and political treatises. In the *Nicomachean Ethics,* he begins with what the well-habituated man thinks to be true about the noble and the just without knowing the reason for this: the "that" but not the "why" is the starting point (1095a31–1095b8). Aristotle believes it is better to begin with what is more knowable to man rather than with what is more knowable simply.[78]

Aristotle thinks that the opinions about goodness and happiness held by the many over a long time or by a few esteemed men are likely not to be wholly mistaken but to be partly or even mostly correct.[79] His procedure, therefore, is to examine the confused and apparently contradictory statements of opinion commonly made about an issue and then by clarification and refinement to determine exactly the points of agreement and disagreement; his ultimate aim is to discover the kernel of truth in each opinion. Aristotle assumes that in most cases of apparent disagreement the opinions on both sides are true, but only partially so; therefore what is needed is philosophic clarification and refinement

through which the partial truths can be combined into a more comprehensive view.

Aristotle practices this method of inquiry throughout the
Nicomachean Ethics, but rarely does he comment explicitly upon the
method itself.[80] At one point (1145b1-7) he says:

> We must, as in all other cases, set the phenomena before us and,
> after first reviewing the difficulties, go on to prove, if possible, the
> truth of all the common opinions [*endoxa*] about the affections of
> the mind, or if not, of the greater number and the most
> authoritative; for if we both solve the difficulties and leave the
> common opinions standing, we shall have proved the case suffi-
> ciently.

At the beginning of the *Eudemian Ethics* (1216b28-35), Aristotle
makes perhaps his clearest statement of the procedure that he follows in
moral inquiry:

> It would be best for all men to be seen to agree to the things that
> will be said, but if not, for all to agree in some manner. They will
> do this if they are led to change their position; for each one has
> something suitable with respect to the truth, from which it is
> necessary to reach a demonstration by some means concerning
> these things; for, advancing from the things stated truly but not
> clearly, there will be clarity, if we always exchange the customary
> confused statements for the more intelligible things.

Later in the same book (1235b13-18), after stating the divergent
opinions about the nature of friendship, he observes:

> An argument must be taken up that best restores the opinions
> about these matters and at the same time solves the difficulties
> and contradictions. And this will be the case if the contradictory
> opinions are seen to be well argued [*eulogos*]. For such an argu-
> ment will be most in agreement with the phenomena; and it hap-
> pens that both contradictories remain if what is said is true in one
> form but not in another.

From these statements it is clear that moral philosophy, for Aristotle, is essentially a refinement of common opinions. The philosopher
must start with what men commonly believe, but he must not be deceived by such beliefs. He must assume that no opinion accepted by a
large number of people or by a few of great esteem can be wholly
baseless; but he must recognize that, although such an opinion contains
some element of truth, the fragment of truth is obscured by the mud-

dled fashion in which it is expressed and by the errors with which it is mixed. Even when they have a grasp of some truth, men tend to distort it because of their inclination to state partial truths without qualification, as though they were simply true, and because of their preference for seeing things in ways that serve their selfish interests. Hence the philosopher must recognize opinion as a cloudy medium from which truth can be extracted only by the careful elimination of many elements of distortion.

The distorting influence of self-interest is made evident by Aristotle in his study in the *Politics* of opinions about justice. Once again he maintains that all the prevalent opinions are somewhat truthful: "all those who dispute about regimes express some part of justice" (1281a9-10; see also 1301a18-1301b4). But men tend to see only that part of justice which favors their own interests and to ignore the rest: "For some think that being unequal in some respect, such as wealth, they are wholly unequal; but others think that being equal in some respect, such as freedom, they are wholly equal" (1280a23-25). The problem is "that the judgment is about themselves, and perhaps most men are bad judges about the things that concern themselves" (1280a10-17).

Aristotle finds a similar combination of truth and self-serving distortion in the opinions of the Greeks who defend the justice of slavery (*Pol.* 1255a3-1255b15):

> they do not mean to say that they themselves [if conquered] would be slaves, but that barbarians are. And yet whenever they do say this, they seek for nothing else than the slave by nature about which we spoke at the beginning; for they are compelled to say that some are slaves everywhere, and some nowhere.

A common opinion, therefore, is almost always dubious, because rarely is it simply true; it is usually distorted by the prejudices and partial perspectives of men. Yet even if it is not simply true, neither is it simply nonsense. One can assume that in some manner it reflects the truth.

Thus, unlike sophistry, rhetoric can depend upon common opinions while still being a genuine form of reasoning. In drawing his premises from common opinions, the rhetorician resembles the dialectician more than the sophist. And yet Aristotle concludes the first chapter of the *Rhetoric* by conceding how difficult it is in some cases to differentiate rhetoric and sophistry.

Rhetoric, Dialectic, and Sophistry (1355b7-24)

Returning to the correlation between rhetoric and dialectic, Aristotle observes (1355b15-22):

> it belongs to rhetoric to see what is persuasive and what is apparently persuasive, just as in dialectic the syllogism and the apparent syllogism. For sophistry lies not in the faculty [*dunamis*] but in the choice [*proairesis*]. But there is a difference in that, while the one according to knowledge and the one according to choice are both rhetoricians, sophistry is according to choice, but dialectic is not according to choice but according to the faculty.

This passage is an excellent example of Aristotle's occasionally elliptical style of writing and of its resultant obscurity. His meaning can be discerned even so.

Rhetoric and dialectic are alike in being faculties for making both genuine and apparent arguments. To be either a rhetorician or a dialectician, one must have a knowledge of invalid as well as valid forms of reasoning. But sophistry arises not from the faculty for making either genuine or merely apparent arguments, but from the "deliberate choice" (*proairesis*) of apparent arguments—that is, arguments that appear to be valid but in fact are not.[81] The invalidity of sophistical inferences, Aristotle explains in *On Sophistical Refutations* (165a37-165b12, 176b29-177a8), consists either in the formal fallaciousness of the syllogism or in the premises appearing to be common opinions (*endoxa*) when in truth they are not.

While the dialectician possesses the *faculty* for using fallacious arguments, the sophist is one who deliberately *chooses* to use them. But such a distinction cannot be so easily made between the rhetorician and the sophist; one with the *faculty* of arguing fallaciously and one who *chooses* to argue fallaciously are both called rhetoricians.

Despite the difficulty in distinguishing rhetoric and sophistry, a problem that may be due merely to the fact that the name "rhetoric" is indiscriminantly applied to both,[82] and despite the fact that rhetoric does resemble sophistry (1. 4. 1359b10-13), Aristotle separates the two. He says that while the sophist employs fallacious arguments as though they were valid, the rhetorician distinguishes true arguments from those that are merely apparent; furthermore, the genuine enthymeme—the fundamental instrument of rhetorical reasoning—is distinguished from the apparent enthymeme of the sophists (see 2. 24).

In this first chapter of the *Rhetoric*, Aristotle has challenged the most common criticisms of rhetoric—particularly those stated by Plato in his *Gorgias*. True rhetoric is the "counterpart" not of "cookery" but of dialectic. It is not an artless "knack" for persuading people; nor is it a collection of sophistical devices using emotional appeals for distracting audiences or for deceiving them with specious reasoning. Rather, it is a mode of argument, an art of reasoning that consists essentially of "proofs" (*pisteis*) as conveyed through the enthymeme, which is the "body of proof." Like many other beneficial instruments, rhetoric can be harmful if it is misused. But the virtuous speaker can be trusted to apply it properly, and the commonsense judgments of men as expressed in common opinion can be depended upon in most cases to restrain the speaker who would misuse it.

The problem remains that, except for his brief references to "proofs" and the enthymeme, Aristotle has not commented on the actual techniques of rhetoric. It is not until the second chapter of his book that he begins the technical exposition of his theory.

The Three Modes of Proof (1. 2)

The Definition of Rhetoric (1355b25-35)

At the end of the first chapter of the *Rhetoric*, Aristotle speaks of the "function" (*ergon*) of rhetoric as being "not to persuade, but to see [*idein*] the existing means of persuasion concerning the particular" (1355b9-11). It is the same with all the other arts. The function of medicine, for example, is not to create health—in some cases this is impossible—but to promote it as much as is possible (1355b9-14). This is then restated in the definition at the beginning of Chapter Two: "Let rhetoric be the power [*dunamis*] of observing the possible means of persuasion concerning the particular" (1355b25-26).

The rhetorician is like all other artists in knowing the means available in any situation for promoting what he aims at but being at the mercy of circumstance as far as whether these means are sufficient for achieving the end in practice. An artist can always be "productive" of the object of his art, but he cannot always "produce" it. A doctor is "productive" of health, a builder "productive" of a house, and a trainer "productive" of a good bodily condition; but in each case possession of the art does not guarantee the actual production of the object.[83]

Aristotle thus denies the assumption of sophists such as Gorgias that since rhetoric is the "artificer of persuasion," the rhetorician can always succeed in "putting persuasion in the soul of the audience."[84] As noted earlier, Gorgias thinks that the best rhetoric exerts a force over the soul of a listener comparable to that of a drug over the body; he implies, then, that a genuine rhetorician always succeeds in persuading his audience. But Aristotle emphasizes that rhetorical persuasion is not compulsion. The power of rhetoric is not irresistible. Even when a speaker has made his case as persuasive as possible, his listeners are still free to accept or reject his arguments.[85]

Aristotle defines rhetoric so as to place the essential activity of the rhetorician not in the realm of practical execution, but in that of theoretical planning. The function of rhetoric is not to persuade but to "observe"—Aristotle uses both *idein* and *theorein*—the means of persuasion possible in each case (see also 1. 2. 1356b33–34). The true art of rhetoric belongs more to the knowledge of the causes of rhetorical activity than to the activity itself.[86]

The theoretical element of Aristotle's definition—rhetoric as "seeing" or "observing"—is not all; a practical element also exists. Rhetoric is a kind of "seeing," but a "seeing" of the means of persuasion appropriate to *particular cases*. The importance of particulars shows the practical character of rhetoric. Rhetoric requires not that one merely discern the principles of persuasion but that one discern these principles in application to particular circumstances.[87]

Although he thus acknowledges the practical nature of rhetoric, Aristotle tends to emphasize its theoretical activity: the study of argumentation is primary, and everything else is secondary. Indeed, one of the common criticisms by students of rhetoric is that Aristotle gives too little attention to the nonrational features of rhetorical activity. Friedrich Nietzsche, for example, regarded the *Rhetoric* as a "purely philosophic" treatment of the subject, arguing that Aristotle had defined rhetoric so as to stress the rational side of the art just as he had done in defining tragedy in the *Poetics*. In both cases, Nietzsche explained, Aristotle considered the effect of the art as independent of the performance, and therefore he handled the techniques of verbal delivery as inessential. For Aristotle, Nietzsche complained, the "discovery" (*theorein*) of arguments was the only essential component of rhetoric.[88]

Aristotle's emphasis on the rational character of rhetoric has been evident up to this point in the *Rhetoric* in his insistence that the rhetorical art rests solely upon "proofs" and upon the enthymeme, the "body of proof." Now he must explain in detail the nature of rhetorical proof.

The Three "Proofs" (1355b35–1356a22)

"Proofs" (*pisteis*) are either "artificial" (*entechnoi*) or "inartificial" (*atechnoi*). "Inartificial proofs" refer to evidentiary material that exists

35

independently of the speaker's actions—such things as witnesses and contracts. "Artificial proofs," on the other hand, are created by the speaker in his speech. Aristotle comments on the "inartificial proofs" at the end of Book One (Chapter 15), but otherwise he concerns himself solely with the "artificial" sources of persuasion; since the latter can be methodically constructed by the rhetorician in his speech, they are more central to the rhetorical art.

The *pisteis entechnoi*, those provided by the speech itself, are of three forms—*ethos, pathos,* and *logos.* A speaker can be persuasive in his speech by displaying his own moral character (*ethos*), by guiding his listeners to certain emotional dispositions (*pathos*), and by proving or appearing to prove something (*logos*).

When he first enumerates the three *pisteis,* Aristotle finds fault with the sophistical rhetoricians for ignoring the importance of the *ethos* of the speaker; he notes once again that they concern themselves only with *pathos;* and he directs the reader ahead to the subsequent treatment of the passions. Thus Aristotle makes clear that his criticism of the sophists is not founded upon a denial of the rhetorical importance of either *pathos* or *ethos.* Rather, what is required—and what they do not provide—is a rational study and application of all three *pisteis.*

A rhetorician is persuasive through *ethos,* Aristotle explains, when he speaks in a way that makes him "worthy of belief" (*axiopistos*). "For we believe good men [*epieikeis*] more and sooner concerning everything generally; and in those things where there is no exactness but contradiction of opinions, we believe them completely"(1356a6-8).[89]

Although the art of rhetoric itself may be morally neutral, the rhetorician is constrained by his audience to exercise his art in a manner that displays good moral character. The bad man can, of course, speak so as to appear virtuous, but the fact remains that he is not free to speak as he pleases—he is forced to speak like a man of virtue. Aristotle's stress on the persuasiveness of the speaker's moral character and his rebuke of the sophistical writers for neglecting this element of rhetoric (1356a10-13) thus fortifies the earlier conclusion that Aristotle presents rhetoric as directed to moral ends.

Aristotle's remarks on *ethos* can be confusing, however, unless one differentiates the various ways in which *ethos* enters rhetoric. Comments on the *ethos* of the speaker have just been noted; later in the *Rhetoric* (2. 1. 1378a6-19), it is said that the most persuasive *ethos* for a rhetorician is a combination of "practical wisdom," "virtue" and "goodwill." But this must be distinguished from the expositions on the *ethe* of regimes (1. 8), on the *ethe* of the three periods of life and of the social classes (2. 12-17), and on the *ethe* expressed by the style of a speech (3. 7. 1408a26-33 and 16. 1417a16-35). While the rhetorician should argue in a manner that manifests his own practical knowledge, moral virtue, and goodwill, he should also speak in a way that conforms to the characters of his listeners (as determined both by the collective character of their regime and by their own individual characters); and to do this he should display the required character not only in the form of his arguments, but also in the style of his presentation.[90]

Aristotle says little in this early portion of the *Rhetoric* about the rhetorical appeal to *pathos*; instead he refers the reader to his treatment of the passions in Book Two (1356a13-19). Yet his observation that "we do not render judgments similarly when we are rejoicing and when we are sorrowing or when we are loving and when we are hating" (1356a14-16), suggests a connection between emotion and judgment, which becomes the underlying theme of his subsequent examination of the passions (2. 1. 1378a20-31).

Finally, persuasion through logical argument (*logos*) is said to occur "whenever we show the true or apparently true from the means of persuasion concerning particulars" (1356a19-21). Thus we are reminded that rhetoric requires a knowledge of merely apparent, as well as true, arguments; for as has been noted, Aristotle considers such knowledge necessary in order that the rhetorician may be well armed against those who argue falsely and unjustly (1355a29-37).

It is surely surprising now to reach the end of Aristotle's initial comments on each of the three *pisteis*—*ethos*, *pathos*, and *logos*—without any reference to the enthymeme, which was previously said to be the "body of proof" (*soma tes pisteos*) and the "most authoritative of proofs." One might, of course, infer that Aristotle identifies the enthymeme with persuasion through *logos*, an inference that has been commonly made by interpreters of the *Rhetoric*. There is justification for this view: Aristotle does speak of the appeal to *logos* as some form of logical argumentation (1356a3-4 and 36-37). But it can also be maintained that a weighing of all the evidence shows that the enthymeme cannot be identified with *logos* because it incorporates all three of the *pisteis*—*ethos*, *pathos*, and *logos*.

Aristotle has previously implied that the enthymeme arises somehow from all three *pisteis* by his statement that a speaker becomes a master of the enthymeme through the *pisteis entechnoi;* that is, he does not restrict the enthymeme to only one of the *pisteis* (1354b20-21).

How can the enthymeme encompass so much? The answer is suggested by Aristotle's reference to the enthymeme as the "body of proof":

the enthymeme can be conceived as the underlying foundation on which the *pisteis* hang like clothes draped on a body. The persuasive power of the enthymeme need not be simply "logical"; it can also be "ethical" and "pathetical." The enthymeme can combine thought and feeling.[91]

At this early point in the study of the *Rhetoric*, it is not possible to examine all the evidence for viewing the enthymeme as comprehending the three *pisteis*. But one should note here Aristotle's reference later in the *Rhetoric* (2. 20. 1393a21–24; cf. 1. 2. 1358a1–2) to the enthymeme and the example as "common proofs" (*koinai pisteis*) in contradistinction to the "particular proofs" (*idiai pisteis*). From this it is clear that an understanding of the relationship of the enthymeme to the three *pisteis* requires a grasp of the different ways that Aristotle uses the word *pistis*.

The primary meaning of *pistis* is "belief," "confidence," or "trust." Aristotle uses the term to refer to any belief that arises either from a syllogism or from induction.[92] But in the *Rhetoric* Aristotle employs *pistis* not only in its fundamental meaning of "belief" (e.g., 1. 2. 1355a6 and 9. 1367b30), but also as referring either to the formal logical process leading to belief (enthymeme or example) (e.g., 1. 2. 1356b6–8 and 2. 20. 1393a21–24) or to the material sources of belief (*logos, ethos,* and *pathos*). The rhetorician creates *pistis* in the mind of his listener by reasoning with the *koinai pisteis* (enthymeme and example) based upon the *idiai pisteis* (*logos, ethos,* and *pathos*).[93]

It is clear, then, that the enthymeme is not one of the three *pisteis*. While the enthymeme is, of course, a logical instrument, it is not restricted to the *pistis* of logical demonstration (*logos*); it can also be stated so as to show the character (*ethos*) of the speaker or to affect the emotional state (*pathos*) of the listener.

Rhetoric, Dialectic, and Politics (1356a23–35)

To be skillful in the use of the three *pisteis*, Aristotle concludes, a speaker must be capable of syllogistic reasoning and must also understand the moral characters and the passions of men. "Thus it happens that rhetoric is some sort of offshoot of dialectic and of the subject of morals [*ta ethe*] which is justly called politics" (1356a25–27). It is wrong, however, for rhetoric to be made to appear identical to politics. Rather, rhetoric is some sort of "part" or "likeness" of dialectic since both are powers of providing arguments that are not restricted to the definite subject of any science.

Rhetoric shows a tension between universality and particularity in its subject matter. Since it is an "offshoot" of dialectic, rhetoric is universally applicable to different subjects; but since it is also an "offshoot" of politics, it is restricted to a particular subject matter. In one sense, rhetoric is comprehensive because it reasons from *endoxa*, which are comprehensive. Yet in practice, rhetoric is usually restricted to politically relevant matters.[94]

The respects in which rhetoric is like and the respects in which it is unlike dialectic are now evident. Neither rhetoric nor dialectic has a specific subject matter; nor do they have special premises. Rather, they both reason from probabilities and common opinions, and they both can prove opposites. Rhetoric nonetheless differs from dialectic in two major respects. Although rhetoric is theoretically capable of dealing with all questions, in practice it handles only political subjects. Also, rhetoric is unlike dialectic in that it deals with *particular* cases of action.[95]

Aristotle begins at this point in the text, however, a detailed discussion of what he regards as the most important resemblance between rhetoric and dialectic, which is the resemblance in their forms of inference.

The Enthymeme and the Example (1356a36–1356b25)

By considering rhetoric in correlation to dialectic, Aristotle introduces his theory of logic into his theory of rhetoric. He establishes a correspondence between induction, syllogism, and apparent syllogism in dialectic and example, enthymeme, and apparent enthymeme in rhetoric.[96] He even refers the reader of the *Rhetoric* to the *Analytics* and the *Topics* for explication of the inductive and deductive forms of inference that are the models for rhetorical reasoning.[97]

After speaking of the three *pisteis*, Aristotle turns to enthymeme and example as the fundamental vehicles of *pistis*. "All rhetoricians produce belief [*pistis*] through demonstration [*deiknunai*] — speaking either with examples or enthymemes — and beyond these there is nothing else" (1356b6–7). The remainder of Chapter 2 of Book One is devoted to a study of induction and deduction in rhetorical argument.

Aristotle gives much more attention, however, to rhetorical deduction (the enthymeme) than to rhetorical induction (the example). The reasons for this are, first, that the enthymeme is more forceful than the example and, second, that the example can be understood as a source for or as arising from enthymematic inference (1. 2. 1357b25–37; 2. 20. 1394a9–18; 23. 1398a31–1398b18; 25. 1402b13–21). Hence the enthymeme can be considered the primary instrument of rhetorical reasoning.

Arguments depending on examples, Aristotle says, are as persuasive as those depending on enthymemes; but enthymemes are more effective in winning the applause of a crowd (1356b18-23). Despite the persuasiveness of examples, enthymemes are more logically compelling before an audience.

The Audience and the Subject Matter (1356b26-1357a23)

Aristotle has stressed the correspondence between rhetorical and dialectical reasoning, but he now comments on the distinctive features of rhetorical logic. He explains how the enthymeme and the example differ from the syllogism and from the inductive inference of dialectic with reference to the audience and the subject matter of rhetoric.

Rhetoric concerns practical matters about which men deliberate; and it is addressed to the common people who must judge these matters, people who cannot follow a long or complex argument. By implication, dialectic is more theoretical in its subject matter and is addressed to small groups of interlocutors rather than to large crowds.[98]

The subject of rhetoric is deliberation about human activity. An enthymeme is a syllogism that concerns the objects of human actions and what things are to be chosen or avoided with respect to these actions. Aristotle observes later in the *Rhetoric* (2. 21. 1394a22-33) that the enthymeme, since it is a syllogism, must show the "cause" (*aitia*) and the "wherefore" (*dia ti*) of the maxims guiding human actions (cf. 1. 1. 1354a7-11, 2. 21. 1395b1-8).

An enthymeme, then, could be called a "practical syllogism."[99] But there are at least two important problems that necessarily arise in connection with the "practical syllogism." The first problem, to which Aristotle draws attention in this section of the *Rhetoric* (1356a14-17, 24-33), is that the objects of deliberation—human actions—are contingent phenomena; therefore, practical reasoning can be true "for the most part" (*to polu*)—since human actions do exhibit regularities—but rarely can it produce *necessary* truths. The second problem, which Aristotle indicates elsewhere in the *Rhetoric* (e.g., 1. 10) and in other writings, is that practical reasoning is not purely intellectual since reason leads to action only in connection with "desire" (*orexis*).

Rhetoric—like ethics and political science—involves reasoning from premises that hold only "for the most part" to conclusions of the same character. This is the case because reasoning rarely attains any greater degree of certainty in the realm of human action. But it would be wrong to conclude that rhetorical argumentation is a defective or invalid form of reasoning since it involves probability but not absolute certainty.

Aristotle would maintain that one should seek whatever degree of certainty is appropriate to the subject matter; and in reasoning about human action, probable knowledge is the most that one should expect.[100]

Since rhetoric concerns deliberation and judgment about practical affairs, it can be assumed to pertain to the practical rather than the theoretical intellect: in short, if rhetoric is to control men's practical decisions, it must combine reason and desire.[101] This explains why the enthymeme must combine *logos, ethos,* and *pathos.* The purely logical form of the syllogism must be infused with emotional or appetitive elements so as to elicit both the intellect and the desire of the listener in support of a conviction leading to action.

Rhetorical reasoning is circumscribed not only by its subject matter, however, but also by its audience. The rhetorician usually addresses large crowds of ordinary people, and therefore he must speak so as to be understood by listeners with limited capacities for following arguments.[102] Since his audiences cannot follow long chains of inferences, a rhetorician cannot construct his enthymemes from premises that are themselves the conclusions of prior inferences (1357a8-13). He must employ premises acceptable to his listeners without proof—that is, premises drawn from "reputable opinions" (*endoxa*).

Aristotle is careful to point out, however, that the rhetorician cannot hope to conform to the opinions of each *individual;* but he should know what opinions are typical of each *class* of people (1356b26-34). A speaker cannot take into account the individual differences among his listeners because they are infinite and thus unknowable, but he can know the fundamental character types among men and how to adapt his arguments to each type.

Some premises are so well known that the listener can be expected to add them himself, and so the speaker should leave them unstated. For this reason, the enthymeme often contains fewer premises than the standard syllogism of the first figure (1357a17-23).[103] As a rule, "enthymemes should be condensed as much as possible" (3. 18. 1419a18-19).[104]

Yet Aristotle does not confirm the common assumption that the enthymeme is by definition an incomplete syllogism.[105] Although he lays it down as a practical maxim that speakers need not verbally express elements of an enthymeme that would be familiar to or easily inferred by the listeners, he does not state this to be a necessary characteristic of the enthymeme. It is a practical rule of procedure that forms no part of the definition of the enthymeme.

41

Aristotle instructs the speaker to abbreviate his enthymeme only when he knows that the listener will add the missing element on his own (1356a19). In such a case the enthymeme is "incomplete" only in its verbal expression; in a deeper sense, the enthymeme is a complete syllogism. Even in the most rigorously demonstrative reasoning, Aristotle thinks, premises that are clear or well known need not be explicitly stated. The justification for this is that syllogistic demonstration concerns the "discourse" (*logos*) in the mind, not that which is "external." A syllogism can be incomplete as stated audibly but complete as stated silently in the mind.[106]

Furthermore, the suppression of premises is not simply a concession to the cognitive defects of the audience. For a good speaker does this knowing that, because of their love of learning, listeners delight in supplying the unstated premises themselves. Men enjoy hearing a syllogism that allows them to discover its full meaning for themselves (2. 23. 1400b28-33). This same point is made in the *Port Royal Logic* with the comment that enthymemes are commonly abbreviated because "this suppression flatters the vanity of those to whom we speak, in leaving something to their intelligence, and by abbreviating the discourse, it makes it stronger and more lively," the assumption being that "the nature of the human mind is to prefer rather that something be left it to supply than that one imagine that it needs to be taught everything."[107]

Also, by abbreviating the enthymeme to two statements, of which one follows from the other, the rhetorician makes his reasoning conform to the natural tendency of the mind to inquire into something unknown by connecting it to something known. This makes the enthymeme more forceful, because "things side by side are more apparent to an audience" (2. 23. 1400b27).

Ordinarily, the enthymeme is more difficult to comprehend than the example, because the enthymeme requires reasoning from the general to the particular, while the example consists of reasoning from one particular to another.[108] But if the general premise of an enthymeme is suppressed (see 1357a20-23), the result is a truncated syllogism that moves from particular to particular with an implicit general principle; the enthymeme acquires the concrete immediacy of an example.[109] In this manner the enthymeme becomes a source of "quick learning" (3. 10. 1410b20-21). The rhetorician can benefit from the logical power of deductive reasoning but without making his argument too difficult for the common audience.[110]

It is clear, therefore, that Aristotle thinks that there are good reasons for stating an enthymeme in a truncated form. But it is equally clear that he does not regard the enthymeme as being essentially an incomplete and thus defective syllogism.

The effect of this section of the *Rhetoric* is to cónfirm that rhetorical argument can be genuinely rational despite the uncertainty intrinsic to its subject matter and the cognitive limitations of the audience. Although the practical life of men allows only a knowledge of probabilities, the validity of this knowledge can be denied only by assuming fallaciously that whatever lacks absolute certainty is necessarily false (see 2. 25. 1402b21–1403a2). And although the listeners have a limited capacity for reasoning, they do have a love of learning that makes them receptive to arguments that are informative without being esoteric.

Probabilities and Signs (1357a24–1357b25)

Aristotle provides one of his clearest expositions of the syllogistic character of the enthymeme in his comments on "probabilities" (*eikota*) and "signs" (*semeia*) as the sources of enthymematic reasoning. His remarks here and the passages that he cites in the *Prior Analytics* make it clear that enthymemes can be classified according to the three figures of the syllogism as analyzed in his logical treatises, which shows once again the falsity of the assumption that enthymemes cannot be complete syllogisms.

Applying his modal logic to rhetorical syllogisms, Aristotle explains that the premises of enthymemes can be "necessary" or "probable," but that they are usually "probable" since the subjects of rhetorical argument generally involve only probabilities.[111] An enthymeme is an inference from "necessary" premises to a "necessary" conclusion and is therefore an irrefutable syllogism if it is founded on a "necessary sign," which is called a *tekmerion*.[112] But most enthymemes are constructed from "probabilities" or "non-necessary signs."

Aristotle's distinction between "probabilities" and "signs" is somewhat obscure.[113] But this passage in the *Prior Analytics* (70a2–10) to which he refers the reader of the *Rhetoric* (1357b21–25) contains the clearest statement of the distinction:

A probability [*eikos*] is a generally accepted premise [*endoxos*]; for that which people know as for the most part happening or not happening, being or not being, this is a probability, such as that the envious hate or those who are loved are friendly. But a sign means a demonstrative premise necessary or generally accepted [*anangkaia e endoxos*]; for that which exists with something else or that which happens before or after something else happens, is a sign of something having happened or being.

An *eikos*, then, is a general principle (see 1357a35-1357b2) as to the probability that something is or is not, happens or does not happen, founded upon the commonsense experience of men. For example, the general premise that those who are loved are likely to be affectionate in return can be joined to the particular premise that this person is loved, which produces the conclusion that this person is likely to be affectionate. A "sign," on the other hand, is something that by its own existence or occurrence signifies the existence or occurrence of that with which, after which, or before which it exists or occurs. For example, when a woman has milk, this is a necessary sign of a recent pregnancy because lactation necessarily occurs upon the cessation of pregnancy.[114] In short, the "sign" is something known that, because of its inner structure, has a relationship to something unknown; the *eikos* has no such relationship but is rather a general probable proposition that yields a probable conclusion when applied to a particular case.[115] But what is the epistemological status of "probabilities" and "signs"? Are they all valid forms of knowledge, or are some of them partially or even totally false?

"Probabilities" can be false, of course, in exceptional cases since by definition "probabilities" apply only "for the most part"; but this does not prevent them from being genuine sources of knowledge (2. 25. 1402b21-37).[116] Furthermore, Aristotle testifies to the epistemological solidity of the *eikos* by defining it as a proposition established as a common opinion (*endoxos*), as something "which men *know* happens or does not happen, is or is not, for the most part in this way."[117]

"Signs," however, are more difficult to evaluate. Aristotle leaves no doubt as to the validity of the "necessary sign" (the *tekmerion*). But while he declares the *tekmerion* to be syllogistic and irrefutable, he describes the "non-necessary signs" as unsyllogistic and refutable (1357b6-21). And although he speaks here of "signs" as sources of enthymemes, later in the *Rhetoric* (2. 24. 1401b8-13) he classifies the "sign" as a fallacious topic from which apparent, rather than true, enthymemes arise.

A clearer view of Aristotle's theory of "signs" can be gained by examining his analysis of "signs" according to the three figures of the syllogism (1357b11-25). This passage is especially instructive when read in conjunction with the parallel passage in the *Prior Analytics* (70a11-70b6).

A *tekmerion* can be expressed as a syllogism in the first figure; and as long as the premises are true, the conclusion of such a syllogism is irrefutable (1357b14-17).[118] But "non-necessary signs" can be expressed only in the second or the third figures, a condition which means that they are imperfect and thus refutable inferences (1357b11–14, 18–21).[119]

The three figures may be differentiated according to the position of the middle term. If one wishes to prove A of B, Aristotle says, one must find something that is common in relation to both; A must be predicated of B through a middle term C. This may be done in three ways—"by predicating A of C and C of B [the first figure], or C of both [the second figure], or both of C [the third figure]."[120]

An example of a "necessary sign" stated as a first-figure syllogism would be: Every lactating woman (C) has recently been pregnant (A); this woman (B) is lactating (C); therefore, this woman (B) has been pregnant (A).[121] Assuming the truth of the premises, the conclusion follows necessarily.

An example of a "non-necessary sign" stated as a second-figure syllogism would be: Every pregnant woman (A) is pale (C); this woman (B) is pale (C); therefore, this woman (B) is pregnant (A).[122] But in fact this is not a valid syllogism at all, because the middle term is undistributed (used particularly) in both premises. The predicate of every affirmative proposition is undistributed, and here the middle term is the predicate of two affirmative premises.[123] A woman's paleness is not necessarily a "sign" of pregnancy, because while some women who are pale are pregnant, some are pale and yet not pregnant. The example in the *Rhetoric* (1357b18–21) of a second-figure "sign"—"it is a sign that this man has a fever, because he breathes hard"—exhibits the same fallacy.

The fallaciousness of these "signs," however, is not due to their being second-figure inferences. Any syllogism in this figure is "imperfect," but it can still be a valid syllogism if it accords with the rules for second-figure syllogisms.[124] By merely negating the minor premise of the above fallacious inference, for example, one could construct the following genuine syllogism: Every pregnant woman (A) is pale (C); this woman (B) is *not* pale (C); therefore, this woman (B) is *not* pregnant (A).

Aristotle's example in the *Rhetoric* (1357b11–14) of a third-figure "sign"-inference can be stated as follows: Socrates (C) is wise (A); Socrates (C) is just (B); therefore, wise men (A) are just (B). If the conclusion is intended to refer to *all* wise men, then the inference is obviously fallacious, since the two particular premises about Socrates cannot entail a universal conclusion as to all wise men.[125] Furthermore, no valid syllogism in the third-figure can have a universal conclusion.[126] This inference would be valid if the conclusion were particular rather than universal. The combination in Socrates of wisdom and goodness does prove that at least some wise men are good.

It should also be noticed that Aristotle's third-figure "sign" is an argument through example transformed into an enthymeme, for it reasons from the particular to the general (1357b11-12). Here as well as elsewhere in the *Rhetoric*—and in the logical treatises—Aristotle assumes that examples can be stated as enthymemes just as induction can be stated syllogistically.[127]

What, then, is the significance of Aristotle's subsequent classification of the "sign" as a fallacy from which only *apparent* enthymemes can arise (2. 24. 1401b8-18)? First, it is evident from the two examples that he uses in this passage that he is referring only to *non-necessary* "signs" (cf. 2. 15. 1402b13-14). The first example—"Lovers benefit cities, for the love of Harmodius and Aristogiton overthrew the tyrant Hipparchus"—draws a universal conclusion from a particular case and is thus comparable to the previous enthymeme concerning Socrates. The second example—"Dionysius is a thief, for he is bad [*poneros*]"—could be stated as a second-figure enthymeme with the same fallacy (an undistributed middle term) as the previous illustrations of second-figure "signs."[128]

But why does Aristotle speak early in the *Rhetoric* of "signs" as sources of enthymemes without explaining until much later that fallacious "signs" can be sources of apparent but not true enthymemes? One answer would be that since he has stressed from the beginning that rhetoric includes a knowledge of apparent as well as true reasoning (1. 1. 1355a29-1355b1, 1355b14-22, 2. 1356a19-21, 1356a36-1356b6) — not for the sake of practicing unjust deception, but in order to be fully informed and capable of counteracting unjust uses of false arguments—Aristotle can assume that his readers will recognize that fallacious "signs" are suitable for only apparent enthymemes.

But although this is probably part of the explanation, it may also be the case that Aristotle is reluctant to dismiss these obviously defective "signs" as totally false. "Necessary signs" are clearly superior to the "non-necessary signs," because the former can be stated as first-figure syllogisms, and reasoning through this figure is "most generally accepted [*endoxotaton*] and most true" (*An. Pr.* 70b5-6).[129] But even "non-necessary signs" contain some truth, for "there is truth in all signs" (*An. Pr.* 70a38). That Socrates was both wise and good does signify that at least *some* wise men can be good, and knowing that a man is bad should justify the *suspicion* that he might be a thief.

It is often difficult to distinguish clearly truth and falsity in rhetorical arguments. Aristotle thinks it is important for rhetoric that such a distinction be made, as is evident in his differentiation of true and apparent enthymemes; but he also acknowledges that in some cases the distinction becomes blurred.

Examples (1357b26–37)

Having spoken about the sources of enthymemes, Aristotle now briefly turns his attention to examples. What he says is sufficient to show that examples may be considered subordinate to enthymemes.

Reasoning through examples requires a relation "neither of part to whole, nor of whole to part, nor of whole to whole, but of part to part, of like to like, whenever both are under the same genus, but one is better known than the other" (1356b27-29). An example differs, therefore, not only from deduction, which moves from whole to part, but also from induction, which moves from part to whole.[130] While induction reasons from all the particulars to a generalization, example reasons from only one or several well-known particulars to a generalization and then immediately applies the generalization to another particular that is less known.[131]

Since reasoning by examples implies general propositions, such reasoning is actually syllogistic. For instance, concluding that Dionysius is seeking to become a tyrant because he asks for a bodyguard, citing the examples of other rulers who have become tyrants after obtaining bodyguards, is a syllogistic inference with the major premise being that rulers who ask for bodyguards are scheming to become tyrants (1357b30-37).[132] Examples, therefore, can be a source for enthymemes by providing probable universal principles that can serve as major premises (2. 23. 1398a33-1398b20, 15. 1402b17).[133] Clearly, then, as was already evident from his illustration of the third-figure "sign" (1357b11-14), Aristotle thinks that argument by example can be understood as one form of enthymematic reasoning.

Specific Topics and Common Topics (1358a1–36)

Rhetoric is the counterpart of dialectic, Aristotle has argued, insofar as the art of rhetoric rests essentially upon the three *pisteis* and upon the enthymeme ("the body of *pistis*"). But except for some brief remarks on the three *pisteis,* Aristotle has devoted his attention primarily to the enthymeme as the vehicle of rhetorical argumentation.

Aristotle now indicates, however, that his previous discussion of enthymemes as syllogisms based on "probabilities" and "signs" did not touch upon an additional point of correspondence between rhetorical and dialectical reasoning. There is a distinction in rhetoric and dialectic between inferences derived from "common topics" and those derived from "special topics"; therefore, there is "a very great difference between enthymemes" (1358a1-2) that has been ignored by almost everyone.

Strictly speaking, dialectical and rhetorical syllogisms are concerned with the "topics" that are "common" to many different arts or sciences. The "topic" of "more and less," for example, can provide syllogisms or enthymemes for law, physics, or politics.[134] As Aristotle has already said in the first line of the *Rhetoric*, rhetoric and dialectic are forms of reasoning that are common to all types of knowledge and known by all, and so they differ from reasoning that is peculiar to a specialized discipline and known only by specialists.

"Topics" that are "specific" (*idia*), on the other hand, are propositions applicable only to a particular "species or genus" (*eidos kai genos*). Such topics are known only by those with specialized knowledge of the particular subject matter.

Oddly enough, in order to employ purely rhetorical syllogisms, a speaker would have to avoid using any of the propositions specifically applicable to the particular subject under discussion. But in the actual practice of rhetoric, this does not occur; more enthymemes are constructed from "specific topics" than from "common topics." The reason for this is that arguments are stronger if they consist not of general topics, but of particular premises inherent in the subject matter.[135]

Thus Aristotle once again brings to light the tension between rhetoric as a universal method comparable to dialectic and rhetoric as restricted to political argumentation. Being an "offshoot" both of dialectic and of politics, rhetoric requires both a general knowledge of what would be persuasive in any situation and a specialized knowledge of the modes of argument appropriate to political matters.

Aristotle concludes this section of the *Rhetoric* (1358a29-36) by indicating that he will speak first about the "specific topics" (*eide*) of rhetoric and then about the "common topics." But before that he must distinguish the "kinds" (*ta gene*) of rhetoric so that his treatment of the *eide* may be organized accordingly.

The Three Kinds of Rhetoric (1. 3)

Aristotle discusses the three kinds of rhetoric with reference to the three kinds of hearers (1358a36-1358b8), to the three kinds of speeches (1358b8-13), to the three "times" (1358b13-21), and to the three substantive ends of rhetoric (1358b21-1359a6).

Of the three elements of the rhetorical situation—the speaker, the speech, and the listener—the listener is the most decisive, because everything else is aimed at him: rhetoric is for the sake of persuading the listener. Previously, emotional appeal (*pathos*) was said to be the element of rhetoric directed to the audience (1. 2. 1356a1–4); but in some sense every element of rhetoric involves the audience. Indeed, most of the *Rhetoric* concerns audiences—their characters, their opinions, and their passions. The display of the speaker's character, the premises of his enthymemes, the style and arrangement of his speech, and, of course, the emotional features of his presentation—all must conform to the nature of the men to whom he speaks.

The listener, according to Aristotle, is either a member of a political assembly, who judges what is to come, or a member of a jury, who judges things in the past, or simply a spectator, who is concerned with the ability of the speaker. In all three cases the listener is some sort of judge (see 2. 18. 1391b7–20), and therefore there are three corresponding kinds of rhetoric, which differ according to the kinds of judgment involved: "deliberative" (*sumbouleutikon*), "forensic" (*dikanikon*), and "epideictic" (*epideiktikon*).[136] In deliberative rhetoric the speaker engages in exhortation (*to protrope*) or dehortation (*to apotrope*), in forensic accusation or defense, and in epideictic praise or blame.

In addition, Aristotle classifies the three types of rhetoric according to the three "times": forensic rhetoric concerns things in the past; epideictic, things in the present; and deliberative, things in the future.[137] By using this tripartition of time, which he also employs in distinguishing the types of audience, Aristotle insures that his classification is comprehensive, because past, present, and future exhaust the possibilities. In some cases, however, the temporal distinctions do not fit exactly. Deliberative rhetoric, for instance, is often concerned with things in the present (1. 6. 1362a16–17, 8. 1366a17–18); and the praise and blame of epideictic rhetoric often depend on past or future deeds (1358b18–21).

Up to this point, Aristotle's differentiation of the three kinds of rhetoric has been largely formal, for he has abstracted from their substantive content.[138] But he now distinguishes them according to their substantive "ends": deliberative rhetoric concerns the expedient or the harmful; forensic, the just or the unjust; epideictic, the noble or the shameful.[139] That the types of rhetoric must be classified according to their respective moral and political subjects reinforces the point noted earlier that rhetoric cannot be entirely a formal discipline abstracted from any particular subject matter since it is closely bound to the realm of politics.

The nature of each of these three ends of rhetoric—expediency, nobility, and justice—can be examined best in connection with the subsequent chapters of Book One, in which Aristotle discusses each in turn. But his initial statement of the tripartition (1358b21–1359a6) raises a question as to the relationship between "expediency" and "justice."

Will the deliberative rhetorician support whatever policy is expedient, regardless of its justice or injustice? Aristotle cites the case of the deliberative speaker who can discuss the enslavement of a neighboring city without considering whether it is just or not (1358b36–1359a1). This apparent reference to the speeches of the Athenian envoys to Melos suggests that war and foreign relations generally might provide the most obvious situations in which justice has to be secondary to expediency.[140] This does not mean, however, that Aristotle considers the deliberative rhetorician to be unconcerned with justice.

In deliberative speech, justice and expediency are commonly assumed to be complementary if not even identical standards for judging political action (1. 6. 1362b28, 15. 1375b3–4, 3. 17. 1417b35–37). This is so because in its political sense, "expediency" (*to sumpheron*) refers to the interest of the community (*to koinon sumpheron*) rather than to the interest of private individuals (*to idion sumpheron*). As long as the politically "expedient" is understood to be what serves the common interest, rather than the private interest of some individuals, expediency and justice are less likely to conflict.[141]

The Three "Commonplaces" (1359a7–29)

It is clear from what has been said that the rhetorician must have propositions (in the form of "signs" and "probabilities") pertinent to the three subjects—expediency, nobility, and justice—of the three kinds of rhetoric (1359a6–12). But in addition, certain types of propositions are required for all three kinds of rhetoric; and these Aristotle calls the *koina*, which may be translated as "commonplaces" (see 2. 18. 1391b22–1392a7).

These "commonplaces" fall into three types, for such propositions deal with whether something is possible or impossible, with whether something has occurred or will occur, or with whether things are greater or less. While saving his detailed comments for later in the book (2. 19), Aristotle does indicate the pertinence of these "commonplaces" to all three kinds of rhetoric. Regardless of whether a speech consists of judging the past, the present, or the future, there must be some consideration of whether something is possible or impossible and of whether or not something has taken place or will take place. Similarly, irrespective of whether the subject is goodness and badness, nobility and ignobility, or justice and injustice, there must be some assessment of how these properties are possessed in greater or less degrees.

The "commonplaces" should not be confused with the "common topics" mentioned earlier. Aristotle distinguishes three kinds of "topics": "specific topics" (*eide*), "commonplaces" (*koina*), and "common topics" (*koinoi topoi*). The *eide* provide premises appropriate to each of the three subjects of rhetoric (1. 2. 1358a16-21 and 29-36). The *koina* provide premises that are not specific to each of the three subjects but applicable to all three in common (1. 3. 1359a7-27, 2. 18. 1391b22-1392a7).[142] The *koinoi topoi*—also called "the topics of enthymemes"—are formal methods of inference according to which enthymemes can be constructed through the use of the premises provided by the *eide* and *koina* (2. 22. 1396b28-1397a6, 26. 1403a16-24).[143] The "topics" can be classified as material or formal. The material "topics" provide premises for enthymemes; the formal ones provide methods of reasoning. The material "topics" are either specific (*eide*) or general (*koina*); the formal "topics" are general lines of argument (*koinoi topoi*).

One of the benefits of being attentive to Aristotle's differentiation of the three kinds of "topics," is that the organization of the first two books of the *Rhetoric* becomes manifest. And at this point in this commentary—after completing Aristotle's general statement of his theory (1. 1-3) and before entering into his studies of the subjects of rhetoric (1. 4-15)—it seems appropriate to examine the organization of the entire book in order to discern what plan Aristotle has for working out in detail the various elements of his theory of rhetoric.

The Organization of the Book

Books One and Two

Aristotle's handling both of the "topics" and of the *pisteis* shows that, after his first three chapters, he organizes books One and Two so as to move from the particular to the general. From Chapter 4 of Book One to the end of Chapter 17 of Book Two, he presents the "specific topics" (the *eide*) and the particular *pisteis (logos, ethos,* and *pathos*); then at the end of Book Two, he considers the general "topics"—the "commonplaces" (2. 18-19) and the "common topics" (2. 22-24) and the general *pisteis*—enthymeme and example (2. 20-26). It could also be argued that this movement is from a treatment of the particular sources of the enthymeme to a treatment of the enthymeme in general.[144]

Yet many of the scholarly commentators on the *Rhetoric* have found the book to lack a unified organization and have concluded that it must be a compilation of different manuscripts.[145] They find the plan of organization I have sketched unintelligible, because it assumes a view of the enthymeme that is unacceptable to them—that is, it assumes that Aristotle's treatments of the characters and passions of men (2. 1-17) comprise a part of his treatment of the materials of the enthymeme. Since they regard the enthymeme as a purely logical proof that is unrelated to the presentation of a speaker's character or to the emotional state of the listeners, the first half of Book Two (2. 1-17) seems to be an unjustified interlude between Aristotle's discussion in Book One (1. 4-15) of the substantive material of the enthymeme and his discussion in the second half of Book Two (2. 18-26) of its formal logical properties.

But Aristotle sees the entirety of Books One and Two as a single unit in which he examines all the elements of the enthymeme. Late in Book Two he sketches his conception of the unity of his work (2. 22. 1396b28-1397a6):

> We now nearly have the topics about each of the specific subjects [*eide*] that are useful and necessary; for propositions about each thing have been selected so that from these topics enthymemes must be derived about the good and the evil, the noble and the shameful, the just and the unjust; also about the characters, the passions, and the dispositions we have similarly selected topics. Let us now take up all these things in another more general way; and let us speak in passing of refutative and demonstrative enthymemes, and of apparent enthymemes, which are not enthymemes since they are not syllogisms. These points having been made clear, let us define the matters concerning solutions and objections, whence they must be derived with respect to enthymemes.

Hence Books One and Two of the *Rhetoric*, from beginning to end, present a theory of rhetorical argumentation founded on the enthymeme as the instrument that combines all the elements of persuasion. Aristotle's procedure in handling the *ethe* and *pathe* is essentially the same as in his handling of the substantive issues of rhetoric, for in each case he is providing topics or propositions from which enthymemes can be constructed (see 2. 1. 1378a28-31, 3. 1380b30-33, 20. 1393a21-24). Once it is recognized that the enthymeme encompasses all three *pisteis* — *logos, ethos,* and *pathos* — that it is the rhetorical vehicle not only for purely logical proof but also for displaying the moral and intellectual virtues of the speakers and for dealing with the emotions and characters of the listeners, the unity of these first two books of the *Rhetoric* becomes apparent.

Book Three, however, presents special problems. But despite its peculiarities, it too can be seen to be an integral part of the *Rhetoric.*

Book Three

Aristotle says that a speech has three fundamental elements: "thought" (*dianoia*), "style" (*lexis*), and "arrangement" (*taxis*) (2. 26. 1403a34-1403b1, 3. 1. 1403b7-13). The first two books of the *Rhetoric* present the "thought" of a speech under all its aspects. (The implicit inclusion of *ethos* and *pathos* as parts of the "thought" of a speech should be noted. See *Poet.* 1450a6-7, 1456a35-1456b19.) The first part of Book Three is devoted to "style" and the second to "arrangement." The last book is thus the natural completion of Aristotle's project; for, after setting forth his theory of rhetorical argument, he must discuss the style and the arrangement of the actual verbal expression of a speech.

But there is an obvious contrast between the stress on the intellectual or even philosophic side of rhetoric in the first two books and the stress on the verbal elements of rhetoric in the final book.[146] Furthermore, Aristotle is clearly reluctant to enter into the material of Book Three: he views much of it as merely a necessary concession to "the corruption of the listener" (1404a8).

Nevertheless, Aristotle believes that even the rules of style and composition should be designed to facilitate the presentation of a speaker's argument. The ultimate aim of good style and good composition is to allow listeners to follow the speaker's reasoning as easily as possible. I shall consider these matters at greater length later. Now it is sufficient to say that, viewed in this light, the material in Book Three is consistent with the emphasis in the first two books on the rationality of rhetoric.

3

DELIBERATIVE RHETORIC (1. 4-8)

Political Subjects (4)

Rhetoric and the Subjects of Deliberation (1359a30–1359b18)

Aristotle begins his treatment of deliberative rhetoric by explaining that the "commonplace" of the possible and the impossible must be employed to determine whether a subject is or is not an object of deliberation. Men deliberate about things that are possible, but not about things that are impossible or things that occur by necessity. Even among possible things, those that occur by nature or by chance are not suitable subjects for deliberative rhetoric; for since such things are not under human control, to deliberate about them would be vain.

Why, then, does Aristotle subsequently discuss certain things that are due to nature or to chance, an example of which is his listing of "good fortune" among the parts of happiness (1. 5. 1361b37–1362a15)? The deliberative rhetorician, it would seem, needs a knowledge not only of the actual subjects of deliberation but also of all the elements of human nature that influence deliberation. This is so even if these elements are not themselves subjects of deliberation. For example, insofar as physical beauty is a gift of fortune, it is not something about which men deliberate; nevertheless, the deliberative rhetorician must take account of the desire for beauty as a motive that affects men's deliberations.

But although things occurring by chance, by necessity, or by nature, may *influence* deliberation, they are not *subjects* of deliberation. For men deliberate only about what is within the realm of human action, "those subjects about which we take counsel; and such are all those which can naturally be referred to ourselves and the first cause of whose genesis is from us" (1359a36–38).

Since deliberative rhetoric concerns the things of human action, it has the same subject matter as ethics and politics. But once again Aristotle must stress the tension between rhetoric as a universal method unrestricted to a particular subject and rhetoric as applied to political

55

subjects, for rhetoric combines dialectical logic and the part of political science that concerns ethics.[1] Hence, rhetoric cannot attain the exactness of political science, although it treats political matters, because otherwise it would be a specialized science rather than a universal faculty of speech (1359b8-17).

For the purposes of rhetoric, Aristotle says, it is not necessary to enumerate and classify with exactness the subjects of political deliberation. Nor is it necessary to define them "according to the truth" (*kata ten aletheian*); for "this belongs not to the art of rhetoric but to one more practically wise [*emphronestera*] and more truthful; and further, more than its suitable subjects of inquiry have even now been assigned to it" (1359b2-7). Thus Aristotle repeats the point made previously that rhetorical syllogisms should be restricted to "common topics" rather than "specific topics" and therefore that rhetorical reasoning "does not make one practically wise [*emphrona*] about any class of things, for it does not concern any particular subject matter" (1. 2. 1358a11-23). Even so, he concedes that he has already violated this principle by giving rhetoric "more than its suitable subjects of inquiry."[2] In other words, viewed from one perspective, the art of rhetoric should not deal with specific political subjects; but from another perspective, the successful practice of rhetoric requires a good knowledge of these subjects (see 2. 22. 1396a4-1396b19).

Aristotle concludes that he must speak about the subjects of political deliberation where these are pertinent to rhetoric. But he indicates that his treatment will be necessarily incomplete since some things must be left for inquiry through political science (1359b17-18).

It is evident, therefore, that the substantive accounts in the *Rhetoric* of ethical and political subjects are not intended to be as rigorous and comprehensive as the treatments of these same subjects in the *Nicomachean Ethics* or the *Politics*. But this need not imply, as some commentators suggest, that the expositions in the *Rhetoric* are thought by Aristotle to be simply false.[3] A close examination of these portions of the *Rhetoric* will show that the analysis of political and ethical subjects is worked out with great care and that it does not radically contradict the arguments of the *Ethics* or the *Politics*. One may justifiably infer that Aristotle regards these discussions in the *Rhetoric*, like the common opinions on which they are founded, as being somewhat defective and yet always in some way reflecting the truth.

The Five Most Important Subjects (1359b19-1360b3)

The five most important subjects about which all men deliberate are revenue, war and peace, the defense of the country, imports and exports (particularly with respect to food), and legislation.[4] The central subject is the military installations for defense of the city against attacks. This is consistent with the character of the list as a whole; for, except for the last subject mentioned, each concerns the material conditions of political life and specifically economic and military strength.

However, Aristotle concludes his remarks about these subjects of deliberation by declaring that the "greatest and most ruling" means of persuasion for the deliberative speaker is a knowledge of how the laws express the character of each regime. Although material conditions are obviously important, the ruling concerns are to preserve the form of the regime so that it is neither relaxed nor strained to excess and to maintain a harmony between the character of the regime and the character of the people (1360a18-36).[5]

The end of deliberative rhetoric is "expediency," but what is "expedient" varies according to the nature of the regime (1360a17-37). Thus Aristotle implies that although he does not analyze the regimes until Chapter 8, he considers the intervening material in Chapters 5 through 7 (on happiness and goodness) to be subordinate to his regime analysis. The deliberative rhetorician must view the end of his regime as architectonic, as that which comprehends happiness and the good.

Furthermore, the character of the regime as expressed in law would seem to be supreme not only for deliberative rhetoric but also for epideictic and forensic. Obviously, forensic rhetoric depends upon the law and thus the nature of the regime. And epideictic rhetoric rests to a great extent upon definitions of virtue and vice and nobility and ignobility that are determined by the law (see 1. 9. 1366b9-15).

Hence, of the five most important subjects for deliberative rhetoric, the subjects that concern the material conditions of a regime—economic and military resources—are essential; and yet the subject of legislation is still in some sense the most critical. The reason is that legislation, which reflects and preserves the character of the regime, regulates the lives of all who live under its authority; and the ends of legislation encompass all the ends of human action, a category so broad as to include the final end of all action—happiness.[6]

Happiness (5)

The Definitions of Happiness (1360b4–18)

The universal end for nearly all men, both as individuals and as members of communities, Aristotle says, is "happiness" (*eudaimonia*).

And all deliberative speakers must present themselves as supporting whatever promotes happiness and opposing whatever detracts from it (1360b4–14). Hence, deliberative rhetoric is the most comprehensive of the three kinds of rhetoric because it concerns the most comprehensive end of human activity.

Although all three types of rhetoric are in some manner political, deliberative rhetoric concerns the ultimate aims of political life as manifest in the character of the regime; for as with the character of an individual man, so too is the character of a political community defined by that conception of happiness or goodness that guides all activity.[7] Therefore, insofar as deliberative rhetoric involves discussion of happiness or goodness, it is the architectonic form of rhetoric.[8]

Aristotle's view of all human action as aiming at happiness could be characterized as a kind of elevated "egoism." "For the most part," W. D. Ross comments, "Aristotle's moral system is decidedly self-centered. It is at his own *eudaimonia* [well-being] we are told, that man aims and should aim."[9] And perhaps in no other work is Aristotle's "egoism" more evident than in the *Rhetoric*; it is surely safe to assume that this explains its influence on Hobbes.[10]

But does Aristotle provide here in the *Rhetoric* a true account of happiness? Or is it the case that the limitations of rhetoric are such that he is compelled to present a view of happiness that is somewhat distorted, if not simply false? This problem arises with respect to all the political and moral subjects handled in Book One of the *Rhetoric*. In each case the reader must wonder whether Aristotle, in dealing with the subject at hand in a manner suitable for rhetoric, has been forced to set aside his own philosophic understanding of the matter in favor of a more popular account that he would regard as partially, and perhaps even totally, false. The fundamental question concerns to what extent, if at all, rhetoric can be a vehicle for truth.

As in his discussion of goodness (6), degrees of goodness (7), injustice (10), and pleasure (11), Aristotle begins his study of happiness with a definition upon which all his subsequent comments depend. Hence, one's evaluation of his treatments of happiness and the other subjects of rhetoric in Book One will be determined largely by how one evaluates his definitions.

Cope judges in his commentary that the definitions in the *Rhetoric* are superficial and incomplete and in some cases contradictory to definitions given elsewhere in Aristotle's works.[11] Cope takes the fact that Aristotle introduces most of his major definitions with the word *esto* ("let it be") to signify the defectiveness of the definitions.[12] He interprets these uses of *esto* as conveying the thought, "let it be assumed that any of these definitions is sufficient; it is not required that they should be exact, so long as they are accepted and intelligible."[13]

Undoubtedly Aristotle considers it sufficient for the purposes of rhetoric to provide definitions that most men will find persuasive, even though they lack the exactness of scientific or philosophic definitions. But Aristotle's concern that definitions be only as exact as is appropriate for the subject matter is evident in other works besides the *Rhetoric*.[14] It is surely true that the rhetorician must often employ whatever definitions are most intelligible to his audience rather than those most intelligible "absolutely" (*haplos*), but this does not mean that his definitions and the reasoning founded upon them must be simply false.[15]

Furthermore, Aristotle's use of *esto* need not be interpreted as signifying that he considers his definitions to be popular but imprecise statements.[16] For example, he introduces his definition of rhetoric at the beginning of the *Rhetoric* (1355b25-26) with *esto,* and he clearly intends this to be a rather precise and technical definition. He even employs *esto* in his *Analytics* for stating premises or terms.[17] In fact, the discussions in the *Rhetoric* that begin with definitions introduced by *esto* are so carefully constructed as to be comparable to a geometric proof.[18]

Aristotle reasons from his definitions in a rigorously deductive manner. Those chapters in Book One that are organized around definitions (5, 6, 7, 9, 10, 11) display almost exactly the same pattern. He begins by explaining briefly why the subject at hand must be taken up. He then gives a definition or a set of definitions. If he gives a series of definitions, he arranges them in the order of their relative comprehensiveness, from the more to the less comprehensive. He then lists particular items in a manner that shows them to follow deductively from the previous definition or set of definitions.

It is clear, then, that Aristotle is here using what he later describes as the general enthymematic topic derived from definition to organize specific topics (*eide*) in an enthymematically deductive manner (2. 23. 1398a15-28).[19] His procedure in each case is first to reason syllogistically by stating a definition, then to state that some particular thing satisfies the definition, and then to conclude that the particular thing in question is a part of whatever has been defined. Although it is rarely necessary for Aristotle to state explicitly the full inferences, the deductive connections are evident in his frequent statements that if the definition is true, then such and such "necessarily" (*anangke*) belongs to the thing defined.[20] Once again the primacy of the enthymeme in the *Rhetoric* is apparent.

The organization of Aristotle's expositions into deductive patterns moving from definitions to conclusions often depends upon a careful use of conjunctions. This is the case with respect to his treatment of happiness. He starts with a series of four definitions linked by the conjunction "or" (*e*) (1360b15-18). Next he lists the parts of happiness, saying that if happiness is as he defines it, then these must "by necessity" (*anangke*) be elements of happiness (1360b19-24). Then he uses the conjunction "for" (*gar*) three times in explaining the specific connections of these parts of happiness to the previous definitions (1360b25-31). He devotes the rest of the chapter to comments on each of the previously listed parts of happiness, and he employs the conjunctions *men* and *de* (1360b32-1362a15).[21] Thus, what might at first glance appear to be a random collection of remarks turns out after closer inspection to be a very carefully organized statement.

Having examined the formal, deductive structure of Aristotle's comments on happiness, one needs now to scrutinize the definitions from which everything else is deduced.

Aristotle states, "Let happiness be well-doing with virtue [*eupraxis met' aretes*], or self-sufficiency of life, or the most pleasant life with security, or abundance of possessions and bodies with power to guard and use them; for nearly all men agree that one or more of these is happiness" (1360b15-19).

These definitions rest upon the common agreement of nearly all men, which is consistent with what Aristotle has said previously about the need for rhetoric to be founded upon *endoxa*.[22] It is clearly indicated, however, that a few men would not accept any of the definitions and that some would accept one or more but not all four. It has already been noted with respect to *endoxa* that not all opinions are reliable; instead, only those opinions held by many ordinary men over a long period of time or those held by a few men distinguished for their practical wisdom are reliable.[23]

But are these definitions consistent with Aristotle's ethical doctrines in the *Nicomachean Ethics?* Cope maintains that the teaching in the *Ethics* that happiness is attained most fully in contemplation is absent from the *Rhetoric*. He concedes, however, that the first three definitions in the *Rhetoric* are consistent with the conception of happiness elaborated in the *Ethics*. The fourth definition, he says, applies only to a community, not to individuals, because the term *euthenia* ("abundance") was commonly employed with reference to the prosperity of an entire city.[24]

Another commentator has suggested that the first definition — "well-doing with virtue" — corresponds to what is described at the end of the *Ethics* (1178a9-24) as "secondary" happiness — that is, the happiness that comes from being morally, but not intellectually, virtuous.[25] But the phrase "well-doing with virtue" can be interpreted as including intellectual virtue. In the section of the *Politics* in which Aristotle applies the teaching of the *Ethics* to political life, he decides that "well-doing with virtue" is an adequate definition of happiness and the best life (1323b21-1324a4). Although initially this might seem inadequate, since "well-doing" (*eupraxia*) seems to apply more to the life of action than to the life of contemplation (1325a17-23), "well-doing," properly understood, includes contemplation. Indeed, contemplation is the highest form of "activity" (*praxis*) (1325b14-31).

The second definition of happiness — "self-sufficiency of life" — is also consistent with the *Nicomachean Ethics* (see 1097b7-21, 1176b4-7, 1177a28-1177b8). Aristotle stresses the self-sufficiency of happiness in the next chapter of the *Rhetoric* when he says that happiness is a good because it is "desirable for itself and self-sufficient and for the sake of it we desire many things" (1. 6. 1362b11-12), which corresponds closely to the definition of happiness in the *Nicomachean Ethics* (1097b20) as "something final [*teleion*] and self-sufficient, being the end [*telos*] of actions."

The third and fourth definitions, with their references to pleasure, security, and possessions, seem rather prosaic. But it should be kept in mind that Aristotle makes it very clear in the *Ethics* that despite the preeminence of the goods of the soul, the goods of the body and external goods are also important, if not essential, for happiness. Thus these latter two definitions, like the first two, should be recognized as fully consistent with the teaching of the *Nicomachean Ethics* about happiness.

The Parts of Happiness (1360b19–1362a15)

After stating the four definitions, Aristotle deduces a list of the parts of happiness. All except two are deduced from the second definition — self-sufficiency — and they are either goods of the soul, goods of the body, or external goods. This leaves only "good fortune," and Aristotle deduces it from the third definition by saying that "good fortune" is necessary for security of life.

But he also mentions "powers" (*dunameis*) as connected with "good fortune," although he does not include "powers" in the initial list or in his subsequent comments in the remainder of the chapter. It is unclear as to whether "powers" refers to capacities of the mind or body or to political "powers" of some sort (see 1. 6. 1362b25-27, 2. 17. 1391a20-29). The latter seems more likely, since this reading would explain the conjunction with "good fortune," political "powers" and "good fortune" both being external goods. (Perhaps Aristotle assumes "powers" to be included among the goods of fortune.) Also, although "powers" are said to provide security for life and thus are connected to the third definition, they might also be based on the fourth definition, in which there is reference to the "power" (*dunamis*) for guarding and using "possessions and bodies."

The greater part of this chapter (1360b32-1362a15) consists of brief comments on each of the previously listed elements of happiness. Rather than considering all of these remarks, I shall direct attention to only one of the items listed—friendship—with the assumption that one can learn something about Aristotle's handling of all of these parts of happiness by generalizing from a single case. The passage (1361b35-38) follows:

> The friendship of many men and of worthy men [*poluphilia kai chrestophilia*] is not unclear from the definition of friendship, because it is that a friend is such a man as is active for the sake of another concerning the things he thinks to be good for him. One to whom many are so disposed has many friends [*poluphilos*], and one to whom good men [*epieikeis andres*] are so disposed has worthy friends [*chrestophilos*].

According to Cope, this definition is deficient in comparison with the study of friendship in the *Nicomachean Ethics*. "The definition is 'rhetorical,' and does not give the 'essence' of the thing, as a scientific definition would." Aristotle shows in the *Ethics,* Cope argues, that the desire for doing someone good for his own sake is not of the essence of friendship, although it is "a necessary accompaniment and consequence of the feeling or affection."[26] For the essence of friendship is the reciprocity of goodwill.[27] Furthermore, Cope declares, Aristotle makes it clear in the *Ethics,* but not in the *Rhetoric*, that friendships vary according to whether they are founded on the good, the pleasant, or the useful, and that the highest and truest form of friendship is that between good men.[28]

Obviously, Aristotle's treatment of friendship in the *Rhetoric*, as with almost all the other moral and political subjects handled in this book, is so brief that he cannot possibly reproduce the detailed and subtle analysis found in the *Ethics*. And perhaps this shows the fundamental defect of rhetoric — that is, that everything must be abbreviated and simplified before it can enter rhetorical argumentation.

Nevertheless, Aristotle's remarks on friendship in the *Rhetoric* seem quite consistent with his account of friendship in the *Ethics*, especially if one considers the passage here in Book One, Chapter 5, of the *Rhetoric* in conjunction with the passages in Book Two, Chapter 4. For example, although Cope correctly indicates the absence of any reference to reciprocity of goodwill in Aristotle's definition of friendship as a part of happiness, Cope fails to notice that when Aristotle elaborates more extensively on this definition in Book Two of the *Rhetoric*, he introduces "reciprocity" as essential for defining friendship; and the term that he uses — *antiphiloumenos* — is the same that appears in the *Nicomachean Ethics* (1157b30–31). Also, in depreciating the *Rhetoric's* account of friendship for not recognizing the superiority of friendship founded on virtue, Cope fails to give due weight to the emphasis in the *Rhetoric* on the importance of having friendship not just with *many* men, but with *worthy* or *good* men (*epieikeis*).[29] Further, it is made quite clear in Book Two (4. 1381a8–13, 18–35, 1381b7–22, 27–33) that friendship requires shared standards and that the friendship between good men is the truest. Finally, the statement in the *Rhetoric* (1. 7. 1364b1–3) that friendship is a good because a friend is desirable in himself, which suggests that true friendship is not a means to an end but an end in itself, accords fully with the conclusion reached in the study of friendship in the *Nicomachean Ethics* (1170b14–19).

One can conclude from the preceding commentary that in defining and analyzing happiness in the *Rhetoric*, Aristotle does not depart in any fundamental respect from his teaching in the *Nicomachean Ethics*. If his remarks appear defective in comparison with the *Ethics*, it is because of the brevity and condensation required for teaching and practicing rhetoric, that necessary abbreviation perhaps being the most serious limitation of rhetoric in contrast to political philosophy. Even though allowances must be made for the limitations of rhetorical reasoning, a careful reading of this chapter in the *Rhetoric* on happiness (in conjunction with relevant passages elsewhere in the text) leads to the conclusion that the commonsense views of happiness manifest in rhetorical argumentation reflect, even if somewhat dimly, the philosophic understanding of happiness set forth in the *Ethics*.

On Goodness (6)

Goodness Defined (1362a16–1362b9)

The deliberative rhetorician must have some understanding not only of the expedient, but also of the good, Aristotle says, because, although the primary concern of deliberative rhetoric is expediency, whatever is expedient is also good (1362a16–21).[30]

After these introductory remarks, Aristotle sets forth a study of goodness with essentially the same logical organization as his study of happiness. He begins with a series of definitions, which are linked by the conjunction *kai* ("and" or "or"), and which are arranged to follow a progression from the more to the less comprehensive (1362a22–29). Having spoken near the end of his list of definitions of things "productive" of good things and of things on which good things "follow," he defines the terms "productive" and "following" (1326a30–34). He then makes four deductive inferences, of which the first two employ the definition of "following" and the last two, the definition of "productive"; in each case, he states a conclusion and then gives a reason for the conclusion, the reason preceded by the conjunction *gar* ("for") (1362a35–1362b9). Next, based upon the preceding definitions and deductions, he deduces a list of particular goods; and again, in each case, he states the good or set of goods and then, with the conjunction *gar,* introduces a clause that explains the deductive connection with the prior definitions and deductions (1362b10–28). Finally, Aristotle gives a list of topics about the "disputed" goods, each one being introduced by the conjunction *kai* (1362b28–1363b5). That these "disputed" goods are not as well grounded as the previous ones is evident from Aristotle's reliance on "sayings" and, particularly, on quotations from poets (three from Homer and one from Simonides) and one "proverb" (*paroimia*). In many cases, however, deductions—introduced by *gar*—are attempted, but they are not as logically solid as the previous deductions.

Thus, as in the preceding chapter, Aristotle carefully presents his remarks on goodness in a logical sequence that moves from definitions of the good to inferences about particular goods that follow "necessarily" (*anangke*) from the definitions (see 1362a34–35, 1362b3, 7, 10). His concern for logical rigor is manifest in his careful separation of those particular goods that clearly follow from the definitions and those things that some think to be goods although they are "disputed" because they cannot be clearly inferred from the definitions.

It is noteworthy that those things logically connected to the definitions of goodness are also the things generally agreed to be goods, while the things that cannot be deduced from the definitions are generally disputed as to their goodness. In other words, there is a correspondence here between logic and common opinions; those things commonly regarded by men as goods can be logically justified by deduction from commonly accepted definitions of goodness, but those things about whose goodness there is disagreement among men cannot be deduced from accepted definitions of goodness. This is not to say that men are generally aware of the logical character of their common opinions as presented here in the *Rhetoric*. But one might say that common opinions possess an *implicit* logic that becomes evident only when Aristotle presents them in a refined and orderly manner. This, then, seems to provide further confirmation for the conclusion that Aristotle considers common opinions, when properly understood, to possess a certain rational solidity, which is the basis for rhetorical reasoning.

Now that we have sketched the formal structure of Aristotle's analysis of goodness, we must examine the substantive content of his remarks. Again, as in the case of happiness, his definitions require the closest scrutiny since it is from them that he deduces his list of particular goods. Aristotle states the definitions in the following manner (1362a22-29):

> Let good be whatever is itself desirable for its own sake, and that for the sake of which we desire something else, and that at which all things aim or all things having sensation or mind [*nous*], or if they receive mind. And whatever mind would give to each, and whatever mind concerning each thing does give to each, this is the good for each; and that whose presence disposes one well and makes one self-sufficient, and self-sufficiency itself, and that which is productive or preservative of such things, and on which such things follow, and the things preventive and the things destructive of the opposites.

Aristotle begins by defining the good in its purest sense as the final end for the sake of which everything else is chosen. This agrees with his opening remarks about the good in both the *Nicomachean Ethics* (1094a1-27) and the *Politics* (1252a1-7).

In some sense the good might be the final end of even inanimate things, but Aristotle is careful to point out that the good is most properly applicable to beings with "sensation" (*aisthesis*) or "mind" (*nous*). The possession of *nous*, or at least the capacity for acquiring it, is perhaps essential. The good in its fullest sense exists only for beings capable of rationally apprehending it.[31]

Moreover, Aristotle indicates that *nous* determines what is good in particular cases for particular people. Clearly, he uses *nous* in a broad sense here to include *phronesis* ("prudence"), which he makes explicit in the succeeding chapter (7. 1363b14-15, 1364b12-20; see also 1. 11. 1371b27-29), just as in the *Nicomachean Ethics* "practical wisdom" is essential for deciding what is good in particular circumstances.[32]

Aristotle next defines as good that which puts a man in a healthy condition, that which makes a man self-sufficient, and self-sufficiency itself. Finally, having begun with things good in themselves, Aristotle concludes by acknowledging the goodness of things good as means — things productive or preservative of goods or on which goods follow and things that prevent or remove evils. After defining the terms "productive" and "following," Aristotle uses these two definitions in conjunction with the definitions of goodness as the basis for four deductions that expand his conception of goodness (1362a34-1362b9). The third deduction is that the virtues are necessarily good, "for those possessing them are well-disposed, and they are also productive of good things and practical."[33] The final inference is that pleasure is a good, "for all living things aim at it by nature."[34]

Nothing in this account of goodness contradicts the *Nicomachean Ethics*. The definitions of the good, although they are necessarily founded on the common opinions of the men to whom the rhetorician must speak, reflect the conclusions reached by Aristotle in his philosophic inquiries.

Particular Goods (1362b10-28)

Aristotle's list of particular goods consists of ten deductions. In each case there is a statement of a good or set of goods, followed by an explanation of the logical connection with the previous definitions and deductions. Although there is no need to examine this entire list, the comments on honor and reputation are worthy of attention.

Aristotle says that "honor" (*time*) and "repute" (*doxa*) are goods, not only because they are pleasurable and productive of other goods, but also because, "for the most part," they are accompanied by the possession of the things for which men are honored (1362b21-23; see also 7. 1365a7-8). Aristotle's respect for common opinions is here apparent, because he assumes that the general opinions of men with respect to honor and dishonor are for the most part true. (Or is it perhaps the case that men who are honored become worthy of their honors through their desire to appear worthy of them? [See 1. 11. 1371a8-23 and 2. 11. 1388b2-7.])

Yet Aristotle is also aware of the defects of the opinions of the many as the following passage (1362b15-18) suggests:

> Health, beauty, and such things are goods, for they are virtues of the body and productive of many things; for instance, health is productive of pleasure and of life, wherefore it is thought [*dokei*] the best of all, because it is the cause of the two things most honored by the many, pleasure and life.

Aristotle would surely agree as to the goodness of health, but he would not endorse the opinion that health is "the best of all," as is suggested by his use of *dokei* ("it is thought" or "it seems") (see 1. 7. 1365b8-12). Health is commonly thought to be the greatest good only because the many honor pleasure and life above all things. The opinions of the many are somewhat distorted by their preoccupation with things of the body.[35]

Disputed Goods (1362b28-1363b5)

Having listed "nearly" all things agreed to be good, Aristotle turns next to listing those things whose goodness is disputed; and his concern is to show what syllogisms can be offered in their favor (1362b28-30). Rather than attempt to study everything mentioned here, I shall consider only a few representative topics.

According to the first topic, "that is good the opposite of which is evil" (1362b30). But, as Aristotle says elsewhere, in some exceptional cases it does not hold that the contrary of evil is good.[36] The opposite of "defect," for example, is "excess," but both are evils. Hence, while this topic is undoubtedly a rather reliable maxim, it is subject to dispute since it is not true in every case.

The second topic is related to the first. That is good "the opposite of which is expedient for our enemies; for example, if it is especially expedient for our enemies that we be cowards, it is clear that courage is especially useful for the citizens" (1362b31-33). First of all, this topic has the same defect as the previous one. Although it may be true in most cases that the opposite of what would help a man's enemies would be good for him, there are obviously circumstances in which a man and his enemies would have a common interest (see 1362b36-38). Also, this topic, as well as others in this section of the *Rhetoric* (1362b30-38, 1363a10-16, 1363a20-22, 1363a34-35), rests upon the questionable assumption that whatever helps one's friends or injures one's enemies is good.[37] But Aristotle implies that such a conception of goodness, as dubious as it might be upon serious reflection, possesses a certain solidity when considered in the context of war and the need for courageous citizens.

The difficulty of deducing these "disputed" goods from the definitions of goodness is illustrated by the following topic (1363a8-9): "And that which the many aim at and which seems to be fought about is good; for that at which all aim, that was the good, but the many appear as though they were all." The attempted deduction is that since the good has been defined as that at which "all" men aim, and since the "many" is equivalent to "all," that at which the "many" aim is good. The argument has some force since what the "many" seek is often the same as what "all" seek. But such is not always the case, and Aristotle indicates the weakness in the minor premise of the above syllogism by using the verb "appear": the "many" *appear* [*phainein*] to be the same as "all," when in reality this is not so.[38]

The final example of the "topics" of "disputed goods" concerns "things for which men happen to feel an appetite, for such a thing appears not only pleasant but also better" (1363a37-38). Once again, Aristotle makes an attempt here to establish an implicit logical connection with the definitions of goodness. If the good is that which is desirable for its own sake, then why should not all the objects of man's appetites be goods? The goodness of such things is questionable, however, because they are objects not of deliberate or rational desire, but of "appetites" that men "happen" to feel; and the result of such random impulses is to make some things "appear" to be pleasurable and better things when in truth they are not.[39]

On the basis of the four examples just examined, one may conclude that Aristotle regards these "disputed" goods as things for whose goodness somewhat plausible arguments may be made. But the arguments are not so cogent, not so logically rigorous, as those through which the prior list of particular goods was deduced from the original definitions. Aristotle's frequent use of words such as "seems" and "appears," in contrast to his previous use of the word "necessarily," is perhaps sufficient in itself to signify the dubiousness of the syllogisms in this final section of Chapter 6.

One of the major theses that I have advanced in this commentary on the *Rhetoric* is that, according to Aristotle's theory, true rhetoric is not an art of deception, but a genuinely rational mode of argumentation. The preceding analysis of Aristotle's chapter on goodness supports this interpretation of the *Rhetoric* insofar as it shows that, far from being indifferent to the validity or invalidity of the arguments he discusses, Aristotle carefully distinguishes those arguments that can be set forth in a logically compelling manner from those that are not so cogent even though they "seem" to be at least partially true. In other words, instead of trying to teach the rhetorician how to make the weaker argument appear to be the stronger, Aristotle sharpens the ability of the rhetorician to discern the superiority of the stronger over the weaker argument. This concern for ranking arguments according to whether they are more or less certain, relative to one another, is also apparent in the next chapter of the *Rhetoric*.

On Comparing Goods (7)

Men often agree as to the expediency of two things, Aristotle observes, and yet disagree as to which is more so. It is necessary, therefore, to speak of the greater good and the more expedient (1363b6-8).

As in the previous chapters, Aristotle begins with a definition: "Let something exceed when it is as much and more, and be exceeded when it is contained in another" (1363b8-9). This definition, in combination with the definitions of goodness stated earlier, is the basis for inferring that a larger number of good things is necessarily a greater good than one or a smaller number (1363b14-21).[40]

The remainder of the chapter consists of a list of topics for ranking good things as greater or less, and all the topics are deductions from the definitions of goodness and from the definition of exceeding and being exceeded.[41] Every topic is introduced by *kai,* and most have a *kai . . . gar* construction; but in those instances where the deduction is obvious, the *gar*-clause is omitted.

The topics are not all of equal certainty. Some are almost indubitable, while others are highly questionable. In some cases, Aristotle makes it clear that equally strong arguments can be made on either side of an issue. In other cases, he says that certain topics "seem" (*phainetai* or *dokei*) valid: although they contain some truth, he implies, they are still quite dubious.

There are a number of cases of contradictory arguments that have equal weight (1364a10-31, 1363a4-6, 1365a19-31). From one viewpoint, the first principle (*arche*) is greater than the end (*telos*); but from another, the end is greater than the first principle. The scarce can be argued to be greater than the abundant, but the abundant can also be argued to be greater than the scarce. One can maintain either that the difficult is greater than the easier or that the easier is greater than the

69

difficult. And finally, that which all share seems greater than that which few or none share, but the opposite can also be argued.

Another way that Aristotle signifies the uncertainty of a topic is by saying that it only "seems" to be true (see 1365a10-19, 1365a38-1365b12, 1365b16-17). Health and wealth, for example, are said to "seem" (*dokei*) to be the greatest of goods because they are useful for pursuing many good ends (1365b7-12). Since they are necessary conditions for achieving many worthy things, health and wealth are surely important; but to conclude that they are therefore the *greatest* goods is dubious.

Aristotle is careful to present deceptive reasoning as being based on what only "seems" so. For instance, "the things divided into parts seem [*phainetai*] to be greater," he explains, "for they seem [*phainetai*] to exceed in more things" (1365a10-12; see also 1. 14. 1375a8-12).[42] Here is an example of the sort of deceptive techniques favored by the sophists; and since he cannot ignore such modes of argument—for the good rhetorician must understand such things if he is to be well armed against them—Aristotle explains the technique, at the same time clearly indicating its "seeming" character.

There is an even more interesting illustration of how Aristotle handles sophistical arguments. Consider the following passage (1365a37-1365b8):

> And things with reference to truth [are greater than] things with reference to opinion [*doxa*], the definition of that which has reference to opinion being that which one would not choose if it were likely to remain unnoticed. And therefore receiving a benefit would seem [*doxeien*] more desirable than confering one; for one would choose the former even if it were unnoticed, but it seems [*dokei*] that one would not choose to confer a benefit unnoticed. And those things [are greater] that men wish more to be than to seem [*dokein*], for they are more with reference to truth. And therefore men say [*phasi*] that justice is a small thing, because it is more desirable to seem just than to be so, but this is not the case with health.

Aristotle here outlines one of the favorite lines of argument for the sophists in their criticisms of ordinary morality. Justice is merely conventional, and therefore unnatural, they contend, because while men desire to *appear* just in public, they secretly desire to *be* unjust when they are unseen by others.[43] But once again Aristotle's use of the words *dokei* and *phasi* suggests that these sophistical arguments are not completely true even though they "seem" to be true to many people. Oddly enough, Aristotle implies, the sophists employ the principle that "being" is superior to "seeming," to justify conclusions that merely *seem* to be true.

A few lines after the passage just quoted, Aristotle says that "those things whose presence is not unnoticed [are greater] than those unnoticed, for these things stretch more toward the truth" (1365b14–16). When compared with the previous passage, this remark suggests that the considerations governing men's public appearances are in some sense closer to the truth than the desires that rule men's actions when they are unseen. As members of communities, men approach the truth more closely than they do as individuals. As individuals, ordinary men often allow their judgments to be distorted by their appetites; but as members of communities, they make judgments that manifest a sense of justice. Perhaps men express their *natural* inclinations better in their *conventional* standards of justice than in their private desires.[44]

In this chapter of the *Rhetoric* Aristotle exercises the utmost care not only in separating valid from invalid arguments but also in differentiating valid arguments according to their relative degrees of certainty. The practical matters with which rhetoric deals can seldom be known with great exactness, and as a result the study of rhetorical reasoning depends less upon distinguishing truth and falsity than upon discerning the subtle *gradations* of truth in rhetorical argumentation.

It is clear, then, that Aristotle is not indifferent to the quality of the arguments he studies. He does not merely catalogue the various rhetorical techniques without concern for whether they are logically compelling or simply fallacious. He instructs the rhetorician in the most rigorously deductive and the most patently sophistical lines of argument, but without blurring the difference between the two.

The Regimes (8)

The Supremacy of the Regime Question (1365b20–28)

Aristotle began his examination of deliberative rhetoric by insisting that, of the five major subjects of deliberation, preserving the character of the regime was the most important. Having spoken about happiness and goodness, he now concludes his section on deliberation by reiterating the primacy of the regime question, thus suggesting that the conceptions of happiness and goodness that guide deliberation both determine and are determined by the nature of the regime.

For deliberative speaking or for persuasion generally, the "most ruling" or "most authoritative" source of arguments is knowledge of the regimes; for all men are persuaded by the expedient, and the expedient is what preserves the regime. Furthermore, the nature of the regime determines the locus of authority (1365b20–28). Hence, the regime is rhetorically important for at least two reasons. First, expediency is the fundamental standard for deliberation, and the expedient is whatever serves the regime. Second, the rhetorician addresses his speeches to the rulers of his community, and the form of the regime settles the character of the ruling group.[45]

The Four Regimes (1365b29–1366a6)

Just as I have argued that Aristotle's studies in the *Rhetoric* of happiness and goodness are in agreement with his teaching in the *Ethics,* despite the simplification and abbreviation required for the *Rhetoric,* so shall I maintain that his comments on the regimes in this chapter of the *Rhetoric* are consistent with his analysis in the *Politics,* although again the account in the *Rhetoric* is highly simplified and condensed.

Aristotle stresses that he does not intend to provide a thorough treatment of this subject in the *Rhetoric* since he has already done this in the *Politics,* and he refers his readers to that work (1. 4. 1360a36–38, 8. 1366a19–23). He states, furthermore, that it is sufficient for the rhetorician to have enough knowledge of the differences among regimes so that he can shape his speeches to conform to the character of his regime.[46]

This explains the obvious incompleteness, which commentators have been quick to point out, of the regime analysis in the *Rhetoric.*[47] In one instance of what has been considered cursory treatment, Aristotle defines the regimes without distinguishing the various forms of each, something he does in the *Politics.* The result is that his definitions are somewhat misleading. This is particularly evident with respect to oligarchy because, by defining oligarchy in the *Rhetoric* simply as rule based on a property qualification, he does not take into account the fact that one type of democracy also has a property qualification.[48]

But despite the existence of the defects that spring from the brevity of the analysis, Aristotle's treatment in the *Rhetoric* of the regimes does not contradict his teaching in the *Politics;* closer examination of his remarks makes this clear.

Aristotle defines four kinds of regimes — democracy, oligarchy, aristocracy, and monarchy (1365b29–1366a2). In a democracy offices are distributed by lot; in an oligarchy they belong to those satisfying a property qualification; in an aristocracy they go to those satisfying an educational qualification; and in a monarchy, one man rules over all and possesses power that is either limited (kingship) or unlimited (tyranny). Each form of government has a particular "end" (*telos*) (1366a3–7). The end of democracy is freedom; of oligarchy, wealth; of aristocracy, things relating to education and legal institutions; and of tyranny, protection. Aristotle does not mention the end of kingship.

Thus, of the six regimes discussed in the *Politics,* two (kingship and tyranny) are considered here to be variations of one form (monarchy), and another (polity) is not mentioned at all. But in one section of the *Politics* (1293a35–1293b2, 1295a1–24), Aristotle says that the four regimes commonly enumerated (which are those listed by Plato) are "monarchy, oligarchy, democracy, and the fourth that which is called aristocracy," and this is the classification that he adopts in the *Rhetoric*.[49] It is understandable that Aristotle does not introduce into the *Rhetoric* his conception of "polity" as a special regime; such a regime is rare and not even commonly recognized as a separate type of regime.

The distinction in the *Rhetoric* between kingship and tyranny is consonant with that in the *Politics.* A king rules according to law over willing subjects for the common good; a tyrant rules without law over unwilling subjects for his own interests.[50] And that the end of tyranny is "protection" is suggested by Aristotle's remark in the *Politics* (1321a1) that "the worst regimes need the most protection."

The differentiation of the ends of democracy, oligarchy, and aristocracy—freedom, wealth, and virtue (or education), respectively—is also to be found in the *Politics* (1294a11–25, 1299b25–28). But further comment is required with respect to democracy and aristocracy.

In the *Politics* (1291b34–38, 1294a13), Aristotle explains that democracy may be defined as aiming either at freedom or at both freedom and equality. In the *Rhetoric* he does not explicitly mention equality as connected to democracy, and he defines its end as freedom simply. But even so, by describing democracy in the *Rhetoric* as founded upon the distribution of offices by lot, he would seem to acknowledge, at least implicitly, the importance of the principle of equality.

According to the *Rhetoric*, the end of aristocracy, which is also the qualification for holding office, is education as prescribed by the laws. "For those who stand by the things prescribed by law are the ones who rule in an aristocracy. And these necessarily appear to be the best [*aristoi*], whence this regime has taken its name" (1365b34–37). Aristotle thus defines aristocracy as founded not on virtue (*arete*) simply, but on the virtue of the citizen, which varies according to the regime, and which requires an education appropriate to the regime. But in the *Politics* (1289a26-34, 1293b1-23, 1279a35-38, 1286b3-8), he explains that the name "aristocracy," which would signify the best regime, is justly applied only to a regime governed by those best in virtue simply, the good citizen also being a good man. But the name is commonly given, Aristotle observes, to regimes governed by those who are best according to a standard of virtue that is relative to the regime. Therefore, it is clear that in the *Rhetoric* Aristotle defines aristocracy not in its strict sense, which would make it the best regime, but as it is commonly understood. The ideally "best" regime is too rare to be of concern to the rhetorician, who must deal with politics as it is ordinarily understood and practiced, rather than as it might be if men and circumstances were better than they usually are. (It should be remembered, however, that Aristotle has referred to the best regime earlier in the *Rhetoric* [1. 4. 1360a24] without any elaboration.)

The Characters of Regimes and the Characters of Men (1366a7-23)

There is a correspondence between the characters of individual men and the characters of regimes. For just as a man manifests his character in his "moral choice" (*proairesis*) with reference to an end, so does a regime (1366a13-17). Further, a reciprocal influence ties the characters of men and the characters of their regimes: the character of a regime determines the character of its citizens, but the character of the citizens also determines the character of their regime.[51] A speaker who would know what sort of character is likely to be found most persuasive by his audience must study not only the characters of the particular people who might compose the audience but also the character of the regime in which he speaks.[52]

What Aristotle says here in his brief sketch of the regimes is consistent with what he says in the *Politics*. If he departs at all from his teaching in the *Politics*, it is not in what he *says* in the *Rhetoric* but in what he does *not* say. That is, he does not discuss either the best regime simply (the true aristocracy) or the best practicable regime (the "polity"). Although some understanding of these two types of regimes may be essential for the theoretical study of politics, the fact that they rarely, if ever, exist in practice makes them inappropriate subjects for the *Rhetoric*, since the rhetorician can deal with political things only as they are known from the ordinary experience and common opinions of men.

That being so, a knowledge of the characters of the different regimes existing among men is the greatest source of arguments for the deliberative rhetorician. And to some extent this is true even in epideictic and forensic rhetoric because, as I shall soon demonstrate, standards of nobility and justice are largely shaped by the laws. Perhaps, therefore, the nature of the regime is decisive for all three kinds of rhetoric. If it is, the architectonic supremacy of politics over rhetoric is confirmed.[53]

4

EPIDEICTIC RHETORIC (1. 9)

Introduction (1366a23-33)

A speaker who praises or blames, Aristotle says, is concerned with virtue and vice, the noble and the disgraceful. He assumes, therefore, that virtue and vice coincide with the noble and the disgraceful and that the latter correspond to the things praised and the things blamed.[1]

Aristotle also indicates that the discussion in this chapter applies not only to the subjects of epideictic rhetoric but also to the persuasiveness of the speaker's *ethos*. By understanding what things are praised and what are blamed, a speaker knows what sort of character he should present in his speech to his audience.

Finally, Aristotle says that he will examine the subjects of this chapter only so far as is necessary for the sake of illustration. As in previous discussions, he does not intend to provide an exhaustive treatment of virtue and vice, nobility and ignobility, presumably because a brief account is sufficient for rhetoric and because he has examined these matters in his ethical treatises.

Aristotle moves in this chapter from the more essential to the more peripheral elements of his subject. The definitions of nobility and virtue are followed first by an enumeration of their parts as deduced from the definitions (1366a34-1366b22), and then by their "signs" and "works" (1366b23-1367a33); finally there is a discussion of the techniques for praising and blaming (1367a34-1368a39).

Nobility and Virtue (1366a34-1366b22)

Aristotle continues to employ the same deductive method used in previous chapters. After defining the noble, he infers, "If this is the noble, then virtue is necessarily noble, for being good it is praiseworthy" (1366a29-31). He then defines virtue and deduces the particular virtues. He reasons that justice and courage—and, next to them, liberality—are the greatest virtues since they fulfill the definition of vir-

77

tue to the greatest extent. He then defines each of the particular virtues, except for "gentleness" (*praotes*) and "wisdom" (*sophia*). With each definition, except that of *phronesis*, he refers to the vice that is contrary to the virtue. Aristotle connects nobility and virtue to happiness and goodness, deriving his definitions of nobility and virtue from his prior definitions of happiness and goodness.[2]

As in previous chapters, a question arises as to whether Aristotle's remarks in this chapter on nobility and virtue contradict his teaching in the *Nicomachean Ethics*. But, as in the foregoing cases, I shall argue here that although Aristotle recognizes the differences between rhetoric and moral philosophy, and although these differences are reflected in his treatment of nobility and virtue in the *Rhetoric*, what he says in the *Rhetoric* does not fundamentally contradict what he says in the *Ethics*. To illustrate an opposing point of view, I shall consider the claim advanced by Cope that the definition of virtue in this chapter contradicts the doctrine of the *Ethics*.

Aristotle states: "Virtue, it would seem [*hos dokei*], is a power that is productive and preservative of goods, a beneficent power for many and great things, even for all men concerning all things" (1366a37–1366b2). Cope dismisses this definition as lacking any of the elements of the definition worked out in the *Nicomachean Ethics*.[3] In particular, he argues that the definition of virtue as a "power" (*dunamis*) rather than as a "habit" (*hexis*) directly contradicts the teaching of the *Ethics*. He also draws attention to the omission in the account of virtue in the *Rhetoric* of any reference to "choice" (*proairesis*) or to the doctrine of the "mean," both of which are essential for the explication of virtue in the *Ethics*.

Aristotle does conclude in the *Nicomachean Ethics* that the virtues are not *dunameis* but *hexeis*. A close examination of his remarks, however, will reveal that he is speaking of *dunameis* only in the particular sense of powers that arise simply by nature rather than through "choice" (*proairesis*).[4] The virtues cannot be *dunameis* in this sense because men are not blamed or praised for powers that they cannot have chosen. But in the *Metaphysics* Aristotle gives one of the possible meanings of *dunamis* as being something through which "one accomplishes something well or according to choice [*proairesis*]" (1019a23–27).[5] So *dunamis* in this sense would be applicable to virtue.

That Aristotle defines virtue in the *Rhetoric* as a *dunamis* only in this latter sense is implied by his comments on praise, in which he assumes the virtues to be *hexeis* and to be founded on *proairesis* (1. 9. 1367b22–26, 1367b32–33; see also 1. 10. 1369a8–9, 1369a15–23; 2. 12.

1388b31-34). In contrast to Cope, Aristotle seems to consider his definition of the virtues in the *Nicomachean Ethics* to be consistent with his
definition in the *Rhetoric* of the virtues as *dunameis*.[6]

But it is true, however, that in the *Rhetoric* Aristotle views virtue
from a perspective that differs, at least in emphasis, from his exposition
in the *Ethics*. In particular, he stresses in the *Rhetoric* much more than
in the *Ethics* the political or legal character of virtue. This is especially
apparent in his list of the virtues in the *Rhetoric*. Consider, for example,
the following passage (1366b4-8):

> The greatest virtues are necessarily those most useful for others, if
> virtue is a power for conferring benefits. For this reason people
> honor just men and courageous men the most; for courage is
> useful to others in war and justice in peace. Next is liberality, for
> the liberal give freely and do not dispute the possession of wealth,
> at which other men aim the most.

Thus Aristotle emphasizes the virtues as being beneficial for others
rather than benefiting the possessor of the virtues. As a result, he ranks
the more political virtues, such as courage and justice, above the others.

Aristotle's stress on the political elements of virtue is also evident in
his definitions of the first three virtues on his list, for in each of these
cases—justice, courage, and temperance—the virtue is defined with
reference to the prescriptions of law. Justice is the virtue through which
each man receives his due "as the law dictates"; courage, that through
which men do noble deeds in dangerous circumstances "as the law dictates"; and temperance, that through which men bear themselves
toward bodily pleasures "as the law dictates" (1366b9-15). In the light
of the *Ethics*, it is clear that Aristotle here defines justice, courage, and
temperance not as virtues simply, but as *political* virtues.[7]

This emphasis in the *Rhetoric* on the close relationship between virtue and the law is actually compatible with the *Nicomachean Ethics*.
Since the law commands actions according to the virtues and forbids actions that display the vices, Aristotle says in the *Ethics* (1130b22-29), actions according to the law are for the most part the same as the actions
according to virtue. The education of citizens by the law, then, tends on
the whole to produce virtue. There can be some discrepancy, however,
since being a good man is not always the same as being a good citizen,
and therefore law cannot always be coextensive with virtue. Even in the
Rhetoric, Aristotle implicitly acknowledges the difficulty of bringing
virtue totally under the direction of the law. For after his definitions of
the first three virtues, Aristotle goes on to define liberality, magnanimi-

ty, magnificence, and prudence, with no reference to the law (1366b16-22). Legal prescriptions cannot be definitive for these virtues.

The tension between virtue and the law is perhaps most evident in the case of wisdom. Although wisdom appears as the last item on Aristotle's initial list of the virtues, it does not appear in the succeeding list of definitions (1366b4).[8] The place at the end of the first list filled by both "prudence" (*phronesis*) and "wisdom" (*sophia*) is filled in the second list by "prudence" alone. The implication may be that it is easier for a rhetorician to praise a man for his prudence than for his wisdom. For men find wisdom a marvelous sort of knowledge, Aristotle says in the *Ethics* (1127b17-23, 1141b2-14); and yet they regard it as useless since, in contrast to prudence, it is not concerned with human goods but with things eternal.[9]

The implicit depreciation of wisdom and elevation of prudence is consistent with the standard of virtue in the *Rhetoric*, according to which the greatest virtues are those most beneficial to others. It is understandable that Aristotle should advance such a view of rhetoric in the context of a discussion of epideictic rhetoric: although all virtues can be praised, a rhetorician is more likely to persuade audiences to recognize the praiseworthiness of virtues beneficial to them (and to the community in general) than of virtues beneficial only to the person praised. According to Cicero, those virtues that show "courtesy [*comitas*] and benevolence" are more fit for praise by the rhetorician than those virtues that consist in "some intellectual ability or in magnitude and firmness of soul"; and this is so despite the fact that perfect virtue is more akin to the latter than to the former (*De Oratore* 2. 343-44; *De Officiis* 3. 13-17).

Aristotle slants his account of virtue in the *Rhetoric*, unlike his teaching in the *Ethics*, with a view to the demands of rhetorical practice. As a result, although he does not have to directly contradict the doctrines of the *Ethics*, he does have to stress those elements of virtue that are in accord with and in service to the community, rather than those elements that are more private and more independent of the community.

The "Signs" and the "Works" (1366b23-34)

Having spoken of virtue and vice in general and according to their parts, Aristotle turns now to the causes and results of virtue. The things that produce virtue and those that come from virtue are necessarily noble, and these are the "signs" and the "works" of virtue. Although in this section of the *Rhetoric* "signs" (*semeia*) seem to refer to things *producing* virtues and "works" (*erga*) to things *resulting* from the virtues, "signs," broadly understood, could include "works"; for as Aristotle says later in this chapter (1367b33), the "works" (or "deeds") of virtue are themselves "signs" of virtue.

Aristotle deduces that, if the "signs" and "works" of a good man are noble, it then follows necessarily that all the "signs" and "works" of courage are noble. The same applies to justice and to all the other virtues. The one exception is just suffering: to suffer justly or to be punished justly is not noble although it is just.

Thus Aristotle applies the technique of reasoning from "signs" to the subject of virtue (see 1. 2. 1357a24–1356b25). The enthymemes that a rhetorician might employ would follow the same general form: the "sign" of a particular virtue is something that arises in most cases in conjunction with the virtue (major premise); if a particular man shows this "sign" (minor premise), it may be inferred that he is likely to possess the virtue in question (conclusion). This would be the form for *probable* "signs." If there are any *necessary* "signs" of virtue, the enthymemes for such "signs" would have necessary major premises, which would allow the conclusions to be certain rather than only probable.

Topics of the Noble (1366b34–1367a32)

Aristotle begins this chapter by defining the noble, but he immediately concludes from this definition that virtue is noble; and this leads him into a discussion of virtue—its definition, its parts, and its "signs" and "works." At this point in the chapter, he returns to the noble as such.[10]

Aristotle's remarks on noble things consist of a list of topics deduced from previous definitions and deductions. Each topic begins with the conjunction *kai*, and some include clauses introduced by *gar* that give the reasons for inferring that the things in question are noble.

Praise and Appearances (1367a33–1367b26)

Having devoted the first half of this chapter on epideictic rhetoric to the objects of praise—virtue and nobility—Aristotle devotes the second half to an examination of the nature and techniques of praise as such. He begins by discussing some of the techniques of praise (1367a33–1367b26). He then distinguishes "praise" from "encomium" and from "blessing" (*makarismos*) and "felicitation" (*eudaimonismos*) (1367b27–36). Next he shows the "common form" of "praise" and "counsels" (1367b37-1368a10). Finally, he explains the importance of the "commonplace" of "amplification" for praising (1368a11-39).

What is most striking about Aristotle's comments on some of the techniques of praise here (1367a33-1367b26) is the attention that he gives to praising men for things that only *appear* to be virtuous or noble, the underlying assumption being that most people assume that things *are* what they *resemble*. This requires some explanation because Aristotle seems, at least at first glance, to be endorsing the sort of deceptive techniques favored by sophistical speakers.

"It must be assumed, for the purpose of praise or blame," he says, "that the things closely resembling the things in question are the things themselves" (1367a33-34). The examples he gives are cases of excessive or defective moral states that are often treated as though they were the mean because they resemble it. For instance, the arrogant man may be praised as magnificent or dignified, the rash man as courageous, and the prodigal man as liberal. "For it will seem so to the many and at the same time there is a fallacy from the cause" (1367b2-7; cf. 2. 24. 1401b30-33). The fallacy lies in the false assumption that the "cause" of rashness, for example, is the same as the "cause" of courage: the "choice" (*proairesis*) manifested in a rash act is not the same as that manifested in an act of courage. But the fallacy is made somewhat plausible by use of the common topic of "more and less" (2. 23. 1397b12-27): if a man faces dangers unnecessarily, he would seem even more likely to face them for the sake of honor.

Aristotle assumes throughout these passages the doctrine of the *Nicomachean Ethics* that virtue is a mean between extremes of excess and defect, which should be sufficient evidence against Cope's claim that this doctrine is absent from the *Rhetoric*.[11] Furthermore, Aristotle's explanations of how an excessive or defective state can be taken for the virtuous mean are consonant with his comments in the *Ethics* (1108b11-1109b26) about the great difficulty of determining the mean, especially in particular circumstances, which stems from the fact that men who err on the side of the defect or on the side of the extreme because of the resemblance to the mean are often praised. Aristotle even uses some of the same illustrations in the *Rhetoric* as in the *Ethics*.[12]

Aristotle continues (1367b7-12):

> It is necessary to consider in whose presence we praise, for, as Socrates said, it is not difficult to praise Athenians among Athenians. We must also speak of what is honored among the particular audience, such as among Sythians, Lacedaemonians, or philosophers, as actually existing there. And generally what is

honored is to be referred to the noble since they seem to border upon one another.

Once again, the principle is that of praising what *appears* noble to the audience; and in this case, Aristotle notes that people tend to assume that what is honored is noble. But the problem is that different nations or communities honor different things and therefore have different conceptions of the noble; and the rhetorician must respect these differences. (Aristotle implies that philosophers are like a separate nation or community in that they have their own standards of honor and nobility, standards that may conflict with those of the cities in which they happen to live.) There is a distinction, then, between what is noble simply, which is common to all men and in some manner grasped by all, and what is noble for certain people; and the good rhetorician must deal properly with each.[13]

Pertinent to this problem is a passage at the end of the previous section of this chapter devoted to the topics of noble things (1367a27-33). "Profitless possessions" are noble, Aristotle says, for they are "more gentlemanly." He then turns immediately to the topic concerning things considered noble only among certain peoples, for which he gives this example: "In Lacedaemon having long hair is noble, for it is the sign of a gentleman, for it is not at all easy to perform a menial task having long hair" (1367a29-31). He then concludes with a final topic, according to which not to engage in mechanical trades is noble since a gentleman does not live for the service of others. In this passage, Aristotle suggests how peculiar customs pertaining to nobility can reflect a universal standard of nobility. For although the association of long hair with nobility is peculiar to the Spartans, this custom is founded on a universal principle—namely, that it is nobler to live the leisured life of a gentleman than to live a life of menial labor. By recognizing how particular standards of nobility point to universal principles, the rhetorician can accept the particular conceptions of his audience in his speeches without losing sight of the universals.[14]

Returning to Aristotle's remarks on the techniques of praise, I shall look at one final passage from this section and then make some general observations.

Aristotle says that since a man's deeds can be praised as virtuous only if they are done according to "moral choice" (*proairesis*), it is useful for a speaker that they should appear so (1367b22-26). "For this reason also one must assume that accidents and things by chance are due to moral choice; if many and similar ones can be adduced they will seem to be a sign of virtue and moral choice." Actions done purely at random can appear to be done according to a moral intention if many of them fall into a similar pattern. (Similarly, chance events that occur so as to be greatly beneficial to men may seem to display the favor of the gods [see 2. 17. 1391b1–4].) Thus, a rhetorician can deceive his audience to think that a man has done things according to a moral intention that can be praised when in reality he has not.

Unlike the first half of this chapter of the *Rhetoric*, this section contains frequent references to arguments that merely "seem" (*dokei* or *phainetai*) to be valid (1367a33, 1367b3–7, 1367b12–13, 1367b23–26, 1368a16, 1368a26). Thus Aristotle is careful to indicate the dubiousness, if not simple fallaciousness, of these deceptive techniques of praise; and he thereby separates them from the valid modes of reasoning in the earlier parts of this chapter.

As in his chapter on goodness, Aristotle's treatment of virtue and nobility moves from definitions to things clearly deducible from the definitions and then to things that only *appear* to be deducible from the definitions. In this way, he distinguishes the "praiseworthy" (*epaineton*), which belongs to the definition of the "noble" (1366a34–37), from the activity of praise as such (*epainos*) (1367a33–1367b7). What is "praiseworthy" is noble by definition, but what is actually praised may appear to be noble without truly being so.

But why does Aristotle even include such deceptive modes of argument? They would seem appropriate only for sophistical rhetoric. There are at least two possible reasons. First, if the good rhetorician is to handle himself properly, he must understand the sort of rhetorical techniques that his sophistical opponents are likely to use against him. Second, in some cases, even the good-intentioned rhetorician might have to resort to these techniques if there is no other way to advance the true and the just against their opposites.[15] The crucial difference between Aristotle's rhetorical education and a purely sophistical training is that Aristotle teaches the sophistical techniques to the extent that this is absolutely necessary, but without obscuring the fallaciousness of these techniques in contrast to the valid forms of reasoning that he prefers.

Encomium, Blessing, and Felicitation (1367b27–36)

Aristotle distinguishes "praise" from "encomium." While "praise" is speech that sets forth the greatness of a man's *virtue* as manifested in his noble "actions" (*praxeis*), "encomium" deals with "deeds" or "facts" (*erga*) as such. That is, "encomium" concerns any great achievements, but "praise" concerns *moral* greatness (see *Eth. Nic.* 1101b32–35).

"Blessing" and "felicitation," Aristotle adds, are identical to one another, but they are higher or more encompassing than "praise" or "encomium"; for "just as happiness [*eudaimonia*] encompasses virtue, so does felicitation [*eudaimonismos*] encompass these" (1367b34–36). Aristotle makes this same argument—that "felicitation" is higher than "praise" just as happiness is higher than virtue— in the *Nicomachean Ethics* (1101b10–27), where he says that praise implies comparison and is thus inappropriate for the best things (such as the gods, godlike men, and happiness), things for which not praise, but "blessing" or "felicitation," is fitting (see *Rh*. 1. 9. 1366a29–32).

Praising and Counselling (1367b37–1368a10)

"Praise and counsels," Aristotle explains, "have a common form, for what you would suggest in counselling becomes encomium by a change in phrase" (1367b37–38). Therefore, "whenever you wish to praise, see what you would suggest; and whenever you would suggest, see what you would praise" (1368a7–9).

These remarks are important because they indicate that Aristotle regards epideictic rhetoric as being founded not just on the *aesthetic* but also on the *educative* uses of speech. It is commonly assumed that since epideictic rhetoric involves only "observation" (*theoria*), whereas forensic and deliberative involve "judgment" (*krisis*) (see 1. 3. 1358a37–1358b7), epideictic requires only "showy" speech, speech that pleases the listeners through its stylistic beauty, as a play pleases its spectators. But this interpretation restricts *theoria* to its theatrical sense without considering that Aristotle may be using it here in a wider sense to include "contemplation" or "comprehension."

Aristotle's stress here on the ease with which speeches of praise can be transformed into speeches of counsel suggests that, by clarifying, reinforcing, and modifying the moral standards of his audience, the epideictic rhetorician provides a basis for judgment and deliberation about moral and political matters. He aims to please; but in the process of pleasing, he also educates.[16]

The Topic of Amplification (1368a11–39)

The aesthetic side of epideictic rhetoric is evident in the prominence of "amplification" (*auxesis*) in epideictic speeches. This "commonplace" is most suited for epideictic, because epideictic speeches "take up deeds upon which there is agreement, so that what is left is to attribute magnitude and beauty to them" (1368a27–29). The concern of epideictic is not with the existence or the nature of deeds, but with whether they are great or small, beautiful or ugly.[17]

Aristotle concludes by adding that while amplification is most suitable for epideictic speakers, examples are most suitable for deliberative speakers and enthymemes for forensic speakers (1368b29–34). This does not mean, of course, that one type of speaker cannot use the mode of reasoning that is "most suitable" for another type. For amplification, examples, and enthymemes must be employed by all three kinds of rhetoric (see 1. 1. 1377b15–21, 19. 1393a9–21, 20. 1393a22–24).

5

FORENSIC RHETORIC (1.10-15)

Injustice and the Causes of Action (10)

Introduction (1368b1-6)

Aristotle turns now to the third kind of rhetoric — forensic — to which he devotes the remainder of Book One. His examination of forensic rhetoric requires that he comment upon many aspects of law, and as a result these chapters of the *Rhetoric* contain some of the most extensive statements of Aristotle's philosophy of law.[1]

"We have next to speak of from how many and from what sort of things it is necessary to construct syllogisms concerning accusation and defence" (1368b1-3). By beginning in this way, Aristotle reminds his reader that his discussions of the three kinds of rhetoric are intended to provide premises for enthymemes (see 1. 6. 1362b28-30, 2. 6. 1377b15-21). It is easy to forget this because, in his characteristically laconic manner, Aristotle sets forth the material for enthymemes but in most cases leaves it up to the reader to actually construct the enthymemes from these materials.[2] Not until he has completed his comprehensive presentation of the topical sources of enthymemes (1. 4.-2. 17) — sources that are not only substantive, but also "ethical" and "pathetical" in character — does he finally provide, in the last chapters of Book Two, a logical analysis of enthymematic reasoning. But with his opening statement in this chapter, Aristotle draws his reader's attention to the primary importance of the enthymeme throughout the *Rhetoric*.

Aristotle goes on to say that three things must be examined: the motives of injustice, the dispositions of the doers of injustice, and the characters of the sufferers of injustice.[3] But, as in previous discussions, Aristotle wishes to begin with a definition, and in this case he insists that the first order of business is to define injustice (1368b3-6).

After the definition (1368b7-26), Aristotle takes up the motives of injustice, to which he devotes the rest of this chapter and all of Chapter 11. In Chapter 12, he studies the doers and the sufferers of injustice.

Then his study of injustice requires an examination in Chapter 13 of the different kinds of law. Finally, he devotes Chapter 14 to a consideration of the degrees of injustice. But since what he calls "inartificial proofs" belong most properly to forensic rhetoric, he takes up this subject in the last chapter of Book One.

Injustice Defined (1368b7–26)

Doing injustice is defined as voluntarily doing injury contrary to the law (cf. 1. 9. 1366b10–11). Aristotle then clarifies this definition by defining the terms "law" and "voluntary." His definition of "voluntary" leads him to explain the relationship between acting voluntarily and acting through "moral choice" (*proairesis*), which in turn requires a comment on why men intentionally do injustice.

Law is divided into "particular" law, which is written, and "common" law, which is unwritten; and while "particular" law is that of a regime, "common" law is that which seems to be agreed upon by all men (1368b8–9). But this subject can be examined fully in connection with Chapter 13.

Men act voluntarily, Aristotle says, when they act knowingly and without being compelled (1368b10–11). He also explains that although everything done through "moral choice" is done knowingly, not everything done knowingly is done through "moral choice," a distinction that he has drawn from his *Ethics* (1109b35–1110a3, 1111a19–1111b11).

Finally, Aristotle indicates that men do injustice through "moral choice" because of "vice" (*kakia*) or "incontinence" (*akrasia*), and he gives illustrations.[4]

The Seven Causes of Human Actions (1368b27–1369b17)

To account for the motives of unjust deeds, Aristotle must comment on the causes of all human actions. He begins by differentiating seven causes (1368b33–1369a7). He then digresses to explain that these seven causes are sufficient for explaining human action even without reference to the characters or moral habits of men (1369a8–31). Next, he comments on each of the seven causes (1369a32–1369b17).

All human actions either originate from man or they do not. Of those not originating from man, some are due to "chance" (*tuche*) and others to "necessity" (*anangke*). Of those arising by necessity, some come by "nature" (*physis*), others by "compulsion" (*bia*). So there are three causes of actions not originating from man: chance, nature, and compulsion. Those actions originating from man are due either to "habit" (*ethos*) or to "desire" (*orexis*), and desire is either rational or ir-rational. Rational desire is "wish" (*boulesis*); irrational desire is "anger" (*orge*) or "appetite" (*epithumia*). Growing out of these distinctions are seven causes of action, which Aristotle lists in the following order: chance, nature, compulsion, habit, reason, spiritedness, and appetite. In this final list, he uses "reason" (*logismos*) to denote "rational desire" (*boulesis*) and "spiritedness" (*thumos*) to denote "anger" (*orge*).

Aristotle acknowledges that human actions can also be explained as due to men's "characters" (*ethe*)—such as whether they are young or old, rich or poor, fortunate or unfortunate—or to their "moral habits" (*hexeis*)—such as whether they are just or unjust, temperate or in-temperate (1369a8-32). But he thinks that any of these "characters" or "moral habits" can be reduced to one or more of the seven causes. He promises, however, to discuss the "characters" of man more fully later (see 2. 12-17).

He now returns to his list of causes and comments on each one. He follows the order of the original list, beginning with the causes outside man and then going through those that are of man himself.

Things that arise by chance are "those of which the cause is in-definite and those that arise not for the sake of something and neither always nor for the most part nor regularly" (1369a33-34). Things that are by nature are "those of which the cause is in themselves and regular; for they turn out thus always or for the most part" (1369a34-1369b2). Things that are by compulsion are "those that arise through the acting of the agents themselves against their appetite or reason" (1369b5-6).

Perhaps the most ambiguous of these three causes is nature. Although Aristotle here identifies nature with what happens either "always" or "for the most part," he subsequently speaks of "nature" as that which happens "always," in contrast to "habit," which happens "often" (1. 11. 1370a6-10). In other works, Aristotle often restricts "nature" to apply only to things happening "always" and "by necessity"; but in some cases he expands "nature" to include things occurring "for the most part" and things that occur only "sometimes."[5]

One must also wonder whether "nature" here includes *human* nature. Are the things that men do according to their "nature" caused by themselves or by something external to them? Presumably, the four "internal" causes of action—habit, reason, spiritedness, and ap-petite—are all elements of the "nature" of man.[6]

Things done by habit are "those that are done because they have often been done" (1369b6-7). Things done by "reason" are those done because "of the goods already mentioned, they are thought expedient either as an end or as a means to an end"; and Aristotle emphasizes that these are done for the sake of expediency and not of pleasure (1369b8-10). Things done through spiritedness or anger are "acts of revenge" [*ta timoretika*] (1369b11-14), and Aristotle notes that he will define anger when he discusses the passions. Finally, appetite is the cause of things being done that are apparently pleasant, which includes things that have become pleasant by becoming customary (1369b14-17).

It is fitting that Aristotle should place habit in the center of his list of seven, with the causes "external" to man on one side and the "internal" causes on the other, since habit, although it is one of the voluntary causes of action, is the one that is closest to the involuntary causes. Habits are voluntary insofar as they originate from human choices; but when they become well established, they become "second nature" and thus almost completely involuntary.[7] Aristotle suggests this later in the *Rhetoric* (1. 12. 1372b16-18) when he observes that men expect to escape punishment for injustice if they appear to act by chance, by necessity, by nature, or by habit, because in each case they appear to be mistaken rather than unjust.[8]

The remaining three causes constitute a tripartition of the human soul comparable to that made by Plato in the *Republic* (435b-442d): reason, spirit, appetite. Aristotle distinguishes rational and irrational desire. He refers to rational desire as "wish" (*boulesis*) and identifies it with "reason" (*logismos*). He divides irrational desire into "anger" (*orge*) or "spiritedness" (*thumos*) and "appetite" (*epithumia*). He thus employs the same analysis of "desire" *(orexis)* as that found elsewhere in his works.[9]

Although *logismos* may be translated as "reason," it might more properly be rendered as "calculation" in order to distinguish it from *nous*. While Aristotle links *nous* to *to epistemonikon*, which is the faculty of the rational part of the soul that grasps invariable first principles, he links *logismos* to *to logistikon*, which is the rational faculty that concerns variable things.[10] Hence, *nous* is more theoretical, *logismos* more practical. As in Aristotle's implicit elevation of *phronesis* over *sophia* in the previous chapter, his reference here to *logismos* rather than *nous* manifests his concern in the *Rhetoric* with practical reasoning: *logismos* can be a cause of human action, *nous* cannot.[11] *Logismos* can be a cause of action because it is connected with "desire" (*orexis*). Although "thought by itself moves nothing," thought can lead to action when it works in conjunction with desire.[12]

In contradistinction to *logismos*, "spiritedness" and appetite are said to denote *irrational* desire. But remarks elsewhere in the *Rhetoric* and in other of his works seem to indicate that "spiritedness" (and perhaps even some forms of appetite) contains elements of rationality.[13] And since "spiritedness" is associated with anger and with the passions generally, the rationality or irrationality of "spiritedness" bears upon the rationality or irrationality of the passions as treated in Book Two.[14] But these questions can be handled best in connection with Aristotle's study of pleasure in the next chapter (especially 1. 11. 1370a19-27).

The Good and the Pleasant (1369b18–33)

From his analysis of the causes of action, Aristotle concludes that all that men do voluntarily is done either for the sake of what is or seems good or for the sake of what is or seems pleasant (1369b18-23), and he understands the good to be equivalent to the expedient (1369b29-32).

From his remarks on the causes of voluntary action (1369b7-10, 14-15), it is clear that Aristotle considers the aim of "calculation" (*logismos*) to be the expedient or the apparently expedient and the aim of appetite the pleasant or the apparently pleasant.[15] But the aims of habit and "spiritedness" are less clear. Habit would seem to be connected to pleasure, however, since Aristotle notes that things familiar and customary are pleasurable (1369b15-17). "Spiritedness" and anger would also seem to have pleasure as their object—the anticipated pleasure of revenge (1369b10-13; see also 1. 11. 1370b10-15, 1370b30-33).

Since men direct their actions according to their conceptions of the good and the pleasant, and since the pleasant has not yet been examined in the *Rhetoric*, Aristotle sees a need for studying the nature of pleasure. But he reminds his readers that, as in previous discussions, he will think his definitions sufficient for the *Rhetoric* if they are "neither obscure nor exact" (1369b31-32).

Pleasure (11)

Introduction

Aristotle's deductive mode of exposition becomes prominent once again in this treatment of pleasure. He begins with a definition, lays down some corollaries of it, and then gives a catalogue of particulars deduced from the definition.

Aristotle's definition and much of what he deduces from it could apply to all sorts of pleasure; however, he concentrates on *mental* pleasures. His list of particular pleasures is devoted almost exclusively to cognitive rather than sensual pleasures, and the central topic concerns the pleasures of learning and wondering.

Upon reflection, it becomes clear why this should be so. Since the rhetorician appeals to men through speech, he can work upon their minds but not their bodies. Aristotle must, therefore, accentuate the pleasures of the mind in his education of the rhetorician, for those are the only pleasures amenable to persuasion. Aristotle later handles the passions in a similar manner. He stresses the extent to which the passions are rational and thus subject to rhetorical persuasion.

The Nature of Pleasure (1369b33–1370b15)

"Let it be assumed [*hupokeistho*] by us," Aristotle begins, "that pleasure is a certain motion of the soul, a sudden and sensible settling down into its natural state [*huparchousa physis*] and pain the opposite" (1369b33–35).

Cope interprets *hupokeistho* as a sign that this is a merely popular definition of pleasure. Aristotle's treatment of pleasure, he argues, is only a survey of the popular opinions on the subject and cannot, therefore, be taken as reflecting Aristotle's own philosophic understanding of pleasure.[16]

There is substantial evidence, however, that Aristotle has drawn his definition of pleasure, as well as much of what follows from it, from Plato's *Philebus*. In this dialogue, Socrates explains pain as a result of the loss of harmony in a living being and the disruption of its natural state; pleasure is, then, a result of a return of a being to its own natural state through which harmony is restored.[17] Godo Lieberg has studied in detail Aristotle's use of the *Philebus*.[18] He maintains that although Aristotle relies greatly on this dialogue, he shapes his material according to his own views. A sign of this, Lieberg thinks, is his insertion of *huparchousa* to modify *physis* in the definition of pleasure, because *huparchein* is an important technical term in Aristotelian logic.[19]

As Plato does in the *Philebus,* Aristotle defines pleasure as a sensible motion through which a natural state is restored. But as Cope is quick to point out, Aristotle explicitly denies in the *Nicomachean Ethics* and in other works that pleasure is a type of motion.[20] Pleasure is not a "process" (*genesis*) or "motion" (*kinesis*) of restoring a natural state, Aristotle argues; rather, pleasure pertains to the unimpeded "activity" (*energeia*) of a natural state, pleasure being either the "completion" of the activity or the activity itself. All men seek pleasure, he says at the end of the *Ethics*, because all men desire life. Life is an activity, and with the perfection of activity comes pleasure. So life and pleasure "seem to be bound up together and not to admit of separation, since without activity pleasure does not arise, and pleasure completes every activity." This seems to contradict the definition of pleasure in the *Rhetoric*; it may seem that Aristotle provides an account of pleasure for rhetorical purposes that he himself thinks to be false.

But on closer examination of the pertinent passages in the *Ethics* one can see that this conclusion is not justified. The pleasure of the *activity* of a faculty or disposition in its natural state is pleasure in its *essence*, pleasure unmixed with pain; the pleasure of the *process of restoring* a faculty or disposition to its natural state is pleasure only by *accident*, pleasure mixed with pain.[21] Aristotle says in the *Ethics* (1154b15-20):

> The pleasures without pain do not admit of excess, and these are of the pleasures by nature and not according to accident. By things pleasurable according to accident I mean curatives, because curing depends upon the activity of something that has remained healthy, and for this reason the curative itself is thought to be pleasurable; but the things pleasurable by nature are those that create the activity of the healthy nature.

If pleasure were only a process of "becoming" (*genesis*), it would not be a good simply.[22] For that which comes into being through a process is always for the sake of that state of being to which it is directed. Hence pleasure must be an "activity" (*energeia*), which is an end in itself, rather than a process of replenishment, which is a means to an end, if it is to be desirable in itself and thus a genuine good.

The definition in the *Rhetoric*, therefore, is not totally false, but it is incomplete; for to define pleasure as a sensible motion of the soul in returning to a natural state is to define "accidental" pleasure rather than pleasure simply. Aristotle must define pleasure in this way in the *Rhetoric* because it accords with the common opinions about pleasure held by the many, and the rhetorician must draw his premises from such opinions. As is usually the case with common opinions, this opinion about pleasure is not totally true; but it is in some sense correct. The view of the many that pleasure is a kind of sensible motion is founded on experience of the sort of pleasures commonly available to men. But through philosophic inquiry, Aristotle determined that the pleasures commonly known by men are impure and that they only reflect more or less accurately the true nature of pleasure as actualized in some activities of the soul that provide pure pleasures, pleasures unmixed with pains.[23]

At this point it is necessary to return to the text of the *Rhetoric*, noting two elements of the definition of pleasure that deserve special attention: the reference to "nature" (*physis*) and the reference to the "soul" (*psyche*). Unlike goodness, nobility, or virtue, pleasure is defined according to a *natural* standard, for pleasure is the restoration of a "natural state."[24] To understand the character of pleasure requires a proper conception of human nature. Also, pleasure is defined as a movement of the *soul:* all pleasures and pains involve the soul in some manner. Although sensual pleasures are obviously connected to the body, even these pleasures could not exist as pleasures if they did not affect the soul in some way. To have a pleasure is to be conscious of it, and without consciousness pleasure cannot exist.[25] But these two elements of the definition — nature and the soul — must be combined because it soon becomes evident that Aristotle considers his study of pleasure to be fundamentally a study of the nature of man as manifested most fully in the human soul: pleasure is the sudden and sensible restoration of the soul to its natural condition.

After stating his definition, Aristotle adds a series of corollaries. If pleasure is such as defined, he reasons, then what produces the stated disposition is pleasurable, and what destroys it or produces its opposite is painful (1369b35-1370a2). Also, while it is a necessary deduction from the definition that to enter a *natural* state is pleasurable, it is also pleasurable to enter a *habitual* state, because habit is like nature (1360a3-10).[26] Therefore, that which does not come habitually or naturally — that which is compulsory or necessary — is painful, and relief from the compulsory or the necessary is pleasurable (1370a10-17).

Everything for which men have an appetite, Aristotle adds, is pleasant, "for appetite is desire for the pleasant" (1370a17-18). While appetite was classified in the preceding chapter as "irrational desire" (along with "spiritedness" or anger), Aristotle now says that some appetites are rational (1370a19-27):

> Of the appetites some are irrational [*alogoi*] and some are with reason [*meta logou*]. I call irrational all those that arise not from assuming something, such as all those that are called by nature, just as those that exist through the body, such as that of food, thirst, and hunger, the appetite for each particular type of food, those concerned with taste, sex, and generally with touch, smell, hearing and sight. With reason are those appetites that arise from being persuaded, for hearing and being persuaded men are appetitive for many things to be seen and to be possessed.

The "irrational appetites" — such as hunger, thirst, and sexual impulse — arise spontaneously from the body without any process of reasoning. The appetites "with reason," on the other hand, depend upon a man's "being persuaded" that something is pleasurable; an element of reasoning is involved. The bodily appetites are called natural because they occur "naturally"; the appetites "with reason" arise only after a man has been talked into believing certain things to be pleasurable.

But some problems immediately come into view. Although the "irrational appetites" are said to be purely physical, Aristotle's subsequent comments on the pleasures connected with the appetites suggest that even the somatic appetites can have psychic components: thirst, for example, is accompanied by the memories of having drunk and hopes of drinking again (1370b16-19). It is very difficult to find appetites that are purely bodily in character.[27]

Also, Aristotle, in the *Ethics* and elsewhere, commonly classifies all the appetites as irrational in contradistinction to anger and the passions generally, which he describes as obedient to or open to persuasion by reason.[28] His characterization here in the *Rhetoric* of the "appetites with reason" thus corresponds in other works to his description of the passions.

It must be inferred, therefore, that Aristotle uses the term "appetite" (*epithumia*) sometimes in a very narrow sense and sometimes in a broader sense. Sometimes "appetites" denote purely physical and irrational impulses, which are to be distinguished from "passions." But at other times the "appetites" are understood to include not only the irrational impulses of the body but also the passions of the soul.[29] In the passage quoted earlier from the *Rhetoric* (1370a19-27), Aristotle uses "appetite" in its broader sense: the "irrational appetites" are "appetites" in the strict sense, but the "appetites with reason" are the same as the passions.

In any case, by describing appetite as "a desire for the pleasant" and then speaking of "appetites with reason," Aristotle suggests the possibility of *rational* pleasures — that is, pleasures whose existence depends fundamentally upon cognitive activity. But before he can list these pleasures of the mind, he must take one more step in his argument by setting forth another deduction from the definition of pleasure.

Since pleasure can be defined as the sensation of a certain effect, and since "imagination" (*phantesia*) is a certain "weakened sensation," as with the man who remembers or hopes and thereby holds in his imagination what he remembers or hopes, it must be concluded that those who hope and those who remember experience pleasure since there is sensation through imagination (1370a28-32). Pleasant things may therefore exist in the past or the future as well as the present: "In general, all the things that give delight by their presence also for the most part give delight when they are hoped for or remembered" (1370b9-11). By thus moving from the pleasures of direct sensation to the pleasures of the imagination, Aristotle opens the way for a list of particular pleasures that is completely dominated by the imaginative pleasures of the mind rather than the sensual pleasures of the body. The importance of imagination in the list is evinced by the frequent references to *phantesia* or *phainomena* (1370b33, 1371a9, 20, 24).

A Catalogue of Pleasures (1370b16–1372a3)

Aristotle lists fifteen types of pleasure:

1. pleasures accompanying appetites (1370b16-29)
2. revenge (1370b30-32)
3. victory (1370b33-1371a7)
4. honor and good repute (1371a8-17)
5. friends (1371a18-23)
6. customary things (1371a24)
7. change (1371a25-31)
8. learning and wondering (1371a31-33)
9. giving and receiving benefits (1371a34-1371b4)
10. things connected with learning and wondering (1371b5-12)
11. things akin (1371b13-26)
12. reputation for wisdom (1371b27-29)
13. criticizing one's neighbors (1371b29-31)
14. doing that in which one excels (1371b31-35)
15. laughter and the laughable (1371b35-37).

Since this list consists largely, if not exclusively, of cognitive pleasures, it is fitting that the central position is held by learning and wondering.[30]

Aristotle's statement that doing the same things often is pleasurable, because the familiar or the customary is pleasurable, is followed immediately by his declaration that change is pleasant, because perpetual sameness makes the established condition excessive. In the *Nicomachean Ethics* (1154b21-31, 1175a3-10) Aristotle explains that the pleasure men have in change is a sign of their defectiveness. There is more pleasure in rest than in motion, but man cannot take pleasure perpetually in the same activity because his nature is not simple; only God can enjoy the same pleasure continually without becoming cloyed. But in the *Rhetoric* the pleasure in sameness is said to arise from habituation while the pleasurable quality of change seems natural.

Aristotle's inclusion of change among the pleasures is consistent with his definition of pleasure as a form of motion; and it is another sign that in viewing pleasure from the perspective of common opinion, which is appropriate for rhetoric, he is concerned not with what would be pleasurable for the best sort of human beings, but with what is commonly pleasurable for ordinary men. Yet even in the *Rhetoric*, he suggests the dubiousness of change by the fact that it is one of the few things mentioned among the pleasant things that is not mentioned among the good things in Chapter 6.

This acknowledgement here in the *Rhetoric* of the pleasure of changing from the familiar routine of things leads naturally into the pleasures of learning and wondering, for learning and wondering arise from discovery, from seeing new things or seeing old things in new ways (see 1371b5-12). Learning requires a break with the familiar and the customary.[31] But the familiar is not discarded completely, because the unknown becomes known only by its connection to what is already known.[32]

Learning is pleasant since it brings one "into that according to nature."[33] The implication is that since man is by nature a rational being, man "comes into his own" by learning—a teaching that Aristotle develops at length at the end of the *Nicomachean Ethics*.

Learning and wondering are connected because wonder implies the desire to learn (1371a32-33). And the numerous references in the list to the pleasures of wondering or being an object of wonder (1371a23-24, 1371b5-12, 27-29) suggest that the pleasure in learning underlies many of the other pleasures.

That the learning leading to "wisdom" is more pleasurable than that leading to "prudence" is implied by the subsequent distinction between *phronesis* as "ruling" and *sophia* as "knowledge of many wondrous things" (1371b27-29). Wonder is the beginning of "wisdom."[34] The pleasure in learning undoubtedly encompasses "prudence," but the learning that arises from wonder aims at "wisdom." It should be noted that Aristotle connects the pleasure of being *thought* wise not to the pleasure of learning but to the pleasure of ruling (1371b27-29). Also, while Aristotle defined prudence but not wisdom in his chapter on virtue, he now defines wisdom in his chapter on pleasure. Does he thereby intend to suggest that prudence is more akin to *virtue* and wisdom more to *pleasure?*

Thus, in the *Rhetoric* as in the *Nicomachean Ethics*, Aristotle indicates, at least implicitly, that the highest pleasures are intellectual. But in the *Rhetoric*, in contrast to the *Ethics*, he speaks of learning and wonder rather than knowledge or contemplation: he stresses the *process* of pursuing and acquiring wisdom rather than the *possession* of it.[35] In this way, he remains consistent to his view of pleasure in the *Rhetoric* as "motion" (*kinesis*) rather than "activity" (*energeia*).

Aristotle's emphasis in this chapter on cognitive pleasures is consonant with his insistence throughout the *Rhetoric* that the true rhetorician must appeal to the natural desire of men to learn.[36] The enthymeme is the instrument of rhetorical persuasion because it satisfies this desire and thus gives pleasure to the listener.

As in preceding chapters, the primacy of the enthymeme is evident in the deductive rigor with which Aristotle presents his exposition of pleasure. He carefully deduces each item in his catalogue of pleasures from the original definition of pleasure. To illustrate his reasoning, consider the pleasure of "reversals of fortune" (*peripeteiai*) (1371a31-33, 1371b4-6, 11-12).[36] Such reversals are said to be pleasurable because they arouse wonder; and since wondering is pleasurable, the things connected with wonder are necessarily pleasurable. Wondering, in turn, is declared to be pleasurable because it implies an appetite for learning. Finally, learning is a pleasure because it consists of a return to that according to nature, which satisfies the definition of pleasure. Thus, through a series of enthymematic deductions Aristotle links reversals of fortune to wonder, then to learning, and finally to the definition of pleasure.[38]

Another good example of Aristotle's deductive procedure concerns the pleasure of children (1371b13-26). As is usually the case, those elements of the reasoning that are obvious are left unstated. If these are stated, it becomes clear that Aristotle's deduction consists of four interconnected enthymemes, with the bracketed material unstated in the text:

> By definition that according to nature is pleasant. Things akin [*ta sungene*] are so according to nature. Therefore, all things akin are "for the most part" pleasant.[39]

> Things akin are pleasant to one another. Each man feels akin to the greatest degree to himself. Therefore, all men are [pleasant to themselves and] more or less lovers of themselves.

> All men are lovers of themselves. [They identify themselves with what belongs to them] Therefore, men take pleasure in what is their own, such as their "works" (*erga*).

Men take pleasure in their "works." [Their children are their "works."] Therefore, men take pleasure in their children.

It is by reasoning through enthymemes that rhetoricians satisfy their listeners' desire for learning. Aristotle is concerned, therefore, to provide instruction in the use of enthymemes. Later in the *Rhetoric* (20. 18-26), he explicates the formal logic of enthymematic reasoning. But even in his expositions of the subjects pertinent to the three kinds of rhetoric, as is evident in the above examples, he sets forth his comments in enthymematic form and thereby instructs by example.

But the crucial point for my argument is the comparison of this rhetorical treatment of pleasure with the account of pleasure provided in the *Ethics*. Pleasure in its essence—pure pleasure unmixed with pain—is found, as explained in the *Ethics*, in the active functioning (*energeia*) of the natural faculties of man; and the highest pleasure is contemplation, because it is the activity of the highest human faculty. Therefore, the pleasure that accompanies the motion (*kinesis*) of the soul toward a restoration of a faculty to its natural state is pleasure only "by accident"; for true pleasure lies not in the process of restoring a natural faculty, but in the unimpeded activity (*energeia*) of the faculty itself. That men take pleasure in motion or change is a sign of their imperfection. But insofar as a man can share in perfection through the divine activity of contemplation, he can enjoy the pure pleasure of self-sufficient activity, which is unchanging.

In the *Rhetoric*, however, Aristotle must adopt the perspective of ordinary men, for whom all pleasure is some form of restorative motion of the soul. (Moreover, he studies pleasure only in the context of discussing the motives for injustice.) His rhetorical account of pleasure is therefore incomplete and thus defective.

But as so often happens in the *Rhetoric*, the common opinions in this case point beyond themselves to the truth of which they are only the partial embodiment. By accentuating here the cognitive elements of pleasure and by drawing attention to the pleasure of learning as that through which men fulfill their nature, Aristotle indicates that even in their pursuit of ordinary pleasures, all men strive to satisfy their natural desire to know. Thus all men aim at that pure pleasure rarely achieved by only a few men.[40] Aristotle assumes throughout the *Rhetoric* that since men are by nature rational beings, they take pleasure in learning. This assumption explains a quality in men—their natural openness to persuasion through speech—that makes rhetoric possible.

The Agents and Victims of Injustice (12)

Aristotle's study of pleasure completes his examination of the motives of injustice. He must turn now to the dispositions of those who commit injustice and of those who suffer it.

The Agents of Injustice (1372a4–1372b23)

Aristotle begins his study of the doers of injustice with a general statement of the conditions that men must think to be satisfied before they will commit injustice (1372a5–8):

> They do injustice whenever they think the action can be done and can be done by them, or if doing it they would escape notice, or if not escaping notice not suffering punishment, or if suffering it but the loss being less than the profit for them or for those for whom they care.

Just as with the definitions in previous chapters, this initial statement is the point of departure for all of Aristotle's comments on the agents of injustice. After referring to the "commonplace" of possibility and impossibility as being relevant to this subject (1372a8–10), he catalogues the particular factors taken into account by the criminal, all of which are somehow connected to his opening general statement.

Aristotle lists circumstances in which men think they can commit injustice without penalty (1372a11–22), or without being detected (1372a23–33), or without suffering full punishment when they are detected (1372a34–37). He then explains that men commit crimes if the profit seems greater than the penalty (1372a38–1372b9). But since men weigh benefits and losses differently, according to their differing characters, he must comment on the effect of a man's character in judging the proper circumstances for crime (1372b9–16). Finally, he explains how the general conditions of a man's life or the particular conditions of specific actions can lead him to think that his crimes will be unnoticed or extenuated by others (1372b16–23).

Criminals feel confident, Aristotle notices, if they are good public speakers. They are more likely to commit a crime if they see an opportunity for protecting themselves by sophistical arguments, and some of the fallacies on which they rely are the same as those listed by Aristotle as topics of apparent enthymemes.[41]

Aristotle's treatment of the dispositions of those who commit injustice is essentially an account of criminal reasoning. He emphasizes the criminal's rational calculation through which possible benefits are weighed against possible losses. He suggests, however, that not all

100

criminals are totally rational because some allow their incontinence or imprudence to distort their calculation.

Since they prefer immediate gratification without regard for the consequences, incontinent men do injustice whenever the pleasure is before the pain or the profit before the loss. But continent and more prudent men do it when the pain or the loss is immediate and the pleasure or the profit is later and more enduring (1372b12-16). While acknowledging that some criminals may allow their judgments to be warped by incontinence, Aristotle in this way increases the possible rationality of crime by assuming that some criminals act not only with continence but also with "prudence" (*phronesis*) (see 3. 16. 1417a26-28).

In the *Nicomachean Ethics* (1144a22-1145a2), Aristotle distinguishes "cleverness" (*deinotes*) and "prudence" (*phronesis*). A bad man can be as "clever" as a good man, in the sense of discovering the best means for achieving one's end. But although it includes "cleverness," "prudence" also requires that the end chosen be good; so one cannot be "prudent" unless one is also virtuous. In the *Rhetoric*, Aristotle sometimes seems to treat "prudence" as being morally neutral and thus indistinguishable from "cleverness"; but at other times he seems to assume the teaching in the *Ethics* that "prudence" implies virtue (see 1. 7. 1363b14-15, 1364b13-20, 9. 1366b20-22).

The Victims of Injustice (1372b24-1373a27)

Aristotle's account of those who suffer injustice consists of a series of nineteen topics. Although the topics are not arranged according to any precise order, a rough pattern is discernible. The first two-thirds of the list concerns primarily the types of people who are likely victims because they are not on guard or because they are unwilling or unable to seek redress for their sufferings (1372b24-1373a9).[42] The final third of the list involves primarily types of people who seem to deserve the crimes committed against them (1373a9-27), the result being that the crimes "appear almost not to be unjust" (1373a11, 15, 20).

Injustices Likely to be Committed (1373a27-37)

Aristotle concludes this chapter by listing four types of crimes that are most likely to be committed: crimes that all or many people commit habitually, thefts of objects easily hidden, assaults that victims are ashamed to disclose, and crimes that seem so trivial or venial that victims who would appeal to the law would appear litigious.

The shift here from *persons* to *deeds*—from the agents and victims of injustice to unjust acts—serves as a transition to the next chapter, in which Aristotle classifies just and unjust actions.

The Kinds of Law (13)

Aristotle begins the chapter by distinguishing two kinds of law (1373b2-10):

> I say that law is particular [*idion*] and common [*koinon*], particular that which is defined by each people with reference to themselves, and this is unwritten and written, common that which is according to nature. For there is, which all divine in some manner, a common just and unjust thing by nature, even if there is neither mutual communion [*koinonia*] nor agreement, of the sort that Sophocles' Antigone appears to say, that to bury Polyneices is justice forbidden, supposing that this is just by nature.

He then quotes Antigone's declaration: "For neither now nor yesterday but always this lives, and no one knows from whence it comes to light."[43] Next he refers to two other examples of appeals to natural justice, one by Empedocles and one by Alcidamus (1373b13-18). Empedocles claimed it was naturally unjust to kill any animate being. The quotation from Alcidamus is not found in the Greek manuscripts; but according to an anonymous scholiast the reference was to the declaration of Alcidamus that God had made all men free and none a slave.[44]

These three examples of appeals to natural justice are quite odd. The validity of the latter two would surely have to be denied by Aristotle, and the case of Antigone is ambiguous.[45] Presumably, the claim of Empedocles that to refrain from killing animate beings is a dictate of nature would be challenged by Aristotle. Indeed, shortly after the quotation from Empedocles, Aristotle cites refusal to serve in a city's army as an example of injustice against the community (1373b24-25). Further, he refers to Empedocles elsewhere in the *Rhetoric* (3. 5. 1407a32-36) as someone who pretended to speak when he had nothing to say. And the declaration of Alcidamus that all slavery is against nature contradicts Aristotle's doctrine of natural slavery, although he does suggest in the *Politics* (1253b15-1255b40) that the existing institution of slavery is "conventional" rather than "natural." Antigone's case is surely the strongest of the three; but while Aristotle might have thought the family to be natural in some sense, it seems unlikely that he would have thought it an absolute dictate of nature to bury one's brother irrespective of the circumstances. All three examples are invocations of things beyond the city; but the true character of natural justice is manifest not so much in the particular examples, all of which are dubious, but in the fact that they are all appeals to the law that is beyond the conventional. There is natural justice, Aristotle seems to say, but to specify what it demands in particular circumstances is difficult.

The example of Antigone deserves further comment. Aristotle's quotations from the *Antigone* are selected so that there is no reference to the gods, and thus he makes of Antigone's appeal to the gods an appeal to nature.[46] Also, Aristotle manages to refer to Antigone without mentioning filial piety. Familial duties can appear to be simply natural because they are old and habitual. Even if some sort of familial institution is dictated by nature, the actual institutions of marriage and the family might be thought by Aristotle to be largely determined by legal conventions.[47]

In addition to the ambiguity of the three examples, Aristotle's remarks on "natural justice" raise two further difficulties: first, it is not clear how "natural justice" can properly be understood as "natural *law*"; second, while Aristotle refers to "particular law" as "written" and to "common law" as "unwritten," he also divides "particular law" into "written" and "unwritten." Although he refers in other works — particularly in the *Nicomachean Ethics* — to "natural justice," it is only here in the *Rhetoric* that he calls this a "law." Most commentators find no difficulty in identifying "natural justice" and "natural law."[48] But at least one commentator argues that while the notion of "natural law" presupposes a divine legislator, which made it attractive to Christian theologians of the Middle Ages, Aristotle's doctrine of "natural justice" does not require such a presupposition.[49] Yet before this problem can be taken up for examination, it is necessary to clarify the distinction between written and unwritten law.

Aristotle has previously differentiated law into "particular law" that is "written" and "common law" that is "unwritten" (10. 1368b7-10), but he begins this chapter by dividing "particular law" into "written" and "unwritten" (1373b4-6). He further complicates things by speaking of two types of "unwritten law." One type involves "an excess of virtue and vice, for which there is praise and blame, honor and dishonor, and rewards — such as to be grateful to someone who has done something good, to requite a good that has been done, and to be helpful to friends" (1374a18-27). The second type of "unwritten law" is "equity," which makes up for the defects of "particular written law." Some interpreters have inferred that both of these types of "unwritten law" belong to the "unwritten" portion of the "particular law" rather than to the "common law."[50] But there is evidence for the view that the first kind of "unwritten law" — "excess of virtue and vice" — is "common law," and that only the second kind — "equity" — belongs to "particular law." The "common law" is clearly said to be "unwritten" (10. 1368b7-10, 15. 1375a27-1375b2); therefore, when Aristotle distinguishes the two kinds of "unwritten law," one would assume that at least one of the two kinds refers to "common law." Moreover, Aristotle clearly connects "equity" to "particular law" by speaking of it as containing what is "omitted from the particular and written law"; but he does not connect "excess of virtue and vice" to "particular law." Finally, Aristotle says in a subsequent chapter that if the "written law" is counter to one's case, one should appeal to "common law and equity" as being more just since "equity remains always and never changes, nor the common (for it is according to nature), but the written many times" (15. 1375a27-1375b2). There is no obvious way of explaining why he does not mention the "unwritten law" involving "excess of virtue and vice" unless one assumes that this sort of law is included within the "common law."

If "equity" is the only kind of "unwritten law" contained within "particular law," then one can explain why Aristotle equates "particular law," in at least one passage, with "written law." Since the "unwritten" portion of "particular law" — "equity" — is only a *corrective* of the "written law," this sort of "unwritten law" is ancillary to and dependent upon the "written law"; and therefore one could speak loosely of *all* "particular law" as "written."

Also, once one recognizes the "unwritten law" concerning "excess of virtue and vice" as "common law," one can have a clearer notion of "natural law." Examples of the "excess of virtue and vice" are "to be grateful to someone who has done something good, to requite a good that has been done, and to be helpful to friends" (1374a23-24). These same examples are cited by other Greek authors who wrote about "unwritten law."[51] But unlike the traditional examples, Aristotle's pertain completely to reciprocity in human relationships and obligations of friendship; he makes no reference to duties toward the gods or parents (unless the gods or one's parents should be considered benefactors whose good deeds should be requited). As in his reference to Antigone, he is unwilling to mention religious or filial piety as part of what is "just by nature."

The "natural law" that is founded upon "praise or blame, honor or dishonor, and rewards" would seem to be a *customary* law, and this would seem to explain why "natural law" is a *law*. Why is it only in the

Rhetoric that Aristotle speaks of "natural justice" as "natural *law*"? Perhaps because the rhetorician appeals not directly to the "just by nature," but instead to the sense of natural justice embodied in the customary moral standards of men. This is suggested by Aristotle's definition of "common law" as being "as many unwritten things as seem to be granted by all" (1368b10); the "natural law" is that part of "natural justice" to which all men have consented through their long-established—that is, customary—moral practices. This may be spoken of as "law" because customs are in a sense *enacted* by men as "unwritten law." The word "custom" does not appear in these passages on "natural law," but the concept is surely implied.[52] For how else except through custom do men's praise and blame, honor and dishonor, become moral law? And furthermore, is it not characteristic of rhetoric to identify the "customary" and "habitual" with the "natural"?

The appeal to what "all somehow divine" as being just by nature shows again the dependence of Aristotelian rhetoric upon men's commonsense perceptions of the true and the just. The ordinary moral sense of men—such as is manifested in the moral indignation of Antigone—is obviously defective in some respects; but it does exhibit at least a partial grasp of "natural justice," which is the essential foundation of a noble rhetoric.[53]

Justice and Injustice with Reference to Persons (1373b1–38)

Considered in relation to persons, unjust actions can be distinguished, Aristotle says, into those committed against particular individuals and those against the community as a whole.

But since injustice is a voluntary act, it is important to distinguish voluntary and involuntary acts, for one accused of a crime has acted "either ignorantly or unwillingly, or willingly and knowingly, and in the later case with premeditation or through passion" (1373b34–36). This fourfold division corresponds exactly to that found in the *Nicomachean Ethics* (1135b8–1136a5).

Defining Crimes (1373b39–1374a18)

When someone is accused of a crime, it is not sufficient merely to know what he has done; one must also know whether what he has done can be properly described as a crime. It is possible, for example, for a man to admit that he has taken something but deny that he has stolen it. To convict a man of a crime, the community must show that he has done something with the "intention" or "purpose" (*proairesis*) of committing injustice. Thus Aristotle introduces his doctrine of *proairesis* from the

Ethics into the *Rhetoric*. But the rhetorical use of this doctrine is rather different from its use in the *Ethics*. For "purpose" as considered by the forensic rhetorician differs from "purpose" considered with respect to moral character, because a man virtuous in his "purpose" might still commit a crime, and a man vicious in his "purpose" might never commit a crime.[54]

Equity (1374a19-1374b22)

Aristotle begins his remarks on "equity" (*epieikeia*) by defining it (1374a25-1374b1); he then indicates, based on his definition, what things and people are equitable and what are not. This passage is especially important because the traditional jurisprudential concept of "equity" originated with Aristotle, and although he comments on "equity" in the *Nicomachean Ethics* (1137a31-1138a4), his fullest account is here in the *Rhetoric*.[55] That Aristotle should insert so important a statement on equitable justice into the *Rhetoric* is both an indication of the seriousness of the book and a tribute to the moral character of rhetoric.

Equity has a specific and a general meaning. Its specific function is to alleviate the defects of the written law that are due to its inevitable generality and the inability of legislators to foresee all circumstances. More generally, it denotes a human attitude that softens the sometimes unduly harsh effects of the written law. The principle underlying equity is that what is just in most cases is not always just for particular circumstances.

The subtlety of Aristotle's comments is well illustrated by his claim that different punishments should be assigned for "errors," "injustices," and "misfortunes" (1374b2-9). "Misfortunes are all such things as are unexpected and not for depravity, errors such as are not unexpected and not from wickedness, injustices such as are not unexpected and from wickedness—for all things done through appetite are from wickedness."

But in reading Aristotle's account of "equity," one should remember his warning in the first chapter about the bad consequences of allowing jurors to set aside the law in favor of their own discretionary judgment (1354a28-1354b16). "Equity" is meant to correct but not to replace the law. He indicates this when he distinguishes between the equitable judgment of an "arbiter" and the strict adherence to law of a "juror" (1374b20-23). A good government is both a government of laws and a government of men, but such a combination is obviously difficult because of the delicate balance of conflicting principles that it requires. Aristotle will soon state this problem more explicitly (15. 1375a25-1375b25).[56]

Degrees of Injustice (14)

In this chapter Aristotle provides "topics" for determining the greatness of unjust deeds. Unjust acts are greater in proportion to the greatness of the injustice of the agent (1374b23-28), the greatness of the injury (1374b29-1375a1), the greater prominence of the unjust act (1375a2-6), the greater brutality of the act, the greater premeditation, and the greater tendency to arouse in listeners fear more than pity (1375a6-8). The crime also seems greater if a rhetorician can divide it into many crimes (1375a8-11; cf. 1. 7. 1365a10-19). It is also greater if it is "most shameful," such as a crime against a benefactor (1375a13-15). Finally, Aristotle concludes by noting that from one viewpoint a crime is greater if it is against the "unwritten law" — "for it is better to be just without being compelled" — but from another viewpoint greater if it is against the "written law" — "for one who commits injustices that involve fear and punishment will commit those that are not punished" (1375a15-22). This final "topic," in which the opposing sides of an issue can be argued equally well, illustrates the sort of "topic" that appears repeatedly in the next chapter.

"Inartificial Proofs" (15)

Introduction (1375a23-24)

Aristotle concludes Book One with remarks on the "inartificial proofs" (*atechnoi pisteis*) of forensic rhetoric. These are the elements of legal argument that are already present in the circumstances rather than provided by the rhetorician himself. Aristotle considers five—laws, witnesses, contracts, torture, and oaths (see 1. 1. 1355b35-38).

In his comments on each of these five, Aristotle gives instructions for arguing opposite sides of the issue, depending upon which side is most favorable to one's case. But lest this appear a purely sophistical exercise, it should be stressed that in each case, there *is* something valid to be said on both sides. Practical matters are so uncertain that in some cases there is equally strong support for opposing arguments, and it is important for the prudence of the rhetorician that he recognize this.[57]

Laws (1375a25–1375b25)

Aristotle begins with laws. If the written law runs against one's case, he explains, then one should appeal to "equity" and the "common law" as being superior to the written law. The true aim of a judge, one should argue, is to decide in accordance with *true* rather than merely *apparent* justice; therefore the written law should be set aside if it fails to support what is truly just. Also, if a law contradicts itself or some other law, or if its meaning is obscure, or if it was enacted for circumstances that no longer exist, then again a judge should decide without reference to the law. But if the written law supports one's case, one should argue that the duty of a judge is only to decide according to the laws, and that "no one chooses what is good simply but rather what is good for himself."[58] To try to be wiser than the laws, one might say, is like trying to be wiser than a physician, "for the error of the physician does not do as much harm as the habit of disobeying the authority" (1375b22–23).

Aristotle is not showing how to make the weaker argument the stronger because here neither argument is the stronger. From one perspective, a government of men is better than a government of laws because men can decide what is just in the particular circumstances of each case. But from another perspective, a government of laws is better because few men are capable of judging wisely and justly; it is therefore best that men be guided by the wisdom and justice of the legislator as embodied in the laws. Considering this even balance between the two sides of the issue, it is best for the opposing rhetoricians to argue their positions as persuasively as possible so that the judges may see both sides and then decide which side should prevail in the particular case before them.

Witnesses (1375b26–1376a33)

Aristotle distinguishes between ancient and recent witnesses, and he distinguishes recent witnesses into those who participate in the trial and those who do not. Witnesses at the trial are convincing with regard to the facts of the case, but not with regard to the justice or injustice, expediency or inexpediency, of what was done. Concerning the latter question, witnesses unconnected to the case are trustworthy; but ancient witnesses are the most trustworthy since it is impossible to corrupt them.

Aristotle summarizes the arguments both for those who have witnesses and for those who do not. Arguing with "probabilities" alone can be defended by noting that "probabilities" cannot be bribed and cannot commit perjury. But on the other hand, someone with witnesses might argue that "probabilities" are insufficient and that they cannot be brought to trial as witnesses can. Once again reasonable arguments can be adduced for both sides.

Contracts (1376a34–1376b31)

The arguments for and against the legal value of contracts are similar to those concerning whether written or unwritten laws are supreme. If one's position in a dispute is favored by a contract, then one might argue that to deny the authority of contracts is to undermine the laws generally and to eliminate the legal instrument by which the social life of men is regulated. But if one wishes to counter the effect of a contract, one can maintain that justice is the ultimate standard irrespective of contractual obligations that fall short of true justice.

Torture (1376b32–1377a8)

With respect to all the other types of "inartificial proofs," Aristotle gives good reasons both for and against the particular kind of evidence in question. But in the case of torture he quietly but clearly indicates that the arguments against evidence from torture are true while the arguments favoring it are at best "seeming." Although he states the argument favoring it—"it seems to be trustworthy because a sort of compulsion is attached to it" (1375b32-33)—Aristotle makes it evident that the "truth" is quite otherwise: in fact, evidence from torture is untrustworthy, because some people lie to escape or end torture and others never speak no matter how much they are tortured.

Although he is careful to show the indefensibility of evidence secured by torture, Aristotle does not openly condemn it, and he even states the sort of argument that is made in its defense. When torture is regarded as acceptable, the Aristotelian rhetorician must be tough-minded enough to know the arguments in its favor in case he is forced to rely on such evidence. A rhetorician concerned with truth and justice need not be naive; indeed he would be worthy of blame if he were unwilling, in especially difficult situations, to employ whatever distasteful means are necessary to achieve his good ends.

Oaths (1377a9–1377b13)

In Attic legal practice, it was possible for the parties in a dispute to challenge one another to take an oath in order to settle the question at issue. "Concerning oaths, Aristotle says, "the division is fourfold: for either we offer an oath and accept it, or neither, or one but not the other, and in the last case we either offer it but do not accept it or accept it but do not offer it" (1377a9-11). He sets forth the arguments for each alternative.

6

THE CHARACTERS AND PASSIONS OF MEN (2. 1-17)

Introduction (1)

In the preceding chapters, Aristotle has discussed deliberative, epideictic, and forensic rhetoric by presenting the "opinions and premises"
(*doxai kai protaseis*) about which and from which the rhetorician can
construct enthymemes suitable for each type of rhetoric (1377b15-20).
But since rhetoric is for the sake of "judgment," he now explains that "it
is necessary not only to see with respect to the speech [*logos*] how it can
be demonstrative [*apodeiktikos*] and convincing [*pistos*], but also to
establish [*kataskeuazein*] oneself to be of a certain sort and the judge [in
a certain disposition]" (1377b21-23). (Aristotle uses the verbs
kataskeuazein and *paraskeuazein* to denote the speaker's "establishing,"
"rendering," or "fashioning" of his own character and of the passions of
the audience in a manner conducive to persuasion [see 2. 2. 1380a1, 3.
1380b32, 5. 1383a8, 7. 1385a32, 9. 1387b18, 10. 1388a27].) Since the
rhetorician has learned how to argue about the subjects of rhetoric, he
must now learn how to display his own character and how to move his
listeners so as to produce conviction.

But why should Aristotle introduce the *pisteis* of *ethos* and *pathos* at
this point in his book? Many commentators find this shift of attention
confusing because they see it as an interruption of Aristotle's discussion
of logical proof.[1] Chapters 4 through 15 of Book One concern the
materials of enthymemes; but the logical analysis of enthymemes does
not come until the end of Book Two (Chapters 18 through 26) so the
chapters on character and passion seem to be out of place. The location
of this treatment of character and passion becomes understandable,
however, if one recognizes that Aristotle is still concerned in these
chapters with the materials of enthymemes. The mistake of the commentators is in assuming that the presentation of a speaker's character
and the handling of an audience's emotions are unrelated to enthymematic reasoning. Whereas in Book One Aristotle provided
premises related to the subject matter of rhetoric, in Book Two he pro-

111

vides premises related to the character of the speaker and the passions of the audience (2. 1. 1377b15-20, 1378a28-31, 3. 1380b30-33, 9. 1388b27-30, 22. 1396b28-1397a6). Thus, he presents material for constructing enthymemes with which a rhetorician can argue about deliberative, epideictic, and forensic subjects and also display his own good character and move his audience emotionally.

It might be argued, however, that since Aristotle speaks of the proof through the *logos* itself, as founded on "demonstration," and distinguishes this from proof through *pathos*, the appeal to *pathos* cannot be a part of rhetorical "demonstration." But such an interpretation is incorrect because Aristotle speaks of his analyses of the passions as providing materials for "demonstration" (*apodeixis, deiknunai*). So even his study of the passions is carried out for the sake of constructing rhetorical syllogisms (see 1. 2. 1356a1-4, 19-21, 2. 1. 1377b21-24, 1378a6-7, 4. 1382a16-18, 7. 1385a30-1385b11, 9. 1387b18-21).

Aristotle deals with the passions in a way that differs from the practice of sophistical rhetoricians. For while the sophists rely exclusively on appeals to the passions to distract listeners from the subject at hand, Aristotle shows how the passions can be handled as an integral part of enthymematic argument. The sophist excites the passions to divert his listeners from rational deliberation; the Aristotelian speaker controls the passions by reasoning with his listeners. Before taking up the passions, however, Aristotle begins Book Two by commenting briefly on what is required for the character of a speaker.

The Character of the Speaker (1)

What Aristotle says here about the character of the speaker should not be confused with his earlier discussion of the characters of regimes (1. 8) or his subsequent discussion of the characters of men in general (2. 12-17). In these other portions of the *Rhetoric*, Aristotle examines the characters of *audiences* as determined both by the characters of individuals and by the characters of regimes. But here he turns his attention to the character of the *speaker*. It surely is true, however, that the speaker must try to present his own character in a way that conforms to the character of his audience (2. 13. 1390a25-27).

A speaker's character will be most persuasive if he shows himself to possess "prudence," "virtue," and "goodwill" (1378a5-19). Audiences believe that speakers without these three qualities are untrustworthy. Without prudence a speaker is unlikely to have correct opinions. But even if his opinions are correct, he cannot be trusted to deliver his opin-

112

ions sincerely if he lacks virtue. And even if he is both prudent and virtuous, he might still mislead his listeners if he is not well disposed toward them. A speaker wins the trust of his audience by showing that he is a good man, that he knows what he is talking about, and that he wishes to do what is best for his listeners.

The three qualities demanded of the rhetorician correspond closely to the qualifications for political rule generally. This is seen when Aristotle lists in the *Politics* (1309a33-38) the following three factors as required for holding the highest offices: "first, friendship for the established regime; next, a great capacity for the functions of rule; thirdly, virtue and justice—in each regime that with reference to the regime."

Aristotle's remarks about the speaker's character are brief because the three qualities he mentions here are studied elsewhere in the *Rhetoric*. To learn how to display prudence and goodness, the reader is referred to the earlier chapter on the virtues. And to learn about goodwill the reader must look ahead to the sections on friendship and kindness. Looking back at the chapter on virtues, one sees that prudence is there defined as the ability to decide well with respect to good and bad things (1. 9. 1366a20-22). From this one might infer that a speaker displays his prudence by judging well the matters about which he speaks, which is to say that prudence demands mastery of the materials presented in Book One of the *Rhetoric*.[2]

That audiences make such demands upon speakers is surely a serious constraint upon sophistical speakers. This explains why the sophistical teachers of rhetoric try to deny the persuasiveness of the speaker's character (1. 2. 1356a9-13).[3] Audiences can, of course, be deceived sometimes by the mere appearance of good character, and they can be misled sometimes by a speaker's genuinely good character; in both cases they will accept incorrect opinions.[4] But the fact remains that men are most of the time intelligent enough to see that a speaker's advice is trustworthy only if he is prudent, virtuous, and friendly toward them. To be successful a speaker must respect this judgment and somehow come to terms with it. In other words, a speaker is unlikely to prosper if he lets it be seen that he thinks his listeners are fools.

Moreover, it is clear that the persuasiveness of a speaker's character cannot be dismissed as irrational. For is it not quite rational to judge a rhetorician's reliability as proportional to his prudence, his virtue, and his goodwill? It would seem, then, that Aristotle's account of this element of rhetoric further confirms the solidity of the commonsense judgments of listeners. But even if persuasion through *ethos* is rational,

113

what about the influence of *pathos?* Initially, the rhetorical appeal to the passions would seem to be an appeal to purely irrational impulses, but an examination of Aristotle's remarks gives grounds for concluding that even the passions can be dealt with in a rational manner and that the rhetorician can include persuasion through *pathos* as an element of his enthymematic argumentation.

Anger as the Paradigmatic Passion (1–3)

Reasoning with the Passions

The success of the rhetorician in handling the passions suggests that the passions must somehow be rational. For in trying to persuade an audience to adhere to some passions and give up others, the speaker must assume that speech alone is sufficient to alter men's passions. And such an assumption is verified not only by rhetorical practice but also by more common experiences: men are continually talked into or out of their passions, either by themselves or by others. Passions do respond to arguments.

Passions are affected by arguments because men agree that passions can be either reasonable or unreasonable and that passions shown to be reasonable should be adopted while those shown to be unreasonable should be rejected. Since a passion is always *about* something, since it always refers to some object, it is reasonable if it represents its object correctly and unreasonable if it does not. This does not mean, of course, that men adhere only to reasonable passions, but it does mean that they must *believe* that their passions are reasonable. That is, even if all passions are *rational,* it does not follow necessarily that they are all *reasonable* or *true,* because what makes the passions rational is that they can be *either* reasonable *or* unreasonable, *either* true *or* false.

It is the rationality of the passions that distinguishes them from purely bodily sensations and appetites. It would be ridiculous to judge an itch or a pang of hunger as true or false, reasonable or unreasonable; and it would be equally absurd to argue with a man who felt an itch or a sensation of hunger in order to convince him that his feelings were unjustified. But it is not ridiculous to judge a man's anger as reasonable or unreasonable or to try to argue with him when his anger is unjustified. A man's anger depends upon his belief that anger is a proper response to something that has occurred, but a man's sensations or physical appetites do not require that he believe this or that.

Reflections such as these might lead one to conclude that passions rest upon judgments about things in the world and that they are true or

114

false depending upon whether they correspond correctly with their objects. Hence a rhetorician can arouse or allay the passions of his audience with arguments: he arouses a passion by showing that the facts of the case justify such a passion, and he allays a passion by showing that the facts do not justify it. The rhetorician changes the passions of his listeners by changing their minds.

This preliminary sketch of what might be called the cognitive theory of the passions suffices for the purposes of this study, for it is now necessary to scrutinize in detail Aristotle's own study of the passions to see that he does in fact take this view of the passions and to see how he applies this to the particular passions that he considers.[5]

Anger is the first passion that Aristotle examines, and he commonly treats it as representative of all the passions (1. 1. 1354a15-17, 10. 1369a3-8, 1369b10-17, 2. 1. 1378a20-31, 21. 1388b33).[6] Anger, it seems, is the paradigmatic passion. One can assume, therefore, that Aristotle's general view of the passions will be manifest in his treatment of anger.

Anger Defined and Analyzed

Aristotle's method of organizing his remarks on anger sets the pattern for his discussions of the other passions. His method combines two principles: deduction from an initial definition and a tripartite analysis.

Each passion, he thinks, may be divided into three parts; for example, with respect to anger, "how angry men are disposed, with whom they are customarily angry, and in what sort of circumstances" (1. 1. 1378a23-26). Thus, one may differentiate the motives (or state of mind) of each passion, its occasions, and its objects.[7]

But also, just as in Book One (particularly chapters 5 through 7 and 9 through 11), Aristotle employs a deductive method, which consists in stating a definition (introduced with the technical term *esto*) and then working out the necessary inferences from it. For each of the passions, Aristotle deduces every statement either from the definition, from one of its parts, or from some inference from the definition.[8]

How Aristotle combines these two principles of organization—the tripartite analysis and deduction from a definition—can be illustrated with regard to anger. He begins with a definition. "Let anger be a desire [*orexis*] with pain for a manifest [*phainomene*] revenge for a manifest slight of oneself or one's own, the slight being undeserved [*me prosekontos*]" (1378a32-33). He next infers that if this definition is so, then it is true by necessity (*anangke*) that anger is directed at individuals but not at men in general; he also infers that anger must be accompanied by pleasure from the hope of revenge. Here he draws upon his study of pleasure in Book One (1. 11. 1378a34-1378b9). Next he defines slighting and lists three types of slight (1378b10-33). Then, turning to another element of the definition of anger—that the slight must be undeserved—amplifies this point (1378b34-1379a8). Having elucidated the definition, he applies his tripartite analysis and comments first on the dispositions of angry men (1379a9-27) and then on those who are the objects of anger (1379a28-1379b35). Finally, he indicates that with this knowledge of the dispositions, the conditions, and the objects of anger, the speaker should be able to handle men's anger (1379b36-1380a4). As with his treatment of the other passions, Aristotle assumes that there is no need for a separate discussion of the conditions or occasions of anger since these are apparent in his discussions of the dispositions and objects of anger.

Aristotle then turns to the opposite of anger—calmness or gentleness (*praotes*). As with anger, his concern is with the disposition of calmness, the persons towards whom men are calm, and the reasons for calmness (2. 3. 1380a5-7). He begins by defining calmness as "the quieting or appeasing of anger" (1380a8). He then discusses those with whom men are calm (1380a9-1380b2) and the disposition of calm men (1380b3-30).

A knowledge of the dispositions characteristic of passions such as anger helps a speaker control the passions insofar as he can control the thoughts or beliefs essential to the dispositions. Aristotle's definitions of the passions commonly rest on men's conceptions of situations; a speaker can influence these conceptions by the arguments he makes. Similarly, the other two dimensions of the passions—the conditions under which and the persons against whom the passions arise—generally depend upon the impassioned man's thought or beliefs, which the speaker can attempt to create or suppress with his speech.[9]

Aristotle conceives of the passions not as inner feelings or sensations, but as opinions or judgments about the world. A man becomes angry when he believes someone has unjustly slighted him. His anger, then, is an apprehension or assessment of something outside himself.[10] This apprehension may be correct or incorrect, but the existence of the anger depends upon the angry man's belief that he has grasped the situation correctly. Anger, therefore, implies some sort of judgment.[11]

That Aristotle regards anger as resting upon an act of judgment is especially apparent in a passage in the *Nicomachean Ethics* (1149a25-1149b3). Incontinence in anger is less shameful than incontinence in appetite, he says, because "while anger follows from reason somehow, appetite does not and is therefore more shameful; for he who is incontinent in anger is conquered by reason somehow, while he who is incontinent in appetite is conquered by appetite but not by reason." How is it that the angry man is "conquered by reason somehow"? To become angry, Aristotle explains, a man must apprehend by "reason or imagination" that he has been slighted, and then he must reason syllogistically that it is necessary to revenge himself for the slight.[12] The fault with acting in the heat of anger, Aristotle indicates, is not the *absence* of reasoning but the *hastiness* of the reasoning.

Anger thus rests upon some sort of reasoning, which allows the rhetorician to control the anger of his audience by reasoning with them. Aristotle provides numerous illustrations of how a speaker can diffuse the anger of his listeners by persuading them that they are mistaken in their judgment of reality and should therefore calm their anger. At one point, for instance, he observes that a rhetorician can use what he has learned in the *Rhetoric* to allay the anger of his audience by showing them that those with whom they are angry are "fearful or worthy of respect or benefactors or involuntary agents or men grieved at what they have done" (1380b30-33). If a group of men become angry at someone who acted involuntarily or who is sorry for what he has done, one has to assume that since they are mistaken they will give up their anger when they are persuaded that the one with whom they are angry acted unwillingly or is sorry for his action (1380a8-14). Anger is inappropirate here because the conditions of anger have not been satisfied; and therefore when the angry listeners are convinced of this, they will be calmed. Also, as Aristotle indicates, anger is logically incompatible with fear (1380a20-23, 32-34). Men cannot feel angry either with those whom they fear or with those who fear them. They cannot be angry at those whom they fear because fear of the harm their enemies can inflict stifles their desire for revenge, and they cannot be angry at those who fear them because they know that they cannot be slighted by those in fear. Therefore, when a rhetorician sees that his listeners are angry at people whom they should fear or people who are fearful of them, he can calm their anger if he can show them their mistake. Not only with respect to anger, but also with respect to the other passions, Aristotle makes it clear that his intention is to show the rhetorician how to "prove" (*deiknunai*) to an audience when a certain passion is or is not justified by the circumstances (see 2. 4. 1382a17-19, 7. 1385a29-35, 9. 1387b17-21).

Of course, the listeners may not be persuaded by the speaker's arguments to alter their passions. But the point here is that the rhetorician handles the passions in the same way he handles any other

117

issue—through some form of reasoning. In any particular situation, his reasoning may not be persuasive enough to be successful; but as Aristotle said at the beginning of the *Rhetoric* (1. 1. 1355b10-14), the act of rhetoric consists not in creating persuasion in every case, but in being as persuasive as possible in the circumstances.

Moreover, the assumption here is that the rhetorician advances his position by promoting those passions appropriate to the circumstances and opposing those passions that are inappropriate. But of course a rhetorician may find himself in a situation where his success would require that his audience either adopt *unjustified* and *unreasonable* passions or give up passions that are *justified* and *reasonable*. Again, this might be a case where the rhetorical situation is so hopeless that the art of rhetoric is insufficient for success. Or it might be a case where the unscrupulous rhetorician would resort to sophistry; but it was noted earlier that even sophistry cannot guarantee success.[13]

Up to this point, an outline of Aristotle's study of anger has been sketched, and it has been noted how his manner of treating anger suggests that the rhetorician can deal with anger through reasoning of some sort. It is necesssary now to examine anger in somewhat greater detail, keeping in mind that it is to be considered paradigmatic for all the passions. Attention will be directed to three elements of the definition of anger that commonly apply as well to the other passions. First, anger is said to be accompanied with pain, and the passions generally are said to involve pleasure and pain. Second, anger is a desire for a "manifest" (*phainomene*) revenge for a "manifest" slight, and the other passions often rest upon "impressions" (*phainomena*) or "imagination" (*phantasia*) of some kind. Third, anger is a response to an "undeserved" slight, and most of the other passions also depend upon some notion of justice and injustice. After examining these points, I shall compare Aristotle's teaching about anger in the *Rhetoric* with what he says in the *De Anima* and the *Ethics*. And since Aristotle often indicates in his other works the deceptiveness of anger and of the passions generally, it is necessary to reflect upon the defects of emotional judgment in the context of rhetorical reasoning.

Pleasure and Pain

As is true of all the passions (1378a20-23), anger involves pleasure and pain. That he has been slighted and that he has not yet revenged himself gives the angry man pain. (Anger is not simply pain, however, because the pain precedes the anger and causes it [*Top.* 125b32-35, 127b30-33].) But at the same time, the hope of revenge—and par-

118

ticularly the image of revenge that this hope brings before his mind—gives the angry man pleasure (1378b4-9).

Also, being in pain disposes men to become angry (1379a8-24). Men are pained when they aim at something they do not yet have; if someone obstructs them or makes light of their condition, they are inclined to become angry with him. This might seem to imply that being thwarted or harmed is sufficient to give rise to anger even without a slight. But perhaps what Aristotle has in mind is that men in need are naturally inclined to interpret being thwarted or harmed by someone as a slight. On the other hand, men who are free from pain are disposed to be calm and not easily angered (1380a2-5). For when men are pleased and when they are confident that their pleasure is secure, they are less likely to think themselves slighted since they do not think themselves vulnerable (1379a36-1379b3).

That anger and the other passions involve pleasure and pain might be taken to indicate the purely bodily character of the passions. But the highly cognitive nature of the pleasures and pains associated with the passions should not be overlooked. The angry man is pained by the *thought* that he has been slighted and has not yet revenged himself. And the pleasure that he experiences comes from the "thought" (*dianoia*) or "mental image" (*phantasia*) of his future revenge (1378b2-9). Aristotle applies here what he has said in Book One about the cognitive and imaginative side of all pleasures.[14] Although the fact that the passions are accompanied by pleasures and pains surely distinguishes the passions from acts of pure contemplation, the passions still seem to be cognitive experiences of some sort.

Imagination and the Passions

That the passions are cognitions, although not cognitions of the purest kind, is indicated by Aristotle's frequent use of *phainomenos* and *phantasia* in defining the passions: the reasoning characteristic of the passions arises largely, it seems, from the imagination.[15]

With respect to anger, Aristotle speaks of the "image" of a slight that arouses anger and of the "image" of revenge that pleases the angry man. Of course, in his use of *phainomene* in this context, Aristotle probably also desires to convey the suggestion of "conspicuous" or "manifest." That is, a man is angered by slights done *in public view,* and he wishes to get his revenge also in public view. Even so, it is still clear that Aristotle links anger to acts of imagination.

Imagination is a rather crude form of cognition in the *De Anima* (427b7-429a9, 434a1-9), where Aristotle describes it as "the movement

119

that arises from the activity [*energeia*] of sensation" (see *Rh.* 1. 11. 1370a27-28). Imagination is the capacity to hold in memory the images of sense-impressions, a faculty possessed even by animals without "intellect" (*nous*), and which must be distinguished from the distinctly human faculty for forming universals.[16] Imagination is essential, however, for the highest intellectual activity, since even theoretical cognition requires "mental images" (*ta phantasmata*).[17] Imagination is also important for practical reasoning. Aristotle use both *phainomenos* and *phantasia* in reference to the conception of the good that guides a man's conduct.[18]

Aristotle's suggestion that the passions are commonly connected to the imagination points to the cognitive character of the passions, at the same time indicating their cognitive limitations. Since the passions arise from "mental images," the rhetorician can handle the passions of his audience by arguing so as to create in their minds the proper "images." Yet he must recognize that to the extent that emotional cognition rests simply upon the imagination without the aid of any higher faculty of reason, it tends to be as unreflective (and thus misleading) as imagination itself. But the limits of emotional judgment are a subject to be considered a bit later in this book.

Anger and the Moral Sense of Men

The final element of anger to consider here is stated by Aristotle at the end of his definition—namely, that the slight that arouses anger must be "undeserved" (*me prosekontos*). Men become angry when they think they are not being treated in accordance with their worth. Anger, then, is a response to injustice in its fundamental sense of not receiving one's due. Indeed, one of the means for the speaker to calm anger is to convince men that they are suffering justly, "for anger does not arise against justice, for they no longer think they are suffering contrary to desert [*para to prosekon*], and this was anger" (1380b17-18; but cf. 1379a36-1379b2, 1381a35-37).

Anger, then, manifests a sense of justice. One might even wonder whether anger shows men's grasp of those unwritten laws of justice spoken of in Book One, Chapter 13. Is it perhaps through anger (and some of the other passions as well) that "all somehow divine" what is just by nature? This seems to be borne out by the fact that some of the prime causes of anger—such as ingratitude, refusal to return good for good, and failure to help one's friends—are the sort of things that Aristotle has identified to be unjust by nature.[19]

That men reveal a natural moral sense in their passions is most evident in the anger of Antigone. Aristotle describes her passion, although without mentioning her explicitly, when he speaks of those who think they are just but have been treated unjustly, and who therefore become fearlessly confident, not only because of their anger but also because they think the gods help those who suffer injustice (2. 5. 1383b2-8).

Moral passions of this sort surely provide a powerful sanction for certain commonly accepted principles of justice.[20] As Aristotle explains, the fearful inclination of most men to commit injustice whenever they can is balanced by the fearful desire of the victims of injustice for retaliation (2. 5. 1382a27-1382b13, 1382b19-22, 6. 1384b6-8). Divine retribution is unnecessary to enforce the unwritten laws of justice so long as the sufferers of injustice are passionately convinced that they are themselves the instruments of divine vengeance.

But even if some of the passions are shown in the *Rhetoric* to manifest a natural moral sense, it is still true that Aristotle does not exhibit the same concern with moral virtue in his study of the passions in the *Rhetoric* as he does in the *Ethics*. Departing from his analysis of the passions in the *Ethics*, Aristotle seems unconcerned in the *Rhetoric* with determining the virtuous mean with respect to each passion. The perspective of the *Rhetoric* seems, then, to be amoral if not immoral. But this must be more closely examined.

Anger in the *Ethics*

Aristotle says in the *Ethics* (1106b16-24) that virtue, with respect to the passions, consists in attaining a "mean" so that each passion occurs at the right time, with the right people, for the right purpose, on the right occasion, and in the right manner. With respect to anger, "calmness" (*praotes*) is the virtue that is a mean between "irascibility" (*orgilotes*) and "inirascibility" (*aorgesia*) (1125b26-1126b10). The "calm" man "is unperturbed and is not led by his passion, but [is angered in the manner and on the occasions and for the length of time] as dictated by reason."

There are two apparent differences between this account of anger and that in the *Rhetoric*. First, the passions appear in the *Rhetoric* as pairs of opposites with no mention of a virtuous mean; anger is treated as the opposite of "calmness." Second, "calmness" appears in the *Rhetoric* as a passion rather than as a virtue. Is this, as many commentators claim, evidence of an intellectually dubious and morally defective method of study such as is characteristic of rhetoric? Let me consider alternative explanations.

Aristotle concedes in the *Ethics* (1108b10-1109a19, 1126a32-1126b10) that it is difficult to lay down a principle for deter-

121

mining the mean because to do so is a matter of judging according to the particular circumstances. Furthermore, one of the extremes can seem so close to the mean that it is hard to distinguish them. This is the case with anger: "To calmness we oppose the excess more than the defect, for it occurs more — for seeking revenge is more characteristic of men [*anthropikoteron*] — and harsh men are worse for living together [*pros to sumbion*]" (1126a29-32). Perhaps this explains why Aristotle treats anger and calmness as opposites in the *Rhetoric*. Since "inirascibility" is a rare defect among men, the rhetorician need not be concerned with it. Also, the rhetorician needs to concentrate his attention on irascibility since it causes more disturbance in political life than "inirascibility." It is sufficient for rhetoric to understand the opposition between irascibility and calmness; "inirascibility" is too rare and too innocuous to be rhetorically interesting.

But why should Aristotle present "calmness" in the *Rhetoric* as a passion rather than as a virtue? First, it should be noticed that in Book One Aristotle lists *praotes* as a virtue (1. 9. 1366b3): even within the *Rhetoric* itself "calmness" is at once a virtue and a passion. Yet does this truly contradict the *Ethics?* Does not Aristotle imply in the *Ethics* that *praotes* is not only a virtue but also a passion? One must remember that *praotes* is not the *absence* of anger, but rather the disposition to become angry with the right person, at the right time, in the right circumstances, and so on. A man becomes virtuous with respect to anger by becoming more reflective about it, by making sure that his anger is always appropriate. Reason rules a passion not by suppressing it, but by transforming it into a reasonable passion.

Still more needs to be said on this point. That Aristotle in the *Rhetoric* includes "calmness" among the passions may suggest that in the *Rhetoric* he depicts the passions not as they are in their raw state, but as they are after they have been tamed by the habituation of law. As Aristotle emphasizes near the end of the *Ethics* (1179a34-1180a14), the passions of the multitude of men are subject not to argument but only to force, and therefore the education of the laws is necessary to create by habituation the proper character among the many. Obviously, so long as men are amenable to compulsion but not to persuasion, rhetoric is ineffectual. The activity of rhetoric presupposes, therefore, that citizens have already been so shaped by the laws that they are open to the appeal of persuasive speech. And this means that their unrefined, and thus unreasonable passions have been transformed into passions that are amenable to argument. It would not be surprising, then, as a result of this habituation of men by the laws, for the virtue of "calmness" to become a passion.[21]

The ultimate conclusion here is that the passions as they appear in the *Rhetoric* are more accessible to reason than are the passions as they arise naturally among men before they are shaped by the laws. This is quite understandable since, as has been argued previously, Aristotle emphasizes in the *Rhetoric* that the speaker must control the passions of his listeners by reasoning with them. But it is now clear that the success of rhetorical appeal to the passions through argument depends upon the prior training of the laws, which direct the passions of the citizens toward reasonableness.

Moreoever, since Aristotle stresses the rationality of the passions in the *Rhetoric*, he abstracts from their physiological character and presents only their cognitive elements. This becomes especially evident when one considers the account of the passions in the *De Anima*.

Anger in the *De Anima*

In the *De Anima* Aristotle regards the "passions of the soul" as both cognitive and somatic. He says (403a16–26):

It is probable that all the passions of the soul are associated with the body [*meta somatos*]—spiritedness, calmness, fear, pity, confidence, and, further, joy and both loving and hating; for at the same time as these the body is affected in a certain way. This is shown by the fact that sometimes when strong and manifest sufferings [*pathemata*] befall us, we are not provoked to exasperation or fear, while at other times we are moved by small and imperceptible sufferings when the body is disposed to anger and is as it is when it is in anger. This is even more apparent; for even when nothing fearful is befalling them, men may come to have the passions of the fearful. If this is so, it is clear that the passions are reasons in matter [*logoi enhuloi*]. Hence the definitions are such as, "being angry is a particular movement of a body of such and such a kind, or a part or potentiality of it, as a result of this thing and for the sake of that."

Passion, then, must be considered to have both a rational or cognitive side—its "reason" or "formula" (*logos*)—and a somatic side—its physiological manifestations.[22] The dialectician, however, stresses the cognitive side, Aristotle goes on to say (403a26–403b9), while the natural philosopher (*physikos*) stresses the physical side. For example, the dialectician defines anger as a "desire for retaliation or something of the sort," while the natural philosopher defines it as "the surging of the blood and heat around the heart." Neither of these two definitions is complete, Aristotle indicates, because the dialectician defines only the "form" (*eidos*) or "formula" (*logos*) of anger, while the natural philosopher defines only the "matter" (*hule*).

When Aristotle in the *Rhetoric* defines anger as the desire to revenge a slight, he clearly adopts the dialectical view of anger.[23] This is altogether appropriate because the dialectician defines anger in accordance with how it exhibits itself publicly in the social relations of men, which is consonant with the political perspective of the rhetorician. The physiological nature of the passions is too private, too hidden from view, to be relevant to rhetoric; in the *Rhetoric* Aristotle almost completely disregards the bodily side of the passions (but see 2. 12. 1389a18-20, 13. 1389b29-33).

Furthermore, the dialectician's definition of anger as a cognitive activity is suitable for the rhetorician since it presents anger as something accessible to persuasion. Insofar as anger is a commotion around the heart, the rhetorician has no means to deal with it; but insofar as it is a desire for revenge, he can control it through argument. By introducing the dialectician's definition into the *Rhetoric*, Aristotle manifests once again his concern for showing the rhetorician that it is indeed possible to reason with the passions.

Nonetheless, the fact that the passions do have a somatic basis of some sort raises questions about their rationality. We have already noted suggestions in the *Rhetoric* itself that the reasoning underlying the passions is often rather crude and therefore quite dubious. And in various places throughout his works, Aristotle speaks of the passions as obscuring and hindering the dictates of reason.[24] It is therefore necessary to consider the limits of the reasoning connected with the passions.

The Defects of Emotional Judgment

We may begin by noting a remark that Aristotle makes in the long passage from the *De Anima* quoted above: "We are moved by small and imperceptible sufferings when the body is disposed to anger and is as it is when it is in anger." Sometimes a man's physical condition is such that he is easily incited to anger by minor occurrences that would go unnoticed if his bodily condition were different. This, then, would illustrate how a passion can distort a man's view of reality because of the passion's close association with the body. But even here the cognitive and rational nature of passion is indicated by the fact that the body can only

124

predispose a man to a certain passion. That is, although a man's physical condition can incline him to a passion, his actual adoption of the passion will require an act of judgment that is not completely determined by his body.

Even when the cause of a passion is physiological, the object of the passion must still be present to consciousness; further, the man with the passion must believe that the conscious *object* of the passion is also the *cause*. Consider the following illustration.[25] A man who has lost a lot of sleep and drunk a lot of coffee is apt to become angry with those around him. If he becomes angry with someone, it is likely that the object of his anger is not the true cause of his anger. But if he comes to believe that the true cause of his anger is too much coffee and too little sleep, not anything done by the one with whom he is angry, then his anger will disappear. A man can sustain a passion only as long as he believes that the object of his passion is the cause of his passion, even if this belief is incorrect. A rhetorician, therefore, can dispel a passion from the souls of his listeners if he can convince them that the true cause of their passion is a physiological state of some sort. (But, as noted previously, it would be only in rare cases that the physical side of the passions would be of concern to the rhetorician.)

But what about those who are from birth naturally disposed to anger? For there surely are men who, either because of their natural constitution or because of their early training, are always inclined to anger. These are those whom Aristotle describes as "irascible men" — that is, men who are inclined to be always angry rather than angry on particular occasions.[26] But presumably even irascible men must go through the process of reasoning required for becoming angry: they must judge that they have been slighted and then reason from the major premise that slights must be revenged to the conclusion that therefore they should desire revenge. As we saw previously, the defect of irascible men is not their *lack* of reasoning, but the *hastiness* of their reasoning. Even the anger of men predisposed to anger is not *irrational* although it is often *unreasonable:* their anger does arise from judgments about the world, but their mistake is in being guided by prejudgments that often do not correspond correctly to the situations at hand.

What makes anger — and perhaps most of the other passions — so often an obstacle to clear reasoning is not, then, an *absence* of judgment, but rather the frequent *inadequateness* of the judgments from which it arises. Why should anger so often involve inadequate judgments? Aristotle may imply an answer to this when he defines anger as a response to a slight of "oneself or one's own." Anger and all the other passions always manifest a partiality for oneself and one's own. Passionate judgments tend, therefore, to be faulty since they depend upon a particular, self-interested perspective rather than a general, disinterested one. The partiality of emotional judgments may reflect the limitations imposed by the bodily nature of men. Because men have bodies, they tend to see things only as these are related to their own concrete and particular existence; this tendency hinders their looking at things from an abstract and universal viewpoint.

The passions exhibit a self-centered perspective not only in the preoccupation with oneself and one's own but also in the concentration on that which is *near* in time and space rather than *far*. For example, men feel pity or fear only for those evils that are present or very near (2. 5. 1382a19-27, 8. 1385b11-15); therefore, a rhetorician cannot arouse fear or pity about distant evils unless he can describe them so vividly that they seem near (2. 8. 1385a26-1385b4; see also 2. 6. 1384b27-36). The passions are largely governed by immediate impressions rather than a general view of things; this is a sign of their dependence on the imagination. The narrowness of the emotional field of perception is, therefore, one of the reasons for the frequent defects of emotional judgments.

The passions are rational in that they are founded on judgments of what the world is like, but they are less than perfectly reasonable to the extent that they are founded on short-sighted, partial, biased, or hastily formulated judgments. Yet the fact that the passions often depend on defective reasoning should not obscure the fact that they do require some sort of reasoning; it is, in fact, this element of reasoning that gives the rhetorician a lever for controlling the passions.

It is possible to avoid the common defects of the passions by becoming more reflective about them, by clarifying and refining the judgments from which they arise. One thereby strives to become passionate in the right way, about the right things, with the right people, and so on; one's passions are then completely reasonable since they correspond truly to the particular circumstances. Although this high standard for the passions is more apparent in the *Ethics* than in the *Rhetoric*, Aristotle does speak in the *Rhetoric* of cases where passions arise simply from good judgment and correct reasoning, saying that the "well-educated" are inclined to pity because they are "good reasoners"; "good and worthy men" are prone to indignation because "they judge well and hate unjust things"; and men in the prime of life are likely to maintain a mean between fear and confidence, "neither trusting nor distrusting all, but judging rather in accordance with the truth" (2. 8.

1385b27-28, 9. 1387b7-9, 14. 1390a30-34). Furthermore, that Aristotle should so rigorously set down the proper conditions for each of the passions and then indicate that the speaker is to show his listeners that their passions are or are not justified suggests that he thinks the aim of the best rhetoric is to make citizens more reflective about their passions than they would otherwise be, and thus to guide them to a position of reasonable moderation.[27]

The Other Passions (4-11)

Exposition of Aristotle's study of anger has brought to light the major points in his comments on the passions. Although it is unnecessary for the purposes of this book to consider the other passions in great detail, a brief survey of his remarks on each of the passions in order will perhaps help the reader discern the most salient characteristics of each and see the recurrence of the general themes that have been discussed.

Love and Hate (4)

"Let us say whom men love and hate, and why," Aristotle writes, "after we have defined friendship [*philia*] and loving [*philein*]. Let loving, then, be wishing [*boulesthai*] for someone the things one thinks good, for the other's sake but not for one's own, actively procuring them in accordance with one's power. A friend is one who loves and is loved in return, and those think themselves to be friends who think themselves disposed so to one another" (1380b33-1381a3). It follows necessarily from this, Aristotle continues, that a friend shares in another's pleasures and pains for the sake of the other, pleased when the other's wish (*boulesis*) is fulfilled and pained when it is not. "And for these men the same things are good and evil, they are friends to the same ones, and they are enemies to the same ones, for they necessarily wish the same things for one another; wherefore one who wishes for another what he wishes for himself appears to be the other's friend" (1381a9-12).

It should be noted that Aristotle restricts his account of love to friendship. Although some of what he says would apply to sexual love, no explicit references to *eros* appear anywhere in his chapter on love.[28] It would seem that while friendly affection is important to the public life of men and thus pertinent to rhetoric, erotic love is too private a matter to be rhetorically interesting (but see 2. 24. 1401b9-12).

Aristotle's preoccupation with friendship to the exclusion of *eros* is indicated by the definition of "loving" (*philein*) as "wishing" (*boulesis*), for "wish" is a rational desire for the good, in contrast to "appetite" (*epithumia*), which is an irrational desire for pleasure (1. 10. 1369a1-5); and *eros* is an "appetite" (2. 7. 1385a22-25, 12. 1389a2-5).[29] This may also show that in the *Rhetoric* Aristotle prefers to discuss the more rational types of passion.

The nature of friendship as Aristotle understands it is suggested by two peculiarities of his exposition. He does not comment, as in his accounts of the other passions, on the disposition appropriate to this passion, indicating perhaps that no special disposition is required, since men are naturally disposed to friendship. And except for calmness and kindness, friendship is the only passion not defined as a pain; this is so because it requires the sharing of both the pleasures and the pains of another.

What underlies this inclination of men to share in the life of another? That friendship is always "for the other's sake but not for one's own" might be taken to indicate an altruistic disposition. Yet it is clear that the love for the other depends upon the likeness of the other to oneself: one loves another because he has the same ideas of good and evil and the same friends and enemies as oneself. One sees oneself in one's friend; a friend, then, is "another self" (see 1381b13-18). Love of others is a refined form of self-love.

The likeness to oneself that one sees in a friend is essentially, Aristotle indicates, a *moral* likeness. There must be agreement about what is good and what is bad. This is why one perfers to be friends with good men, for men show, by their choice to be good, that they share one's conceptions of goodness (1381a15-29, 1381b1-8, 26-31). Since they are recognized by another, one's moral standards are fortified, both because one becomes more confident about them and because one is ashamed to violate them before one's friend; and with a friend one is ashamed, not of what is shameful only "according to public opinion," but of what is shameful "according to the truth" (1381a35-37, 1381b17-22, 28-32, 1384b25-27).

Here, then, is a good example of how the passions reflect and reinforce the natural moral sense of men. Friendship requires moral judgment, because friends must judge one another to be good. This encourages men to be good in order to be judged worthy of friendship and, further, to avoid the shame of doing evil once they have friends. The sense of shame seems to exist at two levels. Men are ashamed of violating the moral standards of public opinion in the community at large, presumably because there is agreement about these standards and men are ashamed not to fulfill the moral expectations of their fellow citizens. But because these standards apply over the whole community, their generality tends to render them somewhat defective. In private, men recognize them as "merely conventional." In men's private lives, it is the more intimate community of their personal friends that provides moral guidance: here they are ashamed of what is "truly" (*pros aletheian*) shameful.

Moral character is manifest also in hatred. Since it is the opposite of love, hatred requires a moral judgment that the people one hates are evil. Hatred, then, involves a more general moral condemnation than does anger; for whereas anger is an unfavorable response to a particular pain that one has suffered unjustly from another, hatred is an unfavorable response to the vices of a man irrespective of whether one has suffered any perceptible pain at his hands; one hates a man simply because he is the kind of man that he is (1382a2-14).

With this understanding of love and hate, the rhetorician should be able, Aristotle concludes (1382a16-18), to "demonstrate" (*apodeiknunai*) to an audience whether men are their friends or their enemies. For the ultimate aim of Aristotle's comments on the passions is in each case to provide material from which enthymematic arguments may be constructed.

Shame and Kindness (6–7)

The next passion that Aristotle takes up is fear. But since he explicitly connects fear and pity, both in the *Rhetoric* and in the *Poetics*, it will be useful to consider these two together after examining shame and kindness.

He defines shame as "a certain pain and uneasiness about evil things, past, present, or future, that appear [*phainomena*] to bring dishonor" (1383b14-16). Aristotle then discusses the objects of shame (1383b10-1384a22), those before whom men are shamed (1384a23-1384b27), and the conditions of shame (1384b28-1385a13). In these remarks, Aristotle does not mention blushing, another bit of evidence that in the *Rhetoric* he chooses to disregard the somatic side of the passions in order to stress the rational. He does discuss blushing in the *Nicomachean Ethics* (1128b10-17).

Aristotle defines "kindness" (*charis*) as "that in accordance with which one who has it is said to render a favor [*charis*] to someone in need, not for something in return, nor for the sake of the one rendering the favor, but for the sake of the recipient" (1385a17-19). He then comments on what makes something a genuine favor (1385a20-29) and concludes by showing how a speaker can prove that someone has or has not acted out of kindness (1385a30-1385b11).

Is there any significance to the fact that of the list of passions discuss-ed by Aristotle, shame and kindness are the central ones? Shame might be of central importance because it is the prime example of how passion can support moral restraint. Moreover, since shame presupposes a prior moral education, the centrality of shame may confirm the earlier con-clusion that in the *Rhetoric* Aristotle depicts the passions not as they are in their raw, unrefined state, but as they are once they have been shaped by the civic training of the laws.[30]

Why should kindness be at the center of the list? Perhaps because it is essential that a speaker show his kindness toward the city. In addition to prudence and virtue, the speaker must display "goodwill" toward his audience, and he can do this only by making his listeners aware that he has done favors for them in time of need, simply as acts of kindness. And it should be added that it is much more likely that a speaker can show his kindness toward his listeners than that he can show friendship toward them, for friendship requires a reciprocity that a speaker is unlikely to achieve with the citizens.[31]

Fear and Pity (5, 8)

"Let fear," Aristotle says, "be a certain pain or uneasiness from an im-pression [*phantasia*] of an imminent evil that is destructive or painful" (1382a19-21). He then takes up the objects of fear (1382a27-1382b27) and the disposition of fear (1382b28-1383a13) and concludes by discussing confidence, which is the opposite of fear (1383a14-1383b11).

"Let pity," Aristotle says, "be a certain pain from the appearance of an evil, destructive or painful, befalling someone undeserving of it, an evil such as one might expect oneself or one's own to suffer, whenever it appears near" (1385b12-15). He then considers the disposition of those who pity (1385b15-1386a2), pitiful things (1386a3-16), and pitiful men (1386a17-1386b8).

Aristotle establishes a number of connections between fear and pity. First, fearful things are pitiful when they happen to others like ourselves, and pitiful things are fearful when they threaten us (1382b26-27, 1386a26-28). Second, both fear and pity require that one be neither hopeless nor overconfident (1382b28-1383a13, 1385b18-23). Third, one capable of pity must be capable of fear, but a fearful man is unable to feel pity if his fear is extreme (1383a7-13, 1385b32-34, 1386a17-28). And fourth, pity is ultimately grounded on the self-regarding attitude underlying fear (1385b15-18, 1386a1-3).

Both fear and pity are aroused by the appearance of imminent evils of a destructive character. When the evils befall others like us in circumstances like our own, we feel pity; but as the evils come nearer to us, we feel fear. If the evils seem inevitable and irremediable, however, we resign ourselves to our fate and feel neither fear nor pity. On the other hand, if we feel so supremely confident as to think ourselves invulnerable to suffering, then we are immune to either pity or fear.

It is clear, therefore, that pity presupposes a capacity for fear. Indeed, one might even say that pity rests upon an incipient fear: it is because the evils suffered by others are of a sort as to threaten us that we feel pity for them. But once the evils come so near to us as to arouse fear, it is difficult to feel pity; and if we are quite terrified, our preoccupation with our own suffering makes us incapable of sympathizing with others. Hence, the other-regarding attitude of pity rests upon the self-regarding attitude of fear. One feels pity for the undeserved suffering of others only if one sees that suffering as something that might happen to oneself. The situation here is analogous to that of friendship, in which love for others arises from love of oneself.

From this sketch of pity and fear, one can begin to see what is required of tragedy if it is to provide a *catharsis* of those emotions. Tragic action must bear a "likeness" to human life in order to evoke fear: if we cannot see ourselves on the stage, the tragedy cannot make us fearful, and thus neither can it make us feel pity, since capacity for fear is the prerequisite for pity. And if men greater and better than ourselves are depicted as suffering an unexpected but inevitable reversal of fortune, then we are likely to feel pity and fear because we are forced to conclude that if such men are vulnerable to suffering, we too are vulnerable.[32]

Some of Aristotle's comments in the *Rhetoric* about fear and pity might well remind the reader of the *Poetics*. The clearest case is at the end of his account of pity where Aristotle explains how a speaker can employ the techniques of the stage to create pity (1386a32-34). Since pitiful things must be near at hand, he notes, suffering in the distant past or distant future cannot arouse pity unless they are made to appear present: "necessarily those who contribute to the effect by gestures, voice, dress, and acting generally are more pitiable; for they make the evil appear close at hand, putting it before our eyes as either future or past" (1386b6-8). Pity is also aroused, he continues, by "signs and actions" such as the dress and the words of suffering men at the point of death.[33] Also, suffering men excite more pity if their "goodness" (*spoudaios*) manifests itself in the midst of their suffering. "For all these things, because they appear near at hand, make the pity greater, both

131

because the suffering is undeserved, and because it appears before the eyes." (This foreshadows the treatment in Book Three of style, the aim of which is to "set things before the eyes.")

Considering the stress that Aristotle places upon pity as a response to *undeserved* suffering, it is clear that both the rhetorician and the tragedian depend upon a certain moral sense in their audiences. Men cannot feel pity unless they share some standard of goodness by which they may determine whether a man's suffering is undeserved. But the moral character of pity is best considered in conjunction with indignation.

Indignation and Envy (9–10)

Indignation and pity reflect the same character, for they both manifest a sense of justice requiring that the good be rewarded and the bad punished (1386b8-16). The difference is that while pity is pain from the sight of undeserved bad fortune, indignation is pain from the sight of undeserved good fortune. Indeed, indignation seems so clearly to exhibit a sense of natural justice that men attribute this passion even to the gods.

The moral principle that gives rise to indignation conforms to the principle of distributive justice as discussed in the *Ethics* (e.g., 1131a24-32) and the *Politics* (e.g., 1281a2-10). The principle is that only a good man is worthy of the goods of fortune, such as wealth and power; therefore, what a man receives "beyond his worth" is unjust (1386b9-17, 1387a13-15). Here, then, is another example of the moral rationality of the passions, of how the passions arise from moral judgments that display a sense of natural justice.[34]

But it might be objected that indignation does not evince a true grasp of the naturally just, and indignation against the wealthy might be cited as a clear example of fallacious moral reasoning (1387a13-28). Indignation is aroused by the belief that the wealthy do not merit their wealth, but it is aroused more often by the newly wealthy than by those of long-established wealth because the newly rich are thought to be less deserving of their wealth. What warrants this judgment? Aristotle explains that the newly rich cause more pain than those with inherited wealth because "the old appears to be something near to the natural"; those rich by inheritance seem to have what truly belongs to them because they have had it for such a long time — "what always appears so, is thought [*dokei*] to be true" (1378a19-27). Old wealth is thought to be natural because it is old, just as new wealth is thought to be unnatural because it is new. The newly wealthy provoke our indignation since we have seen what they have had to do in order to acquire their wealth, but the long-established wealthy appear in a more favorable light since the original acquisition of their wealth is hidden in the distant past. That which has existed for such a long time that its origins have been forgotten seems to be natural.

The moral judgment that distinguishes new wealth from old wealth is grounded, it seems, on a false identification of the natural and the old. This could also be seen as an identification of the natural with the habitual, for as Aristotle has observed previously in the *Rhetoric* (1. 11. 1370a5–8), "as soon as a thing has become habitual it is virtually natural; habit is a thing not unlike nature; what happens often is akin to what happens always, natural events happening always, habitual events often."

Although this preference for old wealth over new wealth rests partially upon an illusion, it is not altogether false. When Aristotle examines the character of the wealthy, he concludes that wealth tends in general to produce the character of a "prosperous fool" (2. 16. 1391a14–19). But he also claims that the newly rich are more foolish than those of long-established wealth since the newly rich have not been "educated" in the use of wealth. Those who have made money love it more than those who have inherited it because people love that for which they have exerted themselves. Furthermore, since those who have inherited their wealth do not have to do all the things necessary for acquiring it, they are free to use it well.[35] The long-established wealthy are thus "educated" in the proper handling of wealth; that is, those who have had wealth for a long time have learned how to appear as though they deserve it (see 2. 11. 1388b2–8).

Thus, there is some warrant for the moral judgment that gives rise to indignation against the newly wealthy. Those with new wealth tend to lack the dignity, the refinement, and the liberality that can be achieved by those with inherited wealth. Even if the identification of the old with the natural is not simply true, it does contain some element of truth. Indeed, is not men's commonsense understanding of the just by nature grounded largely on their assumption that whatever is old is natural?[36] And do they not thus exhibit at least a partial grasp of the truth?

The good moral character of indignation becomes even more evident when it is contrasted with envy. Envy is "a certain pain at the appearance of well-doing in regard to the goods mentioned, concerning those like oneself, and not for the sake of something for oneself, but because it belongs to them" (1387b22–24).[37] While indignation is a reaction against undeserved good fortune, envy is a base resentment that someone who is one's peer enjoys some good fortune.

133

Aristotle's differentiation of indignation from both malice and envy, according to which he distinguishes indignation as founded on good character from malice and envy as founded on bad character, is an improvement upon his unsuccessful attempt in the *Ethics* to conceive of indignation as a mean between envy and malice (2. 9. 1386b17–1387a6).[38]

Emulation (11)

Emulation is like indignation in that it too manifests good character and thus differs from envy. For the emulous man wishes to be worthy of the goods that others possess, but the envious man wishes to deprive others of their goods (1388a34–37).

Aristotle defines emulation as "a certain pain at the apparent presence of honored goods, which are possible for us to obtain, among those like us in nature — pain not because they are another's but because they are not our own" (1388a30–33). He then speaks about those who are emulous (1388a34–1388b9), about the goods of emulation (1388b10–14), and about those who are the objects of emulation (1388b15–30).

In emulation one sees at work once again a natural sense of justice. For instance, in speaking of those inclined to emulation, Aristotle refers at one point (1388b3–7) to

> those to whom belong such goods as are worthy of honored men; for these are wealth, numerous friends, and offices and all such things; for believing that it is fitting that they be good, because it is fitting that these things belong to good men, they seek such things of the goods.

Those who possess the goods of fortune of which only good men are worthy strive to seem worthy of what they have. In order to appear deserving of what they possess, these men act as though they are virtuous, and in the process they become virtuous. (This may explain Aristotle's remark that those of long-established wealth are better "educated" than the newly wealthy in the proper use of their wealth.)

Aristotle puts at the end of this chapter on emulation a brief conclusion to his entire treatment of the passions: "Through what things, therefore, the passions arise and are dissolved, from which the proofs concerning them arise, have been stated" (1388b27–30). This suffices to remind us that Aristotle regards all that he says about the passions as material for the construction of "proofs" (*pisteis*). The rhetorician must handle the passions rationally because he must make his appeals to the passions an integral part of his enthymematic argumentation.

Character and Age (12–14)

Introduction

The passions and the characters of men are interrelated.[39] On the one hand, a man's character disposes him to certain passions; but on the other hand, his passions help to constitute his character. It is fitting, therefore, that Aristotle takes up the characters of men immediately after his account of the passions.

The theme to be stressed here is analogous to that of the previous section regarding the passions. For our concern will be to show that Aristotle presents the characters of men as sufficiently rational so as to be amenable to rhetorical reasoning. Characters are like passions in that they too arise from judgments about the world; and although these judgments are commonly defective, they usually reflect some element of truth and thus provide some access for the rhetorician's appeal through argument.

The characters of men are determined by their passions, their dispositions, their ages, and their fortunes (1388b31–1389a2). The passions have already been examined, and the discussion of the virtues and the vices is adequate for the dispositions. That leaves the ages—youth, old age, and the prime of life—and the fortunes of men—good birth, wealth, power, and their opposites, and good and bad fortune generally.

The Young, the Old, and Those in Their Prime (12–14)

For the young, Aristotle says, the past is short but the future long. They live in hope since they have little to remember but much to hope for. Their expectations are great because their experience is small. And it is common for them to prefer the noble to the useful.

It is characteristic of the young to be excessive and vehement in their passions. They "think they know everything, and they are confident about this, and this is the cause for their excess in everything" (1389b7). Loving victory and honor, they are easily angered because they cannot endure a slight. Being overly confident, since they have not yet experienced failure, they are immune to fear. But they are inclined to pity because they think all men better than they really are. In general, they are more apt to commit injustice through insolence than through wickedness.

For the old, on the other hand, the past is long but the future short. They live in their memories since they have little to hope for. They are cautious and do not have high expectations, having experienced many disappointments. And they commonly prefer the useful to the noble.

It is characteristic of the old to show in their passions their lack of energy. Having experienced many deceptions and mistakes, they are always suspicious: "they love as if they may some day hate, and hate as if they may some day love." Since they are acquainted with suffering, they are inclined both to fear and to pity. And they are more likely to commit injustice through wickedness than through insolence.

Part of the explanation for the differences between the emotions of the young and those of the old may, of course, be purely physiological, as implied by Aristotle's references to the heated desires of the young in contrast to the cooling desires of the old (1389a18-20, 1389b30-33, 1390a12-16); but this by itself is insufficient. Aristotle's frequent use of the word "experience" (*empeiria*) draws attention to the fact that the differing emotions of the young and the old reflect differing amounts of experience: the young have too little experience, but the old have too much; and while the *lack* of experience in the young produces an *excess* of emotional energy, the *excess* of experience in the old produces a *lack* of such energy (1389b2-7, 16-17). The passions of both the young and the old emerge in response to the world as they know it; a difference in how the *feel* about the world evinces a difference in how they *understand* it; and the defects in the emotional attitudes of the young and the old show the defects in their views of reality.

In contrast to the extremes of youth and old age, men in the prime of life adhere to a proper "mean" in their emotional life, based on a fuller grasp of reality than is possessed either by the young or by the old.[40] Aristotle describes these men as "neither extremely confident (for such is of rashness) nor too fearful, but they bear themselves nobly towards both; nor are they trustful in everything nor distrustful in everything, but judging rather according to the truth; and living neither for the noble alone nor for the useful, but for both" (1390a30-1390b1). The emotional bearing of those in their prime displays a proper balance that is attuned to the full reality of human life because, instead of seeing the world from a partial and thus distorted perspective, they judge things "according to the truth."

As described in the *Rhetoric*, men in their prime satisfy the highest standards for moral virtue that Aristotle sets down in the *Ethics*.[41] For example, in being given "neither to parsimony nor to prodigality, but to what is right and fit" (1390b2-3), men in their prime satisfy the definition of liberality in the *Ethics* (1107b8-11, 1119b20-1122a18). And more generally, since men in their prime can find the mean in each case and judge what is truly good, they fulfill the standards in the *Ethics* for the "good man" (*spoudaios*) (1113a23-1113b2).

136

But Aristotle's comments on the character of those in the prime of life are very brief; they do not exhibit the same richness of detail found in his sketches of the young and the old. This may imply that, unlike the character types of youth and old age, the character type of those in their prime is rare. It is easier, and thus more common, to look at life from the partial perspective of an old man or a young man than to take the comprehensive perspective of a man in his prime. Indeed, is it not true that many men advance from youth to old age without ever reaching their prime?

The rarity of men in their prime is not surprising. For it is only philosophic souls that can combine the exuberance of youth with the steadiness of old age.[42] But still the best rhetorician will strive to create, as much as possible, a balance in the dispositions of the citizens so that they avoid excesses of daring or caution.

The divergent emotional attitudes of the young and the old are caused by divergent judgments about the world as these are drawn out by divergent kinds and quantities of experience. The passions thus manifest once again their rationality, since they appear as responses to the world as it is revealed to men in their experience. The passions of the young or the old reflect judgments about human life that are founded on some partial grasp of the truth; the man in his prime attains the whole truth not by rejecting the contrasting judgments of the young and the old, but by combining them. Yet most men most of the time have only partial views of the world, and therefore their emotions are not fully harmonious with reality. Only rarely does a man have that comprehensive view of the truth that allows a balanced emotional life that harmonizes with the whole of human existence.

Character and Fortune (15–17)

Aristotle turns now to the characters of fortunate men. (The characters of unfortunate men may be inferred by implication [1391b4-7].) He describes the nobly born (15), the rich (16), and the powerful (17. 1391a20-29) and he concludes with brief remarks about the effects of good fortune in general (1391a20-1391b3).

Aristotle is bluntly critical of all these character types. Men favored by fortune, he says, are generally inclined to be arrogant and thoughtless (1391b2-3). Yet he also ranks these characters as better or worse with a progression from the nobly born, who are worst, to the rich, who are better, and then to the powerful, who are the best of the three types. Political rule is elevating in a way that noble birth and wealth are not.

The Nobly Born (15)

Those who are nobly born think themselves worthy of honor because their ancestors were honored. But what is important to the nobly born is not just the honorableness of their ancestors, but the remoteness of this honor. For they disdain those among their contemporaries who are equal to their ancestors, because past honors seem superior to present ones. The mere fact of the antiquity of their noble line tends to become more important to them than the virtue for which their ancestors were first honored (see 2. 23. 1398a17–23).

But Aristotle questions the claims of the nobly born by distinguishing between "noble birth" (*eugenes*) and "noble character" (*gennaios*). "Noble birth" refers to the excellence of a man's family, but "noble character" refers to the fact that a man displays the excellence of his family in his own character. It is possible, then, to be nobly born and yet ignoble in one's own character: personal merit, not familial relationship, confers true nobility. In fact, Aristotle indicates that since families quickly deteriorate, the nobly born are for the most part "worthless."

The Wealthy (16)

The wealthy are insolent, arrogant, and incontinent. They think they possess everything that is good since they believe they can buy everything, and so they think they possess what all men seek.

Aristotle concedes that, insofar as many men do need the wealthy, there is some truth to their claims. Even the wise, as Simonides observed, are seen to wait at the doors of the rich. Even so, the essential character of a wealthy man, Aristotle concludes, is that of a "fortunate fool."

Aristotle does add the qualification, already referred to, that those of long-established wealth are better than the newly wealthy. But his point is not that the former are free of the vices of the latter, but only that they have these vices to a somewhat lesser degree.

The Powerful (17. 1391a20–29)

Though the wealthy think that their wealth makes them worthy to rule (1391a12–14), Aristotle makes it clear that the politically powerful are generally better than the wealthy. The exercise of political rule requires that powerful men be "more manly" (*androdesteroi*), "more serious" (*spoudastikoteroi*), and "more dignified" (*semnoteroi*) than wealthy men. "They are more dignified rather than more pompous, for their reputation makes them more visible, so that they observe a mean; and this dignity is a mild and becoming pomposity" (1391a27–28).

Public responsibilities call forth exertions of human capacities and impose standards of conduct that are unequalled by the activities of wealthy men.[43] This is not to deny, however, that politically powerful men promote greater mischief than do wealthy men. In fact, as Aristotle notes, precisely because powerful men are never satisfied with petty things, their injustices are never small, but always great.

The Piety of the Fortunate (17. 1391a30–1391b3)

"Therefore, men are more arrogant and more thoughtless due to good fortune," Aristotle concludes, "but one of the best characters accompanies good fortune, because such men are lovers of the gods and are disposed in a certain way toward the divine, trusting due to the goods that have arisen from fortune."

Oddly enough, the things most accidental can seem to be entirely predetermined, even providential. The man who has benefited from good fortune can infer that it was due to divine favor. Perhaps this is not surprising; for when a man sees that a long series of events, each of which could have turned out differently, has conferred extraordinary and unexpected benefits upon him, it is understandable that he might discern a divinely ordained plan at work.

Since Aristotle speaks so rarely about piety and the gods, one must wonder why he brings up this subject, even if only very briefly, in this context. Why, for instance, should he speak of the piety founded on love of the gods due to good fortune rather than the piety founded on fear of the gods due to bad fortune? Does he think the piety of the fortunate arising from gratitude to be better than the piety of the unfortunate arising from fear and need? It may be instead that Aristotle has already acknowledged the piety of fear by noting that indignation is the one passion commonly attributed to the gods.[44]

Conclusion

In delineating the character types due to good fortune, Aristotle has repeatedly drawn the rhetorician's attention to their moral defects: those favored by fortune are all more or less inclined to be arrogant and thoughtless. Aristotle does conclude, however, that the politically powerful commonly display a character of noble dignity and moral stature that distinguishes them from the nobly born and the wealthy. And among the wealthy he is careful to note the superiority of those "educated" in the use of wealth to those of recently acquired wealth. Still, those with political power often commit great injustice, and those with inherited wealth show the vices of wealth despite their "education."

Aristotle's view here is in accord with what he states in the *Nicomachean Ethics* (1124a28-1124b7). Those without virtue find it difficult to bear good fortune becomingly; they are apt to become insolent, imitating the magnanimous man's disdain for others but without the great virtue that justifies his disdain.

What we have seen in this section of the *Rhetoric* should confirm the earlier conclusion that Aristotle presents rhetoric as guided by certain moral standards. An understanding of the characters of men sufficient for the purposes of rhetoric requires that these characters be morally judged and ranked. A rhetorician is not fully prepared for his work until he can differentiate the virtues and the vices of his listeners.

7

ELEMENTS AND STRUCTURES OF RHETORICAL
INFERENCE (2. 18-26)

Introduction

At this point in the *Rhetoric*, Aristotle's perspective shifts from the particular and substantive aspects of rhetorical argument to its general and formal aspects. In the preceding parts of the work—from Chapter 4 of Book One to the end of Chapter 17 of Book Two—he has provided the rhetorician with the materials or sources of enthymematic reasoning; in the remaining chapters of Book Two, he discusses the logical structure of such reasoning (see 2. 22. 1396b28-1397a6). The primacy of the enthymeme is again apparent, for one might say that while the previous chapters concern the premises of enthymemes, these final chapters of Book Two concern the organization of these premises into syllogistic form.

The "Commonplaces" (18–19)

After a brief digression in which he reminds the speaker that the aim of rhetorical persuasion is to reach some sort of judgment, Aristotle takes up the "commonplaces." It is appropriate that he should discuss the "commonplaces" here after presenting the "specific topics" and before presenting the "common topics" (2. 23). As I have shown (see "The Three Kinds of Rhetoric" in Chapter 2), both the "commonplaces" (*koina*) and the "specific topics" (*eide*) bear upon the subject matter of rhetoric, while the "common topics" (*koinoi topoi*) pertain to the *formal structures* of inference. Unlike the "specific topics," which differ for each of the three kinds of rhetorical subject matter, the "commonplaces" are common to all three. To move from the "specific topics" to the "commonplaces" is to move from the *specific* to the *general*; and to move next to the "common topics" is to move from the *substantive* to the *formal*.

The "commonplaces" are the "topics" of whether something is possible or impossible, of whether something has happened or not, of whether something will happen or not, and of whether something is important or not. Although these "topics" involve the substantive issues of rhetorical argument, they apply to all three kinds of rhetoric. For to argue about expediency, nobility, or justice, a speaker must be able to determine what things are possible, what things have happened or will happen, and what things are important. A deliberative speaker, for example, cannot successfully advocate a course of action unless he can show that his proposal is possible, that it is consistent with past experience, that it is likely to turn out as he predicts, and that it is politically important. But although these "topics" are relevant to all three types of rhetoric, there are differences in emphasis. The importance of things is the primary concern of epideictic rhetoric; things past are primary for forensic; and the possible and the future are especially important for deliberation (1392a2–7).

Aristotle lists fifteen "topics" of the possible, leaving the reader to infer the corresponding "topics" of the impossible (1392a8–1392b13). The underlying principle in most cases is that something is possible (or impossible) if it is connected to something that is possible (or impossible). For instance, if of two things that are alike one is possible, so also is the other (1392a12); or if the beginning is possible, so is the end, and the reverse is also true (1392a15–16, 19–20). A rhetorician shows something to be possible by showing that it is linked to something known to be possible. Thus he makes the unknown known by connecting it with something that is already known, which is the logical movement at work in enthymematic and metaphorical reasoning.[1]

It is not necessary to examine each of the "topics" of possibility individually, but perhaps one should look at the one that is central on the list (the eighth): "And those things are possible of which love [*eros*] or appetite is by nature; for no one, for the most part, loves or desires the impossible" (1392a24–26).[2] First of all, this "topic" holds only "for the most part," and this is true of many of these "topics." For as is characteristic of enthymematic inferences, some of these deductions are "necessary," but most are only "probable" (1392b31–32). Also, this "topic" concerns a human inclination that is "by nature" (*phusei*), and things that occur "naturally" occur in most cases but not in all.[3] Moreover, the frequency with which the word *phusis* appears throughout all the "topics" in this chapter indicates that Aristotle views these lines of reasoning as founded upon regularities in nature (see 1392b3–5, 15–16, 26–31, 1393a6–7).

Aristotle lists six "'topics" pertaining to what has happened. (As in the foregoing section, he leaves the reader to figure out for himself the corresponding "topics" for determining what has *not* happened.) Except for the first one, all these "topics" are based on reasoning that if something's natural antecedent or consequent has happened, it also has happened.[4] As with the "topics" of possibility, there is a logical movement from the known to the unknown: one infers that something has happened if it is naturally connected to something else already known to have happened.

Since the lines of reasoning about what *will* happen are essentially the same as those about what has happened, Aristotle lists only four "topics" pertaining to the future; and even these exhibit the same types of reasoning as the previous ones (1393a1-8).

The remaining "commonplace" concerns the greatness and smallness, the importance and unimportance, of things. But here Aristotle refers the reader to his earlier remarks on greater and less goods in the section on deliberative rhetoric (1. 7). Since the particular ends of the three kinds of rhetoric — the expedient, the noble, and the just — are all goods, the "topics" of amplification can be derived from this previous discussion.

On Examples (20)

Aristotle's treatment of the "commonplaces" completes his account of the substantive elements of rhetoric; he turns now to a study of the formal logic of rhetorical reasoning. He states (1393a22-26):

> It remains to speak about the common proofs [*koinai pisteis*] for all, since we have spoken about the particular ones [*idiai*]. And the common proofs are of two types, example and enthymeme (for the maxim is part of an enthymeme). First therefore let us speak about the example; for the example is like induction and induction is a beginning [*arche*].

Everything previously examined — the "specific topics" (*eide*) for the three kinds of subject matter (1. 4-15), persuasion through *ethos* and *pathos* (2. 1-17), and the "commonplaces (2. 18-19) — pertains to the *material* of *pisteis*, but now Aristotle will consider how *pisteis* are logically constructed out of this material. Thus the enthymeme provides the organizing principle for the first two books of the *Rhetoric*, in which Aristotle moves from the premises of the enthymeme (1. 4-2. 19) to its formal structure (2. 20-26).[5]

Of the two "common proofs"—the example and the enthymeme—Aristotle clearly regards the enthymeme as the more important, for he understands the example as a source for or as arising from enthymematic inference.[6] But he does start with the example, and he considers it the "beginning" (*arche*) of all reasoning insofar as all reasoning could be said to originate as induction.[7]

Examples are drawn, Aristotle says, either from what has happened previously or from what one makes up oneself, and the latter type is divided into "comparisons" (*parabole*) and "fables" (*logoi*). He lists six examples; the first two are historical examples, the second two comparisons, and the last two fables. The two historical examples concern Darius and Xerxes. Since both attacked Egypt before attacking Greece, a Greek orator might cite these facts as showing that the Greeks should not allow the king of Persia to subdue Egypt. The two comparisons are from Socrates: to select rulers by lot rather than by their knowledge was said to him to be as foolish as it would be to select athletes or the helmsman of a ship by such a procedure. The two fables are by Stesichorus and Aesop. Stesichorus, warning the people of Himera not to give a bodyguard to their dictatorial ruler Phalaris, told them a story about a horse who allowed a man to mount him: the horse foolishly permitted this to happen in order to get the man's help in revenging himself against a stag, and the people of Himera would be equally foolish to enslave themselves to Phalaris in order to avenge themselves on their enemy. Aesop defended a demagogue on trial in Samos by telling a fable about a fox with fleas: the fox would not allow a hedgehog to remove the fleas since he thought that the fleas he had would not draw any more blood now that they were full, while new fleas would drain away more blood. Similarily, politicians already wealthy from public money should be considered less of a drain on the treasury than would be the case with poor men newly arrived in office.

All except the first two of these examples concern the problem of selecting good rulers, and even the first two may fit into this category since they suggest the threat of conquest by foreign rulers. It is perhaps appropriate that the Socratic attack on Athenian democracy should be central on the list, for the political weakness of Athens makes it vulnerable both to foreign conquest and to the domestic predacity of tyrants and demagogues.

The centrality of the Socratic examples might also imply that Socrates' use of comparisons provides the model for the skillful employment of examples. But the other references to Socrates in the *Rhetoric* suggest that Aristotle thought Socratic rhetoric to be founded not only upon reasoning through comparisons but also upon reasoning through definitions and through questioning.[8]

Moreover, Aristotle says that philosophy fosters an ability for creating examples because philosophy requires a keen capacity for seeing the likeness of one thing to another (1394a4-7). Similarly, he notes later that this same philosophic ability for seeing likenesses is necessary for making metaphors (3. 11. 1412a9-12). Philosophic training does contribute, then, in important ways, to rhetorical skill.[9]

Even though examples invented by the speaker are useful, examples drawn from history are still more so, especially for deliberative rhetoric, because "for the most part the things that will happen are like those that have happened" (1394a7-8). Aristotle concludes by advising that if a speaker has both enthymemes and examples, he should put his examples after the enthymemes so that they serve as evidence for the truth of the enthymemes (1394a9-18).

Maxims (21)

Before taking up the enthymeme, Aristotle gives an account of the "maxim," which is closely related to the enthymeme. He begins with the following definition (1394a22-28):

> A maxim is a statement, not however about things in particular, such as what sort of man Iphicrates was, but of a general kind; and yet not about all things of a general kind, such as that the straight is the opposite of the curved, but about the things of conduct, and the things to be chosen or avoided with reference to action. And since the enthymeme is the syllogism about these things, it is nearly the case that maxims are the conclusions of enthymemes or the premises without the syllogism.

A maxim states a general principle of action, but the "cause" (*aitia*) and the "wherefore" (*dia ti*) of the principle must be added for it to be an enthymeme (1394a31-32). This view of the maxim throws light upon Aristotle's theory of the enthymeme, because it confirms the argument made earlier in this commentary that the enthymeme is not a defective or incomplete syllogism; for in distinguishing the maxim from the enthymeme by saying that the maxim lacks the complete form of a syllogism, Aristotle presupposes that the enthymeme is a complete syllogism. This becomes quite apparent when he differentiates the four types of maxims.

Maxims that are contrary to common opinion or otherwise subject to dispute demand demonstration and therefore an epilogue that states the reason for the principle. Of those with epilogues, some are part of an enthymeme, and others are enthymematic in character but not part of an enthymeme. Those without epilogues do not need them, either because the maxims are already known or because they are accepted as soon as they are heard. Since Aristotle assumes that a maxim with an epilogue falls short of being a true enthymeme, one must conclude again that he considers an enthymeme a complete syllogism.

Aristotle says (1395b1-3): "Maxims are of great assistance in speeches, first, through the vulgarity of the listeners, for they are delighted if someone speaking generally happens upon opinions of which they have a partial grasp." Even the crudest listener is still a rational animal. Even the person unable to generalize from his particular experiences is pleased by the generalizations of a rhetorician; such a person delights to have what he only vaguely senses in particular cases raised to the level of a universal principle.

Maxims are also useful to manifest good character because by appealing to maxims to support his case, a speaker shows that his reasoning is guided by commonly accepted moral principles (1395a18-1395b19). Aristotle comments further on this point in Book Three, where he says that maxims can exhibit a speaker's character or create the proper emotions in cases where enthymemes would not achieve the same ends (3. 17. 1418a8-21). Yet even in such cases, what is required is not to avoid all reasoning of an enthymematic character, but rather to transform enthymemes into maxims (3. 17. 1418b33-38).[10]

A maxim is a substitute for an enthymeme in those cases where the complete logical form of an enthymeme would be unnecessary and tedious. A maxim is a principle that is agreed to by listeners either without argument or with only an incomplete argument; the principle could be supported with a complete enthymematic arguement, but the argument is so obvious to the listeners that there is no need to state it in full.

A Note on the Enthymeme (22)

Aristotle now turns his attention to the enthymeme. He begins with two rules that were stated at the beginning of the *Rhetoric* — namely, that enthymematic reasoning should not be so long and complex as to be obscure to the audience and that whatever is already obvious to the audience should not be stated verbally lest it seem to be idle talk. Educated speakers violate these rules, Aristotle says (1395b24-30), and this is what makes these speakers less persuasive than the uneducated.[11] Does not philosophic reasoning become long and complex precisely because it does not take for granted what is usually thought to be obvious? Is it not the characteristic defect of popular reasoning that the familiar is unexamined and the problems inherent in the familiar are thus overlooked? The rhetorician must build upon common opinions; to question those opinions belongs to a realm of inquiry beyond rhetoric.

Educated speakers also make the mistake of speaking in generalities without the support of facts closely connected to the subjects under examination. But the successful speaker is well provided with topics that concern the particular matters he discusses. The more facts a speaker has, and the more closely connected they are to the subject, the easier it is for him to prove his case (1396a4-1396b19).

Thus, having insisted that the rhetorician must not state the obvious, Aristotle himself states the obvious rule that a speaker should know the facts about the subject of his speech. Aristotle must state the obvious here because his study of rhetoric is itself theoretical rather than rhetorical.[12]

Aristotle is emphatic about the importance of factual argument: "all demonstrate in this way, whether their syllogisms are rigorous or loose; for they do not derive their arguments from everything but from what concerns each particular subject, and by reason it is clear that it is impossible to prove something any other way" (1396a33-1396b3). There is among men a natural proclivity to demand that rhetorical appeals be relevant to the subject at hand. It would thus seem that except with the most corrupt listeners, sophistical techniques for distracting attention from the substantive issues under discussion are unlikely to be successful, a condition that confirms the rational solidity of the commonsense reasoning of most men (see 1. 1. 1354a18-24, 3. 14. 1415b2-8).

"Topics" of Enthymemes (23)

Rhetoric, Socrates, and the Gods of the City

Having restated the general rules for the construction of enthymemes, Aristotle sets out here to list their "common topics." Like some of the other chapters in the *Rhetoric*, this one consists of a list of "topics" without any easily discernible order. The lack of any apparent order is indicated by the fact that Aristotle introduces each "topic" except for the first with the word "another" (*allos*)—as though to say, "Here is one topic, and here is another . . . and another . . . and another."

A reader might wonder whether the arrangement of the "topics," the way they are illustrated, and the relationships between the list of formal "topics" and the list of examples might be intended to convey a teaching of some sort. One notices, for instance, that this chapter contains a large number of references to the conflict between wise men and the cities in which they live, including a series of references to the trial of Socrates. By tracing these references through the chapter, a reader can see certain patterns that suggest a teaching about the nature of rhetoric as illustrated in Socrates' rhetoric in defense of philosophy.

I shall argue that this chapter of the *Rhetoric*, more than any other, points to the problem of Socratic rhetoric — that is, the problem of how a philosopher should speak to his fellow citizens so as both to protect his philosophic life and to benefit rather than harm his city. When I say that Aristotle "points" to this problem, I mean that he quietly evokes thought about the issue in the mind of the attentive reader but without explicit discussion. Much of what follows, therefore, will be rather conjectural; and although there is solid evidence, I think, for the interpretation that I advance, there is still room for doubt.

Aristotle lists twenty-eight "topics" in this chapter. They may be classified into three groups: antecedent-consequent or cause-effect (7, 11, 13-14, 17, 19, 23-24), more-less (4-6, 20, 25, 27), and some form of relation (1-3, 8-10, 15-16, 18, 21-22, 26, 28).[13] They all assume a form of inference that moves from one thing to another: if this, then that. From what is known a conclusion is drawn that applies to what is unknown.

Examining Aristotle's illustrations of these "topics," one sees that he mentions either the conflict between the philosopher and the city in general or the trial of Socrates in particular in *eight* of the "topics": 4, 7, 10-13, 17, and 23.[14] In *four* of these eight, the name of Socrates appears: 7, 11, 12, and 17.[15] Also, of the *nine* "topics" with examples referring to the gods — 4, 7, 11, 12, 14, 17, 19, 26, and 28 — *five* correspond to "topics" with references to the problem of the philosopher in the city; and all of the "topics" in which the name of Socrates appears are also "topics" with references to the gods.

It should also be noticed that *six* of the *eight* "topics" containing examples of the philosopher's conflict with the city fall under the classification "antecedent-consequent or cause-effect." *Three* of the *four* "topics" that mention Socrates fall under this classification. One must also consider whether this has any significance. I shall look now at each of the examples that pertain to the tension between philosophy and the city.

The fourth "topic" is that of "more and less," of which the first example is the argument, "if not even the gods know everything, then hardly can men" (1397b13). Subsequently, Aristotle adds the following examples: "If other experts [*technitai*] are not contemptible, neither are philosophers. And if generals are not contemptible because they are often defeated, neither are the sophists" (1397b23-25).

The parallel construction of the latter two examples may suggest that philosophers and sophists are similar, from the perspective of rhetoric, in the accusations they arouse and the arguments advanced in their defense. Both philosophers and sophists are "experts" (or "men with an art"), but other "experts" are not so unpopular. Therefore, they can try to defend themselves by stressing their similarities to those "experts" who are more respected.

It is fitting that the sophists are compared to generals, since sophists were known to seek victory in argument above all else and to consider their opponents as enemies against whom they were to practice every sort of deception. But perhaps there is an implicit criticism here—that sophistry is appropriate against one's enemies, but not with one's friends.[16]

What explains the prejudice against philosophers and sophists? Maybe it is because of their claim to know, or at least to desire to know, everything required for knowing the nature of the whole, which is a form of impiety insofar as it is a claim that men can know more than the gods. That the animus against philosophers does arise from their supposed impiety is borne out by the reference in the seventh "topic" to Socrates's *Apology*. This is the "topic" of reasoning from definitions. Of the four examples of this "topic," Socrates is the source of two, the first and the last. Also, of the four "topics" with references to Socrates, this is the only one with two references and the only one that has examples of arguments *by* rather than just *about* Socrates. Maybe the proper inference would be that Aristotle regards argument by definition to be the most characteristic form of Socratic reasoning. (Aristotle says in the *Metaphysics* [987b1] that Socrates "fixed thought for the first time on definitions.")

The first illustration of this seventh "topic" is the argument of Socrates that he cannot be charged with denying the existence of the gods since he is also charged with believing in his own *daimonion,* which is something divine (1398a15-17). Aristotle seems to be quite impressed with this argument because he sets it out in more detail later in the book where he uses it as an example of arguing through interrogation (3. 18. 1419a6-13). It is clear from Plato's *Apology of Socrates* (26a-27e) that

Socrates meets the charge of impiety only by a cleverly deceptive move in his interrogation of Meletus. He is charged in the indictment with denying the *gods of the city,* but he gets Meletus to change the charge to an accusation of denying *all gods.* It is then easy for him to show that this accusation contradicts the accusation that he has introduced new gods — or, more precisely, new *daimonia.* Thus Socrates is able to evade the question of whether he denies the gods of the city.

The second Socratic illustration of the "topic" of definition is the argument that Socrates made to justify his refusal to visit the tyrant Archelaus. It would be an "insult," he said, to be unable to return a favor as well as an injury (1398a23-26).[17]

One of the illustrations of the tenth "topic," which concerns inductive reasoning, is from a speech by Alcidamus, who tries to show, by listing nine examples, that everyone honors wise men (1398b9-18). Of these nine the first three cases are of poets — Archilochus, Homer, and Sappho — who were not statesmen and who were honored despite certain defects that each was thought to possess. The last three are of wise statesmen — Solon, Lycurgus, and some unnamed Theban leaders (probably Epaminondas and Pelopidas) — who were honored for making their cities happy and about whom no misgivings are indicated. Of the three men central on the list — Chilon of Sparta, Pythagoras, and Anaxagoras — the latter two would seem to be the only ones mentioned that would be considered in the strict sense philosophers. Pythagoras is central in the list, and the reference to him is the briefest — only three words. (One might consider the appropriateness of this for someone who kept his most serious teachings secret.)

Of the eight "topics" with illustrations of the philosopher's conflict with the city, the central four are clustered near the center of the list of twenty-eight — that is, "topics" 10 through 13. And of these "topics," the eleventh and twelfth are the central pair of the list of four "topics" with references to Socrates.

The eleventh "topic" includes the appeal to authority, such as that of the gods, a father, or instructors. One example of arguing from the authority of a teacher is used: Aristippus's reproaching Plato for violating Socrates' example and speaking too presumptuously or dogmatically (1398b28-31). The key term — *epaggellesthai* — can mean "to profess publicly" or "to announce" or "to promise." It can carry, as it probably does here, a suggestion of presumption or pretension, or perhaps dogmatism. Aristotle uses the same word in the next chapter with reference to the false promises of Protagoras (1402a24-28). Socrates could be for his students what the authority of gods or fathers was for other men.[18] But the impiety in such a situation was perhaps moderated, at least in its public appearance, by the modest and un-pretentious manner in which Socrates taught and by the calming effect that this example had on his students.

That such restraint was needed in the public presentation of Socratic philosophy is emphasized in the twelfth "topic" by another reminder of the charge of impiety against Socrates. This is the "topic" of reasoning based on the enumeration of parts. One of the two examples of the "topic" is the argument of Theodectes that Socrates was innocent of impiety since he had neither profaned any holy place nor refused to honor any god of the city (1399a7-8). But the weakness in this reason-ing, which resembles the case for Socrates' piety made by Xenophon in the first chapter of his *Memorabilia*, is that one must assume that impie-ty consists *only* in *publicly* refusing to observe the *outward* rituals of the city's religion.[19] That Socrates might have maintained a pious ap-pearance in public matters only to hide the impiety of his private life is not considered. But the accusers of Socrates relied largely on the mere *appearance* of a resemblance between Socratic teaching and sophistry, and therefore it is perhaps only just that the defenders of Socrates should reply by appealing to the *pious appearance* of his public life.

This reference to the trial of Socrates is immediately followed by the "topic" of reasoning from the consequences. The one example of the "topic" concerns the good or evil of education: it is good insofar as it results in wisdom, but it is evil insofar as it arouses envy (1399a9-17). Thus, Socrates' trouble was not peculiar to him, but a necessary result of the philosophic life and how it appears to others.[20]

Aristotle links the thirteenth "topic" with the one that follows because they both involve matters with good and evil consequences. In the fourteenth "topic," the example is an argument of a priestess advis-ing her son not to speak in public: if he speaks for justice, men will hate him; if for injustice, the gods will hate him. But on the other side, she argues, he *should* speak since he will be loved by the gods for saying what is just or loved by men for saying what is unjust. To decide to speak or not to speak is difficult, then, because either saying what is just or saying what is unjust will make one both loved and hated.

Thus, at the center of his list of "topics" in this chapter, Aristotle points both to the difficulty of public speaking and to the difficulty of living as a wise man. Further, he connects the two, for in the trial of Socrates both problems combine to become the problem of Socratic rhetoric.

Essentially, the problem concerns the conflict between the just speech demanded by the gods and the unjust speech demanded by men. In Plato's *Phaedrus* (273d–74a), Socrates explains that *true* rhetoric—that is, *philosophic* rhetoric—would be addressed not to men but to the gods. Recognizing at his trial that his reliance on truth and justice might be unpersuasive, Socrates can only appeal to the gods with the hope that the jurors will feel bound by their sacred oaths to judge according to what is just rather than according to their own inclinations.[21]

Oddly enough, although accused of impiety, Socrates had to rely upon the sense of justice sanctioned by piety. The significance of this comes into view in Aristotle's fifteenth "topic" (1399a28–33):

> Again, since men do not praise the same things openly and secretly; but, on the one hand, openly they praise mostly just and noble things; yet, on the other hand, in private they wish more for the expedient things, another topic is to attempt to infer from each of these the other. For of the paradoxical ones, this topic is the most authoritative.

Pointing out the contrast between men's noble words in public and their ignoble wishes in private was a favorite move of the sophists, for in this way they could challenge public standards of justice as merely conventional. In fact, Aristotle illustrates this "topic" in his dialectical treatise by referring to the argument of Callicles in the *Gorgias*.[22] But Plato shows in the *Gorgias* (461b–c, 482c–83a) that Socrates can use this same line of argument against the sophists by invoking the moral sense that men display in their public standards: most men come closer to the truth in their public praise than in their private desires because as a community they must restrain the ignoble desires by which they are moved as private men.[23]

Socrates and the sophists are alike in differentiating nature from convention; but unlike the sophists, Socrates thinks that certain ends of nature require the aid of convention for their fulfillment. The problem is that most men presume that to distinguish between nature and convention implies that convention should be set aside completely in favor of nature. This presumption leads to the tendency of most men to confuse Socratic teaching with the doctrines of the sophists, for both seem to undermine the city by upholding nature rather than convention. (Aristophanes, for example, depicts Socrates in *The Clouds* as a sophist who teaches his students to use deceptive arguments to attack conventional moral standards as contrary to nature.) Socratic philosophy and sophistry are assumed by such men to be the same since they seem to have the same practical results; this situation leads one to Aristotle's seventeenth "topic" (1399b4–12).

This is the "topic" of reasoning from identity of results to identity of antecedents. The first example concerns impiety: to assert that the gods die and to assert that they are born are equally impious since both result in the conclusion that it is possible for the gods not to exist. The second example is from Isocrates' *Antidosis* (173): "You are about to judge not about Isocrates but about a pursuit, whether one should philosophize." Once again impiety and the conflict of a philosopher with his city appear side by side.

It is noteworthy that all the versions of the second illustration found in the Greek manuscripts have the name "Socrates" rather than "Isocrates." The change to "Isocrates" was made only after philologists noticed that the quotation was nearly the same as one in the *Antidosis*. But Aristotle might have intended to attribute to Socrates this quotation from Isocrates in order to remind the reader that these two men were similar in more than their names: both were charged with practicing sophistry by teaching how to make the weaker argument the stronger. Socratic philosophy and Isocratean rhetoric aroused the same popular prejudices because they seemed to have the same dangerous consequences for the city.[24]

The various ways in which Aristotle alludes in this chapter to the problem of Socratic rhetoric have been indicated. I shall now summarize these points.

Both the life and the teachings of Socrates draw attention to the differences between convention and nature and between the public and the private. Unlike the sophists, however, Socrates does not want to undermine the public conventions—particularly with respect to piety—because these are necessary for supporting standards of justice that could not be maintained for most men in any other way. But most people would interpret Socratic philosophy as leading to the same consequence as sophistry, which is to legitimate the private desires of men as superior to the merely conventional standards of the community.

A noble rhetoric depends upon the widespread and unquestioning acceptance of certain standards of public morality. Although these standards may be unable to withstand rational examination, they are the only standards acceptable for most men. For if one demanded that all men rationally examine their opinions about morality, the result would be not to create rational morality, but to throw most men into such doubts about public morality that they would tend to yield to their ignoble private desires.

153

Such a man as Socrates cannot fail to see the flaws in the moral standards of his community and in the piety upon which such standards rest. But if he goes too far in questioning the public orthodoxy, he runs the risk not only of arousing moral indignation but also of undermining the public sense of justice upon which any rhetorical defense of his life would depend. The success of Socratic rhetoric requires a prudent restraint upon the continual examination of common opinions that characterizes the Socratic life.

Although Aristotle does not say any of this in any clearly explicit way, the unusual number of allusions in this chapter to Socrates' defense of philosophy invite the reader to work out an interpretation such as the one just stated. Having done this, one must return to the text in order to consider one of the more obvious problems.

On Distinguishing True and Apparent Enthymemes

In this chapter, Aristotle sets forth the "topic" of true enthymemes in contrast to the "topic" of apparent enthymemes, which appear in the next chapter. The arguments in this chapter should be valid; the arguments in the following chapter should be invalid. This distinction holds in most cases, but some of the arguments in this chapter seem to resemble some of the fallacies of the next chapter.[25] Without trying to examine each instance in which this problem arises, one can consider an example.

In both this and the following chapter, Aristotle mentions arguments used to justify Paris's abduction of Helen. To illustrate the "topic" of definition, Aristotle cites the argument by Polycrates in his *Alexander* that Paris must have been temperate since men who are not temperate are not satisfied with one woman (1398a22-23). But in the next chapter, Aristotle illustrates the fallacy of the consequent with another example from the same speech: "Paris was magnanimous, for he scorned the society of the many and spent his time in Ida alone. For because the magnanimous are of such a sort, he must be thought magnanimous" (1401b19-23). The first argument seems to be just as unconvincing a proof of Paris's temperance as the second is of his magnanimity, and that they come from the same source only reinforces this impression. But on the other hand, the first inference is clearly not so blatantly fallacious as the second; for while the first is at least formally valid, the second is formally invalid. One might infer from this that although the "topic" of true enthymemes can produce highly dubious arguments, the reasoning from these "topics" is still not so

evidently fallacious as the reasoning from the "topic" of apparent enthymemes.

Aristotle is careful to maintain a clear distinction between these two
sets of "topics." For example, at two points in Chapter 23, he indicates
how a misused "topic" may lead to fallacious reasoning
(1397a28–1397b6, 1398a8–14, 1400b1–3); but in each case, he explains
the source of the mistake so that it may be avoided. In one instance, he
warns the rhetorician against using a certain type of false argument lest
the man make himself appear ridiculous before his audience
(1398a8–14). This is quite different from Aristotle's account of the
"topics" in the next chapter, each of which is fallacious by its very
nature.

"Topics" of Apparent Enthymemes (24)

The major argument of this commentary is that Aristotle views rhetoric
as a genuine form of reasoning and that the solidity of rhetorical reasoning is manifest in the enthymeme. I have argued, therefore, that the enthymeme is a true syllogism, that it is not, as is commonly assumed, a
defective or incomplete inference. Aristotle's distinction between true
and apparent enthymemes provides strong evidence for my interpretation, for such a distinction would make no sense unless the enthymeme
were assumed to be a genuine syllogism.

An "apparent enthymeme," Aristotle says, "is not an enthymeme
since it is not a syllogism" (2. 22. 1397a3–4). An enthymeme is a
syllogism with premises that are drawn from common opinion and that
are either probable or necessary but usually only probable. An apparent
enthymeme is false either in its content or in its form. It is false in its
content when one of its premises *appears* to be a common opinion but is
not and *appears* to be probable or necessary but is not. It is false in its
form when it *appears* to be a valid syllogism but is not.

This chapter on apparent enthymemes is to the rest of the *Rhetoric*
what *On Sophistical Refutations* is to the *Topics*. For just as the dialectician must recognize and defend himself against the sophistical use of
dialectical syllogisms, so the rhetorician must guard against the
sophistical use of rhetorical syllogisms. And in both cases sophistry involves either a material or a formal fallacy, either a false premise or an
invalid syllogism.[26]

Aristotle lists nine or ten "topics" of apparent enthymemes, depending on how one counts them. The problem is that he begins with two
types of fallacy in "style," and one may count this as one "topic" with

two parts or as two separate "topics." In *On Sophistical Refutations*, he classifies the fallacies as verbal or nonverbal. Here in this chapter of the *Rhetoric*, the first two or three of the fallacies—again, depending on how one enumerates them—are verbal, and the last six starting with the "sign"-fallacy are nonverbal. Between these two groups is the fallacy of exaggeration, which is not mentioned in *On Sophistical Refutations*, but which seems to be a peculiarly rhetorical fallacy. If one counts the "topics" as ten, then the "sign-fallacy and the accident-fallacy share the center of the list. If one counts them as nine, the accident-fallacy takes over the center. In *On Sophistical Refutations*, Aristotle does not consider the "sign"-fallacy separately, but treats it as one type of the fallacy of the consequent; if one here classified the "sign" under the consequent-fallacy, the center would shift between the accident-fallacy and the consequent-fallacy. Furthermore, the example of the "sign"-fallacy used in *On Sophistical Refutations* appears here as the second of three examples of the consequent-fallacy. Twenty-six examples of the different types of fallacy are given here. The central examples are the two examples of the "sign"-fallacy. If the "sign"-examples were classified as examples of the consequent-fallacy, then the central examples would be the two examples of the accident-fallacy. At least two conclusions might be drawn from all of this. First, the "sign"-fallacy holds an ambiguous position in the list. Second, the accident-fallacy and the "sign"-fallacy may be of central importance. I shall now go through each of the fallacies.

The first "topic" concerns "style" or "diction" (*lexis*), from which two types of fallacy may arise. The first type is to argue in a pithy, epigrammatic style that appears to be syllogistic when in fact it is not (1401a1–12). A conclusion is stated as though it were the result of a syllogism although no syllogistic reasoning has taken place. This same effect is achieved by stating the conclusions of previous syllogisms so as to give the false impression that a new syllogism, leading to a new conclusion, has been set forth. Thus, the sophist imitates the enthymeme by speaking in an epigrammatic style that is, Aristotle says, the "seat" or "region" (*chora*) of the enthymeme. But a concise, balanced style of argument does not create an enthymeme unless the argument contains a syllogism. The second type of fallacy in style is argument based on a single word with a double meaning (1401a13–23). The inference is invalid because the middle term is equivocal. Of the two kinds of reasoning with which Aristotle begins, the first is false because there is no syllogism, and the second is false because it is founded on a formally invalid syllogism.

156

The second "topic" of apparent enthymemes is the practice of combining things divided or dividing things combined (1401a24-1401b3). Like equivocation, the fallacy here lies in using different meanings as though they were identical — that is, in assuming that something considered separately is the same when it is in a combination. One of Aristotle's examples is the argument that "one who knows the letters also knows the word, for the word is the same as the letters" (1401a28-29). Such an inference is fallacious because it is formally invalid.

The third "topic" is that of sustaining or refuting an argument with exaggeration (1401b4-8). This occurs, for instance, in a judicial proceeding when a deed is exaggerated without the demonstration that the accused did or did not commit it. Aristotle observes: "there is no enthymeme, for the listener reasons fallaciously that someone has or has not done it without it having been proved." This "topic" resembles Aristotle's "commonplace" of amplification and depreciation. Thus, this "topic" is like the first one in that it imitates an element of Aristotelian rhetoric but without fulfilling Aristotle's requirements for the enthymeme. The "sign"-fallacy is next, but I shall reserve it for later discussion since it raises some special problems.

The fifth "topic" is the accident-fallacy (1401b14-19). It involves falsity in one of the premises of the inference — that is, falsity in the *content* rather than the *form* of the inference. This is clear from Aristotle's two examples. If one argued for the greatness of mice, using the premise that they helped a people by gnawing the bowstrings of their enemy, or if one reasoned that dinner invitations were most honorable, using as a premise the insult felt by Achilles at not being invited to a dinner, one would in either case employ a false premise, one that confuses the true cause with a merely accidental fact.

The sixth "topic" is the fallacy of the consequent, which rests upon a formally invalid syllogism (1401b19-29). Aristotle's first example can be understood as an invalid conditional syllogism: if a man is magnanimous, he avoids the company of the many; Paris avoids the company of the many; therefore, Paris is magnanimous. This is fallacious because the necessary connection between the antecedent and the consequent in the major premise is not convertible. That A entails B does not neessarily imply that B entails A. To put it another way, the fallacy results because B is not coextensive with A. The other two examples manifest the same logical defect.

The mistake of taking what is not the cause for the cause is the seventh "topic" (1401b30-33). This "topic" seems to involve a false premise arising from the familiar fallacy of assuming that what comes

157

after something occurs *because* of the preceding thing, a defective form of reasoning common among politicians. The example — the policy of Demosthenes which preceded the war with Philip and which, therefore, was said to be the cause of the war — is noteworthy since this is the only place in the *Rhetoric* where the name of Demosthenes is used.

The eighth "topic" is the use of general premises without the necessary qualifications as to time and manner, which results in a formally invalid syllogism (1401b34-1402a2). This fallacy of "omission" resembles the previous fallacies of combining and dividing and of the consequent and the ninth fallacy pertaining to absolute and non-absolute meanings.

Before going to the last "topic," I wish to return to the fourth, the "sign"-fallacy. I have argued that the distinction between the true enthymeme and the apparent enthymeme assumes that the true enthymeme is a genuine syllogism. But why, then, does Aristotle list the "sign" as a source of apparent enthymemes? Since he speaks of "signs" at the beginning of the *Rhetoric* as sources of enthymemes, his reference here to "signs" would seem to obscure the difference between true and apparent enthymemes. It would further seem to throw into question the syllogistic character of the enthymeme.

First, it should be noted that Aristotle commonly uses the term "signs" to refer only to *probable* "signs," thus excluding *necessary* "signs" (*tekmeria*). The *tekmerion* is clearly not in question here, since it is not only a syllogism but also a necessary syllogism (see 2. 25. 1403a10-16).

The question, then, is whether Aristotle considers the probable "sign" to be necessarily unsyllogistic. Although a probable "sign" is of course fallacious when it violates the standards of syllogistic reasoning, Aristotle does not wish one to conclude, I think, that every probable "sign" is by its very nature fallacious. Consider the two examples that he gives (1401b10-14):

> For instance, if one were to say, "Lovers are useful to cities, for the love of Harmodius and Aristogiton overthrew the tyrant Hipparchus"; or if one said that Dionysius is a thief, for he is wicked; for here again it is unsyllogistic, for not every wicked man is a thief, but every thief is wicked.

The particular case of Harmodius and Aristogiton surely does not show any *necessary* or *probable* connection between love and the overthrowing of a tyrant, but it surely does show a *possible* connection: a tyrant might quite reasonably infer from this one incident that erotic attachments among his subjects are a possible threat to his rule.[27]   The second example is a false inference because its major premise — "Every wicked man is a thief" — is false. But notice that in dismissing this "sign"-inference as unsyllogistic, Aristotle suggests a probable "sign"-relationship that could be the major premise of a valid syllogism: "Every thief is a wicked man." With this premise, one could validly conclude from the fact of a man's being a thief that he is wicked. It is possible, therefore, for a probable "sign"-inference to be a valid syllogism. Indeed, Aristotle provides another example in the *Prior Analytics* (70a24–28): lovers of honor are high-minded; Pittacus is a lover of honor; therefore, Pittacus is high-minded.[28]

Aristotle's brief comments here on the "sign"-fallacy are certainly ambiguous enough to leave room for doubt about his intended meaning (see also, in the next chapter, 1403a2–4). But one can reasonably conclude that in listing "sign"-inferences as sources of apparent enthymemes, he did not mean to imply that *all* probable "signs" are fallacious. For if a probable "sign" is properly stated, it can be syllogistically valid and thus a source of a genuine enthymeme.

The final "topic," the ninth, remains (1402a2–28). In some respects, it is the most interesting, since it is said to be the most common fallacy used by sophists in both dialectic and rhetoric. The fallacy arises from using a term in an absolute sense and then in some particular, restricted sense without distinguishing the two. Aristotle gives two illustrations from dialectic and one from rhetoric. In each case the conclusion is an identification of opposites — in dialectic, being is equated to nonbeing and knowledge to ignorance; in rhetoric, the probable is equated to the improbable. "For instance, in dialectic it is argued that that which is not *is* that which is not, also, that ignorance is knowledge, for there is knowledge that ignorance is ignorance." And in rhetoric, it is argued that since improbable things do happen many times, the improbable is probable. In each case deception results from confusing the general meaning of a word with a particular meaning. Aristotle goes on to illustrate how this sort of argument can be used in the courtroom. If a weak man is accused of assault, his defense is that it is improbable that a weak man would assault a stronger man. But if a strong man is accused, his defense is that it is improbable that he would have committed the assault since he would have known that his guilt would appear probable (see 1. 12. 1372a12–14, 23–28).[29]

Aristotle concludes by associating this sort of argument with Protagorean sophistry:

And this is to make the weaker argument the stronger. And for this reason men were justly annoyed with the claim of Protagoras; for it is false, not a true but an apparent probability [*eikos*], and it is in no art except rhetoric and eristic.[30]

One sees here the prudent balance in Aristotle's account of rhetoric. For he acknowledges on the one hand that fallacious arguments are a part of the rhetorical art; but he stresses on the other hand the popular resentment against such arguments. Thus, he makes it clear that the good-intentioned rhetorician has the advantage over the sophist. In particular circumstances with particular audiences, of course, false reasoning might triumph, and even the noble rhetorician might have to resort to such reasoning. But in general the more effective speaker will be the one who can support his own case with solid argumentation and expose to the view of the audience the fallacies of his opponent. The noble rhetorician is not just morally superior; he is also more successful.

This final "topic" thus confirms the evidence in the previous "topics" that to reason fallaciously is to use apparent rather than true enthymemes. The implication is that to reason enthymematically one must use syllogisms that are both true in their premises and formally valid. By founding rhetoric on the enthymeme, therefore, Aristotle affirms the rational solidity of rhetorical reasoning.

Modes of Refutation (25–26)

Having instructed the rhetorician in the use of argumentation to prove his case, Aristotle concludes Book Two with remarks on how the rhetorician can refute the case of his opponent. Refutation is either by "counter-syllogism" or by "objection." Refutation by "counter-syllogism" occurs when a speaker reasons enthymematically to a conclusion that is the opposite of what his opponent has argued. Refutation by "objection," on the other hand, is not a full enthymeme but an "opinion" that shows the opposing argument to be unsyllogistic or to be founded on some false premise (1402a29-34, 1403a25-34).

Aristotle goes on to distinguish four ways in which "objections" may be raised (1402a34-1402b12) and to indicate how different types of enthymemes may be challenged (1402b13-1403a16). But even without examining these passages in detail, it is clear that rhetorical reasoning may be judged by the standards of syllogistic logic. It is further clear, therefore, that to refute an argument a speaker must show it to be either false in its premises or invalid in its logical form.[31]

Having reached the end of Book Two, Aristotle states rather abruptly that he has spoken so far only about the intellectual components of rhetoric (*ton peri ten dianoian*) and that it remains to speak about the style and arrangement of speeches. This completely unexpected shift of attention is initially quite confusing, and the reader must wonder how Book Three is connected to the first two books. The particular difficulty is that while Books One and Two can be understood as a coherent account of the materials and the logical structures of enthymematic reasoning, the subjects of the last book seem extraneous to the enthymeme. It will be my aim in the next chapter to show that Book Three is, in fact, an integral part of Aristotle's theory of rhetoric as rational discourse.

8

THE STYLE AND ARRANGEMENT
OF SPEECHES (3. 1-19)

Introduction (1)

At first glance Book Three seems an unfitting conclusion for the *Rhetoric*. Having defined rhetoric as the discovery of arguments appropriate to each subject, Aristotle has set forth in Books One and Two a comprehensive treatise on the content and form of rhetorical arguments, thus stressing the rational side of the art. Indeed, critics of the *Rhetoric*, such as Friedrich Nietzsche, point to Aristotle's emphasis on argumentation and his neglect of the techniques for the delivery, style, and arrangement of speeches as showing the excessively philosophic or rationalistic character of his work.[1] In this respect, Aristotle's treatment of rhetoric in the first two books resembles his account of tragedy in the *Poetics:* in both cases, the effect of the art is independent of the performance. But in this final book of the *Rhetoric* Aristotle takes up the very elements of oratorical performance that he has previously neglected — the style and arrangement of speeches. He has denounced sophistical speakers for being so preoccupied with verbally charming and diverting their listeners that they ignore the primacy of "proof" and of the "body of proof" — the enthymeme. Now he seems to be introducing the same devices of verbal ornamentation that are favored by the sophists. And while the preceding books could be said to be founded upon the centrality of the enthymeme, Book Three seems to present those parts of rhetoric that are unrelated to the enthymeme.

But I shall argue that Book Three is consistent with the teaching of the first two books. To devote so much attention to matters of style is necessary, as Aristotle himself admits, only as a concession to corrupt listeners. Yet he manages even here to accentuate the *rational* character of the subject. He strives throughout this final book of the *Rhetoric* to show how the style and arrangement of speeches can sustain, rather than undermine, the practice of rhetoric as a form of *reasoning*.

163

Style concerns not *what* one should say, but *how* to say it (1403b15-17). Hence it has little influence with good listeners because they are more interested in the substantive argument of a speech than in its manner of presentation; "and rightly considered it is thought vulgar" (1403b37-1404a2). But the "corruption of regimes" and the concomitant "corruption of the listener" make it necessary for the rhetorician to be careful about style. Since it is important for speaking clearly, the rhetorician needs to consider it somewhat in any type of instruction. It assumes great importance, however, only for the sake of diverting the listener with pleasing imagery; "wherefore no one teaches geometry this way" (1403b32-1404a12).

It seems, then, that to be overly concerned with style runs contrary to common opinion, for "it is thought [*dokei*] vulgar" (cf. 1. 1. 1354a18-23). But when a regime becomes utterly corrupt, resulting in the corruption of opinion, then even the noblest rhetorician must turn his attention to style in order to hold the interest of his listeners. Thus the character of a regime determines the character of rhetoric. And Aristotle wishes his rhetorician to know not only what would be possible in the best regime and what is commonly required in most regimes but also what is demanded in the worst regimes.[2]

Still, Aristotle states often in Book Three that good style and the proper arrangement of speeches please listeners by instructing them.[3] Metaphor, for example, the most important instrument of rhetorical style, provides listeners, in a manner similar to the enthymeme, with "quick learning," thus satisfying their natural desire to know. Also, Aristotle insists that the best arrangement for a speech is that which presents the substantive argument as clearly and directly as possible—a speaker should first state his case and then prove it. Style and arrangement can, therefore, be aids to argumentation rather than merely techniques of verbal ornamentation and artifice.

Before moving into Aristotle's treatise on style, one should give some attention to a remark at the beginning of Book Three that has been interpreted by at least one commentator to suggest that success in the verbal execution of a speech cannot be taught at all.[4] Rhetorical "acting" or "delivery" (*hupocrisis*), Aristotle says, has the "greatest power" for winning the approval of audiences; those skilled in "acting" receive all the prizes (1403b20-35). But Aristotle observes that "acting is a natural capacity and therefore "less artful," thus clearly implying that it cannot be taught (1404a15-16). Similarly, metaphor, which is the most important element of style and has the "greatest power" in both poetry and prose, is a "sign of natural genius [*euphues*]" and "cannot be received from another."[5] These remarks might well be taken to mean that the most successful elements of rhetoric are natural capacities that are unteachable and therefore that rhetoric is not an intelligible art but merely a natural instinct.

When the passages in question are read more carefully, however, it is not clear that they support such a radical conclusion. After commenting on the importance of style, Aristotle says (1404a12-19):

> When these [the principles of style] come to light, it will have the same effect as acting. Some have attempted to say a little about it, such as Thrasymachus in his *Eleoi*. Acting is by nature and is less artful, but in regard to style it is artful. Wherefore those capable of this [style] obtain the prizes in their turn, just as those capable of acting; for written speeches are strong more because of their style than because of their sense [*dianoia*].

Artful style can duplicate the effects of the naturally talented "actor." Rhetorical success does not, therefore, depend upon an unteachable, instinctive capacity. But the question of metaphor remains. For if the most effective element of style is unteachable, then style itself is "less artful" than it would otherwise be. First of all, in saying that metaphor "cannot be received from another" (*labein ouk estin auten par' allou*) (1405a9), Aristotle is not necessarily saying that it cannot be taught. He might mean instead that since metaphor always violates the normal rules of language, it cannot be acquired from the ordinary linguistic practice of men. The making of metaphors surely does require a special ability, since one must discover metaphors for oneself; one who repeats the metaphors originated by others cannot reproduce the vitality that the novel metaphors had. But even if one cannot learn metaphor by memorizing lists of particular metaphors, one can learn something about the principles involved in discovering them. Aristotle seems to indicate this when he speaks of "smart and popular sayings," which include metaphors, and says, "They are made either by natural genius or by practice, but to show the method is our concern" (1410b6-9). Not only "natural genius" but also "practice" can provide this skill. Furthermore, one can study the way in which this skill is exercised. An innate capacity for making metaphors is important, but a good rhetorician can be taught a great deal about the nature of metaphors and about the principles involved in discovering them; and it is to provide such a teaching that Aristotle writes his treatise on metaphor.[6]

General Rules of Style (2)

"Let the virtue of style be defined as clarity" (1404b2). Aristotle begins Chapter 2 by stating as his fundamental principle that the function of good style is to present clearly the speaker's meaning. The ultimate aim of style, then, is to convey thought; hence, it contributes to the intelligibility of rhetorical argument.

Clarity should be combined with the appropriate dignity, for a good speaker will strive to be clear without being commonplace. "Wherefore it is necessary to make our discourse 'foreign' [*xenos*]; for men wonder at things remote, and what is wonderful is pleasurable" (1404b11-13). When this remark is considered in connection with Aristotle's earlier observation (1. 11. 1371a31-33) that wonder implies a desire to learn, it becomes evident that the pleasure style gives is the pleasure that comes from learning something. When a speaker's language is sufficiently clear as to be easily understandable and yet sufficiently "strange" as to be novel, it gives listeners the pleasurable feeling of learning something new; and such a style of discourse appeals to all men because learning is naturally pleasurable to all (see 10. 1410b9-11).

If a rhetorician goes too far in elevating his discourse and giving it a "foreign air," he runs the risk of making his style seem too contrived. A style that appears natural is persuasive (1404b14-26), while one that appears artificial is not. Rhetorical style should be appropriate to the subject matter. Therefore, a poetic style of language is usually unsuited to rhetoric because the subjects of poetry generally have about them a grandeur that rhetorical subjects have not. One sees here Aristotle's insistence that style cannot be separated from subject matter. Sophistical rhetoricians who would try to employ a grandiloquent style to distract attention from the subject at hand are not likely to be successful, it would seem, for listeners are more easily persuaded when there is a conformity between style and substance.

Although many of the elements of poetic style are inappropriate for rhetoric, metaphor is nonetheless as applicable to rhetoric as it is to poetry. Indeed, metaphor is the chief element of rhetorical style; more effectively than anything else in rhetoric, metaphor can combine clarity with "foreignness" in a pleasing way. Since Aristotle does not discuss metaphor fully until later in the book (Chapters 10 through 12), I shall reserve my comments on his introductory remarks here in Chapter 2 until I discuss the later chapters. It is sufficient here to say that his account of metaphor sustains the prevailing theme of his study of style, which is that a speaker's language should strike a mean between the unintelligi-

166

ble and the commonplace so that it is clear without being ordinary and informative without being recondite.

Frigidity of Style (3)

Frigidity of style is due to the improper use of compound words, strange words, epithets, or metaphors. In each case, discourse becomes obscure because a speaker does not observe a due mean and does not consider what is appropriate.

Aristotle is here attacking some of the sophists' favorite techniques, as indicated by the fact that most of his examples are from the speeches of Gorgias and his student Alcidamus. The sophists use language to confuse their audiences, to blanket them in an impenetrable fog of verbiage and thus divert attention from the subjects under consideration. Aristotle criticizes such techniques because, as has been shown, he maintains that the aim of style is to clarify rather than to obfuscate the issues being discussed.

Similes (4)

"The simile also is a metaphor," Aristotle says, "for it differs little." In fact, a simile is only a metaphor to which the word "like" has been added. To say of Achilles, "he rushed on like a lion" is a simile; to say "a lion, he rushed on" is a metaphor (1406b20-24).

This point is significant in the interpretaton of Aristotle's view of metaphor, for it means that he sees metaphor as being a comparison — that is, one can always explicate a metaphor as saying that one thing is *like* another in some respect. Metaphor is a comparison based on resemblance; it differs from simile only in the directness and brevity of its expression: a simile states that one thing is *like* another, while a metaphor states that one thing *is* another.

Correctness of Language (5)

"The first principle of style is to speak Greek." In this statement Aristotle calls attention to the fact that, unlike the strictly logical elements of rhetoric, style requires some rules peculiar to a particular language; they are not universal. The general principles of style are universally applicable, but in practice they must be applied to the conventions of particular languages.

Even so, the rules Aristotle lists here for good Greek have obvious analogues in other languages. The first rule is to use connecting particles properly; the second is to call things by their special names rather than by vague general ones; the third, to avoid ambiguous terms; the fourth, to distinguish the genders of words; and the fifth, to differentiate plural, dual, and singular words. "Generally what is written should be easy to read or easy to utter, and this is the same thing" (1407b11–12).

Each of these rules is designed to foster clarity of expression. It is therefore fitting that the avoidance of ambiguous language is central to the list of five. The rule is "that there not be ambiguities, unless you would deliberately choose [*proairetai*] the opposite, just as those who have nothing to say pretend to say something" (1407a32–34). After citing examples from Empedocles and the soothsayers, Aristotle concludes: "All of these ambiguities are alike so they should be avoided except for the sake of something such as indicated" (1407b5–7).

Aristotle's attitude toward sophistry in rhetoric is implicit in the way that he states this rule. He sets it down as a principle of good style that ambiguities are to be shunned. But he acknowledges that those who "choose" to be sophists (see 1. 1. 1355b16–22) will violate this rule, because they will wish to appear to say something when in fact they have nothing to say. The good rhetorician must again be reminded of the sort of deception that his sophistical opponents practice so that he can guard against them. And Aristotle might also be suggesting here, as he has elsewhere in the *Rhetoric*, that the noble rhetorician should be prepared to use the sophists' own techniques against them when it is necessary for achieving his good ends.

Grandeur of Style (6)

Aristotle states eight ways in which to give a speech an air of grandeur. 1. A speaker can use the definition rather than the name of something. 2. If he wishes conciseness, a speaker can do the reverse — use the name rather than the definition. These first two rules are important for avoiding indecent language, for sometimes the name of something is obscene; at other times the definition will be. 3. Metaphors and epithets can give grandeur. 4. Speaking of a single thing in the plural is a poetic way of creating grandeur. 5. Giving each word its article — for example, *tes gunaikos tes hemeteras* — is effective in this respect. 6. But also the reverse gives conciseness — for example, *tes hemeteras gunaikos*. 7. "Also speak with a connecting particle, or do without it if conciseness is wanted; but avoid disconnection; for example 'having gone and having conversed' or 'having gone, I conversed with him' " (1407b37–1408a2).

168

8. Finally, one can speak of something by referring to those qualities it does *not* possess.

Propriety of Style (7)

"Style is proper if it is pathetical, ethical, and proportionate to the subject matter [*pragma*]" (1408a10–11). Thus style should be an integral part of the substantive argument of a speech, for it should support all three *pisteis* — *pragma, pathos,* and *ethos*. It should be appropriate to the subject; it should express the proper emotion; and it should manifest the speaker's character. It has been argued previously in this commentary that Aristotle views the enthymeme as integrating *ethos, pathos,* and *pragma;* now it is clear that he requires this same integration for style.

With respect to passionate style, Aristotle states:

> Style is passionate if one speaks with anger of outrage, with disgust and restraint of impious and shameful things, with admiration of things praiseworthy, with lowliness of things pitiable and likewise in other cases. Suitable style also makes the case [*pragma*] persuasive; for the soul [of the listener] makes a logical error [*paralogizetai*] as though the speaker were speaking truly, because in such circumstances men are disposed in the same way; so that they [the listeners] think, even if it is not so, that the facts [*ta pragmata*] are as the speaker says; and a listener always shares the passion of one speaking passionately even if there is nothing to what he says. For this reason many overwhelm their listeners with confused noise. (1408a16–25)

One sees here that a speaker's style, the emotions he expresses, and the subject matter of his speech are intertwined. A speaker cannot express in the style of his discourse any passion he wishes; to be persuasive the passion must be appropriate to the object. It would be absurd, for instance, for a rhetorician to try to express anger in talking about things worthy of praise. But oddly enough, it is precisely the objective reference of passions that leads to deception; for if a speaker argues a case and expresses the passion that would be the appropriate response if the case were as he claims it is, then listeners are likely to infer from the speaker's passion that his case is true. That is, they reason that since a certain set of facts creates a certain type of passion, the existence of the passion implies the existence of the facts. They are deceived by the fallacy of the consequent (see 2. 24. 1401b19–29) because they assume that if the existence of the passion follows from the existence of the facts, the converse must also be true. Although their inference is not necessarily true, it may still be true and perhaps even true in most cases. The inference is not true if the speaker's passion is sincere but falsely grounded or if he is only pretending to have the passion. The inference is true, then, if the speaker's passion is sincere and well grounded.

This reasoning could also be described as a "sign"-inference; that is, the expression in style of a speaker's passion is regarded as a "sign" of the existence of the circumstances to which the passion would be an appropriate response. Similarly, when a rhetorician manifests his character through his style, he relies on a "proof from signs" (1408a26-27). In either case, the listeners reason to a conclusion that is not a necessary truth although it may be a probable truth. In fact, this is the sort of reasoning that all men employ every day—to judge a man's character from the style of his speech and to judge the truth of what he says from the emotional firmness with which he says it—and although it is obviously fallible, it is indispensable.

Rhythm (8)

Rhetorical prose, Aristotle explains, should be rhythmical but not metrical. If it is metrical, it seems too artificial to be persuasive because a metrical style is appropriate for poetry but not for prose. But rhetorical language should be rhythmical, for without rhythm it will be "unlimited," and the "unlimited" is "annoying" and "unknowable." "All things are limited by number, and the number belonging to the form of style is rhythm" (1408b22-29).

These comments on the "limited" and the "unlimited" might well be intended to evoke in the reader's mind certain Pythagorean and platonic doctrines.[7] But without going too deeply into these matters, it is sufficient here to note the fact that what is finite commonly seems intelligible to men while what is infinite seem unintelligible. The boundless is incomprehensible; the mind cannot comprehend something unless it is bounded by a shape that differentiates it from everything else. Number provides the patterns that the mind seeks: a formless mass becomes knowable when the mind discovers in it a numerical structure. For this reason, rhythmical speech is more pleasant than speech without rhythm because rhythm organizes the words according to a numerical pattern, making them easier to grasp.

Thus does Aristotle show rhetorical style in the service of reason. Far from interfering with rhetorical reasoning, proper style provides the intelligibility requisite for deliberation. Listeners cannot judge the truth or falsity of a rhetorician's argument unless he speaks in such a way as to make himself easily understandable.

Periodic Style (9)

Another way for the rhetorician to make his speech "limited," Aristotle adds, is to speak in "periodic" sentences, in which the parts of the sentence are tightly combined in a compact form rather than loosely connected in a continuous fashion. A loosely connected sentence has "no end in itself," and "it is annoying because it is unlimited, for all wish to have the end in sight" (1409a28-33). A period is just the opposite (1409a35-1409b6):

> By a period I mean a sentence having a beginning and an end in itself and a magnitude that is easily seen together [*eusunopton*]. Such a style is pleasurable and easy to learn, pleasurable because it is the opposite of the unlimited, and because the listener thinks that he has got hold of something for himself by reaching an end [or conclusion]; for it is annoying neither to foresee [*pronoein*] anything nor to complete anything. It is easy to learn because it is easily remembered. This is so because in periodic style there is number, which of all things is most easily remembered.

A sentence in which the parts come one after another without any clear starting point or conclusion is difficult to comprehend because it cannot be grasped as a structured whole. A periodic sentence, however, is organized so that its parts exhibit a development from a definite beginning to a definite end; its parts are tightly interrelated so as to compose a whole. Just as does rhythm, a periodic style makes discourse more intelligible by organizing words into numerical patterns that are readily grasped by the mind; this comprehensibility makes speech more pleasing to the listener.

Aristotle makes a similar point in the *Poetics* (1451a2-6, 1459a30-35) with respect to the structure of a plot. He says that a properly constructed plot should be a whole of ordered parts with a beginning, a middle, and an end, and that it should have such a magnitude as to be "easily seen together" (*eusunopton*). He illustrates his thought by referring to one of the characteristics of beautiful things: a thing of beauty must be neither so small that its parts cannot be distinguished nor their relations seen (a one without a many?) nor so large that it cannot be seen altogether at once (a many without a one?). A good plot and periodic style are alike in that they both give to an audience the intellectual pleasure of seeing a many as a one.

171

Periodic style is even more effective when it is structured antithetically. "Such a style is pleasurable because contraries are most knowable, and even more knowable side by side, and also because this style resembles a syllogism; for refutation is a bringing together of opposites" (1410a19-23). Style gives pleasure by making speech more "knowable" than it would otherwise be; thus it contributes to the rational character of rhetoric. Some of the best techniques of style even manifest the same rational structure as the syllogism. The antithetic period is one example of this. But an even more striking case of an instrument of style that resembles syllogistic reasoning is the metaphor.

Metaphor (10-11)

Aristotle is ambivalent about metaphor, for he is at once suspicious and respectful of it. While in the *Posterior Analytics* (97b28-38) and the *Topics* (139b34-35) he denigrates metaphorical speech as "unclear" (*asaphes*), he speaks of metaphor in the *Rhetoric* (3. 2. 1405a7-9) as a primary source of "clarity" (*saphes*). Sometimes he warns against the deceptive results of metaphor in scientific and philosophic reasoning. An example of this is found in his criticisms of Plato's doctrine of the Ideas: to speak of the Ideas as patterns in which all things "participate," Aristotle complains, is "to speak in empty words and poetic metaphors" (*Metaph.* 991a21-23, 992a25-29). But he also compares metaphor to philosophic reasoning: to be a master of metaphor is a sign of philosophic genius.[8] And in the *Rhetoric* he insists that a good metaphor gives listeners the pleasure of learning something.[9]

This apparent contradiction in Aristotle's view of metaphor can be resolved, I think, in the following way. Aristotle thinks that metaphor is an important, if not essential, instrument of thought although it lacks the certitude and exactness of the highest form of reasoning. Metaphor can be a useful tool of reason, but only so long as one carefully avoids being deceived by it. For, as Aristotle says in the *Topics* (139b34-35, 140a8-12), although metaphorical speech is always obscure, it does convey some knowledge of what it signifies through "likeness." It is this element of "likeness" or "resemblance" that makes metaphor rational; for insofar as a metaphor reveals a "resemblance" of one thing to another, it gives new knowledge. But what precisely is the nature of metaphorical "resemblance"? And how does it contribute to an understanding of reality?

In the *Poetics* (1457b7-8), Aristotle says that using a metaphor is giving something a name that belongs to something else, the transference being from genus to species, from species to genus, from species to species, or by analogy. In the *Rhetoric* he considers only one of the four types — metaphor by analogy — because it is the most popular (1411a1-2).

One of the examples of analogical metaphor is Pericles' remark that the youth who died in the war vanished from the city as though the year had lost its springtime (10. 1411a1-3). To say that youth is springtime is not to use the word "springtime" in its literal sense. Literally, spring is a season of the year, not the first period of human life. But metaphorically, one may say that youth is springtime because there is an analogical resemblance between them. Youth is to human life what spring is to the year: both are times of growth and freshness. And since there is this similarity of proportions, youth and springtime are metaphorically interchangeable.

Another example is Homer's calling old age "stubble" (10. 1410b13-16). At the level of literal speech, this utterance is absurd. The difference between an elderly human being and a withered stalk is too great for the two to be equated. But viewed as a metaphor, the statement by Homer makes sense; it even instructs us: "he teaches us and informs us through the genus, for both have lost their bloom" (1410b14-16). "Lost bloom" connects the two otherwise disparate realities.

Metaphor, then, requires a linking of one thing to another founded upon some resemblance between them. But one must go farther than this to understand the nature of this connection. The success of metaphor depends upon combining the familiar with the unfamiliar, because metaphorical resemblance should be neither too familiar (and thus commonplace) nor too unfamiliar (and thus obscure).[10] There are definitions for "old man" and "stubble"; but when Homer says that old men are stubble, he contradicts established definitions and creates a statement that is absurd at the level of ordinary speech. But reexamination of the ordinary meanings of "old man" and "stubble" to see whether there is any way they can be meaningfully linked shows that some of the connotations of "stubble" do apply to old men; something is clear that was unseen before. By combining familiar words in unfamiliar ways, Homer forces us to apply our old knowledge to gain new knowledge. Thus, a good metaphor uses what men know to illuminate what they do not know, thereby giving the pleasure of new learning.

When the connection of two things is so completely strange and novel that men have no prior knowledge that would allow them to make sense of it, then it must be regarded as pure nonsense rather than as a true metaphor. This is what Aristotle means when he says that a metaphor must be sufficiently clear as to be understandable.

But Aristotle also insists that good metaphor should combine clarity with "strangeness" so that it is clear without being ordinary. For a metaphor to be clear, there must be an easily discoverable resemblance between the things connected; but this resemblance should not be so obvious that the listener is deprived of the pleasurable sense of wonder at discovering the hidden connection between remote things. Moreover, the philosophic character of metaphor is here quite evident because the pleasure that men take in seeing the likeness in things that are far apart is a philosophic pleasure.[11]

For Aristotle, then, a good metaphor should teach something; for this reason, it should be neither too familiar nor too strange. If it is too familiar, it presents something already known and thus teaches nothing new. And if it is too strange, it is incomprehensible and therefore cannot teach anything at all.

Aristotle restates this point in a somewhat different way when he suggests that a good metaphor teaches men by presenting them with a riddle—a riddle that perplexes them momentarily without completely baffling them.[12] Initially a metaphor appears as an absurd combination of words; but as soon as one goes beyond the level of ordinary speech and considers the various connotations and subtle associations of the words, a hidden meaning, an intelligible connection that was not evident at first glance is discovered; and this discovery gives pleasure—the pleasure of seeing likeness where previously only unlikeness had been seen.

Metaphor thus illustrates the famous paradox about knowledge that is discussed in Plato's *Meno*—that apparently we can learn only what we already know. For if we were completely ignorant of something, we could not learn anything about it because we would not know where to look to find out about it. In order to inquire about something, we have to ask the right questions, but to ask the right questions we must have some prior knowledge about the subject of our inquiry. In the *Meno* the discussion of this problem leads into Plato's doctrine of reminiscence, according to which all learning is a process of recollection. Aristotle's answer to the problem in the *Posterior Analytics* (71a1–71b8) is perhaps implied here by his discussion of metaphor; for, as has been shown, he describes metaphor as an instrument by which we use prior knowledge to gain new knowledge by combining what we know with what we don't know so that the known can illuminate the unknown.

Furthermore, Aristotle suggests, I think, that the metaphorical movement from the known to the unknown by means of a resemblance between the two is the underlying structure of all human reasoning. All human knowledge is metaphorical because the fundamental characteristic of knowledge is to know one thing through its likeness to something else. This point is most evident in Aristotle's suggestion that in order to be skillful in making metaphors, one must have the philosophic ability to see the likeness in things far apart. Indeed, to be able to see whether things are alike or unlike, the same or different, is the foundation of all philosphy.[13] In this sense, philosophy could be said to be inherently metaphorical.

Moreover, the logical instrument of thought—the syllogism—also exhibits a metaphorical structure. In a syllogism one term is shown to be predicated of another term through a middle term predicated of both; stated somewhat differently, one thing is conjoined to another through some third thing that they share.[14] This syllogistic movement from one thing to another is structurally rather similar to metaphor, in which one thing is connected to another through some resemblance between the two. In addition, the sharpness of mind required to hit upon a middle term without hesitation parallels the mental ability to discern quickly the likeness between remote things.[15]

Aristotle draws attention to the correlation between metaphorical and syllogistic reasoning by noting that the fundamental rules for the rhetorical use of metaphors are the same as those for the use of en-thymemes. Both metaphors and enthymemes are most effective when they are neither too distant from the listeners nor too obvious, for the aim in both is to use what is familiar to illuminate what is unfamiliar so as to give the listeners the pleasure of "quick learning." It seems that metaphor is as much a form of reasoning as the enthymeme, for it is characteristic of all rational inference to discover the likenesses among things and to view one thing through the mirror of another.[16]

But even if metaphor is a form of reasoning, it does not follow that all the characteristics of metaphorical speech can be translated into abstract, literal speech. Good metaphor possesses a vividness, a beauty, and a multiplicity of meanings that cannot be duplicated in nonmetaphorical language. Aristotle notes the vividness of metaphor, speaking of its capacity for "setting things before the eyes" by putting things into a state of "activity" or "actuality" (*energeia*) (11. 1411b21–1412a8). In particular, this vividness occurs when inanimate things are presented as if they were animate. Homer's poetry is full of this sort of metaphor: spears and arrows, for instance, are depicted as

175

"shameless," "eager," or "ruthless" in their flight. Homer thus makes things vivid by infusing everything with life and motion.

Aristotle also recognizes the purely sensuous beauty of good metaphor. Metaphors should be drawn, he says, "from things beautiful either in voice, or in meaning, or to sight, or to some other sense" (2. 1405b17). Finally, one of the pleasures of metaphor is surely its delightful ambiguity—the ambiguity that comes from its evocation of multiple meanings. Any good metaphor will have such a rich variety of associated meanings that it is impossible to explicate all of them; thus one understands why its "clarity" is mixed with "strangeness." To claim that metaphor can be understood as a form of rational inference is not to say that every metaphor can be restated completely as literal discourse. It is to say, however, that metaphor is one means for reasoning about the world and that the pleasure men derive from metaphor is ultimately the pleasure of learning something new about reality.

Styles for Different Kinds of Rhetoric (12)

Aristotle concludes his comments on style by noting the variations in style required for different types of rhetoric. He distinguishes between the style of written compositions and the style of public debates and between deliberative and forensic style.

Written compositions show the greatest precison in their style, while the style of public debates allows the greatest opportunity for delivery (1413b9-10). The speeches of writers seem stiff in public debate, and the speeches of public debaters seem trivial when they are read.

The style of written discourses is most suitable for epideictic rhetoric, but it is also appropriate for forensic. Deliberative rhetoric requires a loose oral style because, since it is directed to a large crowd, it must be like a rough sketch that is meant to be viewed from a distance. Forensic rhetoric exhibits a more exact style of presentation since it is intended for a small audience. Also, there is less room in forensic for the techniques of delivery that depart from the subject at hand because in the circumstances of a trial strict standards of relevance are upheld (1414a8-18).

This appears to contradict Aristotle's explanation at the beginning of the *Rhetoric* that deliberative rhetoric is governed by more rigorous standards than those employed in forensic. But this earlier distinction was based on the *subject matter* of the two kinds of rhetoric: the subjects of deliberative rhetoric tend to be of greater concern to the entire community than are the subjects of forensic, which tend to be rather narrowly private matters. But here in his discussion of style Aristotle is concerned not so much with the *subjects* as with the *style* of speeches; and with respect to style, forensic rhetoric tends to be more exact, more finished, than deliberative.

Aristotle closes this section of the *Rhetoric* on style by explaining that he does not need to set down the rule that style must be pleasant since this has been presupposed throughout his discussion. To speak so as to be neither too obvious nor too obscure and thus to combine clarity with "strangeness" — this in itself gives pleasure; this pleasure that style gives an audience is the pleasure of learning.

The Two-Part Arrangement of Speeches (13)

"A speech has two parts," Aristotle says, "for it is necessary to state the case [*pragma*] and then to demonstrate [*apodeixai*] it" (1414a30–31). Thus he begins his remarks on the arrangement of a speech by clearly indicating that he disapproves of the popular rhetorical theories requiring the division of a speech into many parts. His departure from these doctrines shows again his emphasis on the rationality of rhetoric. According to the traditional theories, a speaker should restrict the proof of his case to one part of his speech, with the other parts being devoted to emotional and other sorts of appeal. But it has been shown that Aristotle would require that *ethos* and *pathos* be integral parts of the rhetorician's argument of his case, and confirmation of this appears in this chapter. The rhetorician's statement and proof of his case, according to Aristotle, are not just two parts of his speech among many; they are the only parts. If any additional divisions of the speech are made, they must somehow assist the argument of the case. Hence, as with his treatment of style, Aristotle's rules for the proper arrangement of a speech show his preference for rhetoric that is concerned with arguing about the subject at hand rather than with techniques for distracting the attention of listeners or arousing their emotions in a way that is unrelated to the subject.

He acknowledges that in some cases a speech might have to be divided into four parts: "proem" (*prooimion*), "statement" (*prothesis*), "proof" (*pistis*), and "epilogue" (*epilogos*). But even here the proem and epilogue should support the statement and the proof by serving as aids to memory (1414b8–13).

Nevertheless, in subsequent comments Aristotle makes concessions to the established practice in these matters. Although he clearly prefers speeches that simply state and then prove the case, he admits that in particular circumstances with corrupt listeners a rhetorician might have to devote parts of his speech to techniques of persuasion that do not contribute to the rational content of his presentation. As in other parts of the *Rhetoric,* Aristotle's concern here is that the rhetorician combine a preference for noble rhetoric with an ability to resort to less noble techniques when they are dictated by practical necessity.

The Proem (14–15)

Proems are apparently more important for forensic rhetoric than for either epideictic or deliberative rhetoric. Although Aristotle comments briefly on epideictic proems at the beginning of this chapter (1414b22-1415a7) and on deliberative proems at the end (1415b31-1416a2), the rest of his remarks concern the forensic uses of proems.

After showing how a forensic proem can introduce the subject of a speech so that the minds of the listeners can quickly grasp what is to follow, Aristotle says: "This, therefore, is the most necessary and the special function of a proem — to clarify what is the end or purpose of the speech; wherefore when the subject [*pragma*] is clear or short, a proem should not be used. The other forms of proems in use are remedies and are common [to all forms of rhetoric]" (1415a21-26). Thus he concedes that although the essential function of proems is to clarify a speaker's argument, proems are also used as "remedies." He explains that by "remedies" he means those cases in which proems are designed to deal with circumstances and audiences that are not conducive to noble rhetoric.

Used as "remedies," proems are related either to the speaker, to his opponent, to the listener, or to the subject. In a proem a speaker can eliminate the prejudices created by his opponent against him and create new prejudices unfavorable to his opponent (1415a27-33). Or the speaker can use his proem to make the listener well disposed, to arouse his passions, or to make him either attentive or inattentive to the case (1415a34-1415b4). "But it is necessary not to forget," Aristotle insists, "that all such things are outside the speech [*logos*], for they are addressed to the weakness of the listener who will listen to what is outside the subject; for if he were not such a sort of listener, a proem would not be necessary except to state the subject in summary fashion so that, like a body, it may have a head" (1415b5-8). Finally, those who "have or seem to have a bad case" can use the proem to direct attention away from the subject so that the weakness of their case will not become apparent (1415b21-24).

Thus, while Aristotle sets down as the norm for proems that they be employed only to prepare an audience for the statement and proof of the case, he also concedes that in some circumstances with corrupt listeners proems might have to be used as a means for deception. With the worst audiences prudence demands that even the noblest rhetorician resort to practices that he would otherwise shun; it should be emphasized here, though, that Aristotle thinks that in most cases audiences are not so corrupt as to require these techniques. For example, for listeners to be ready to listen to what is outside the subject goes against the inclination of men to demand that rhetorical argument be based upon facts inherent to the subject at hand (see 1. 1. 1354a18-24, 3. 14. 1415b2-8).

For a rhetorician to begin his speech by removing the listeners' unfavorable prejudices about him is one of the most common uses of a proem as a "remedy." In Chapter 15 Aristotle lists eleven types of arguments that may be employed in such cases.

The Narrative (16)

Just as in his account of the proem, Aristotle begins his treatment of the narrative with a brief section on epideictic narrative (1416b16-29) and closes with a brief section on deliberative narrative (1417b13-21), devoting most of his attention to the forensic use of the narrative.

A narrative should show what has happened, of what sort (just or unjust), and of what importance. Thus in forensic rhetoric a speaker must give an account of the facts so as to indicate what was done, whether it was a just or unjust action, and whether it was important.

Aristotle also indicates that a narrative should be presented in a way that displays character (1417a16-35) and emotion (1417a36-1417b7). In other words, persuasion through *ethos* and *pathos* should be integrated into the factual statement of the case.

Proofs (17)

"Proofs," Aristotle says, must be "demonstrative." And "proofs" concern what has happened or will happen, whether injury has occurred or will occur, whether the events are important, and whether they are just (1417b21-27).

He explains the variations among the different kinds of rhetoric. The epideictic speaker assumes the facts but goes on to show the nobility, usefulness, and importance of the deeds that he praises (1417b30-34). The deliberative rhetorician will either deny that what

179

his opponent recommends can occur or argue that the opponent's course of action is unjust, inexpedient, or unimportant (1417b35-1418a1). Deliberative rhetoric involves the future, and examples are the best form of reasoning here because one can infer from what has happened what will happen. But forensic rhetoric involves the past, and enthymemes are best for reasoning about the past because the past can be known with enthymematic rigor (1418a2-4). Deliberative is more difficult than forensic rhetoric because the common good, which is the subject of political deliberation, is less clearly defined than the law. But since forensic is founded on such a clear standard, it is higher than deliberative rhetoric because forensic reasoning can be more rigorous (1418a22-28).

The most puzzling portion of this chapter is Aristotle's differentiation of enthymematic reasoning from persuasion through character (*ethos*) and through passion (*pathos*) (1418a5-21).

> Nor should you seek enthymemes about everything. If you do, you will do just as some of the philosophers, who prove syllogistically things better known and more plausible than the premises from which they speak. And whenever you wish to arouse passion, do not use an enthymeme, for it will either drive out the passion or it will be useless; for simultaneous movements drive each other out, the result being their mutual destruction or weakening. Nor should you look for an enthymeme at the time when you wish to make the speech ethical [*ethikon*]; for demonstration involves neither character [*ethos*] nor moral choice [*proairesis*].

To express character or to create passion, Aristotle concludes, a speaker should argue with "maxims" (1418a8-21). He later adds: "If you have demonstrations, you ought to speak ethically and demonstratively, but if you do not have enthymemes, ethically; it is even more suitable for a virtuous man to appear good than that his speech be exact" (1418b1-3).

I have previously maintained that Aristotle handles persuasion by means of *pathos* or *ethos* as an integral part of enthymematic reasoning; to appeal directly to the passions of the listeners without the use of enthymemes is, I have argued, the kind of sophistical technique that Aristotle rejects. But the passages just quoted seem to contradict this interpretation, for they seem to show Aristotle quite willing to encourage direct appeals based on character or on emotions without the mediation of enthymematic argument. But two points should be kept in mind.

Aristotle's remarks in this chapter might be explained as just the sort of concessions to practical necessity that have already been noted in Book Three. This may certainly be part of the explanation, but a more adequate answer seems available. Aristotle says that character can be exhibited or passion controlled through the use of maxims. But he has taught earlier in the *Rhetoric* that a maxim is a "part of an enthymeme" (2. 20. 1393a25): "maxims are more or less the conclusions of enthymemes or the premises with the syllogistic form removed" (2. 21. 1394a27-29). The thought, then, is that the rhetorician, in order to be most effective in his ethical or emotional appeals, should transform his enthymemes into maxims. Aristotle says this explicitly later in the chapter when he advises that speakers can sometimes show their character best by changing enthymemes into maxims (1418b33-37). The best way to be ethically or emotionally persuasive is to support one's case with principles that are familiar and widely known to the audience. But when a principle is obvious and clear to the listeners, it is unwise to become tiresome by stating the complete inference underlying the principle; therefore, in such a case, the rhetorician should reduce his enthymemes to "maxims." Aristotle is not saying that "proofs" founded on *ethos* or *pathos* should be completely independent of enthymematic reasoning. Rather, he is saying that such "proofs" are most successful when a speaker supports his case with "maxims," which rest upon enthymematic inferences; these are, however, so obvious that to explicitly state the full underlying reasoning would be too tedious for the audience. The enthymemes in such a situation are implied by what the speaker says, but they are stated only incompletely. Here, then, Aristotle is applying his rule from earlier in the *Rhetoric* that enthymemes should be abbreviated as much as possible.

That Aristotle does not intend to deny in this chapter the primacy of the enthymeme for rhetorical persuasion is suggested by his references to the popularity of syllogistic refutations. Enthymemes used in attacking an opposing case are more popular than those used in building one's own case, he says, because in the former the syllogistic reasoning is more apparent (1418b2-11). He then goes on to explain that refutation should consist either of objections or of counter-syllogisms (1418b11-23).

Interrogation and Jesting (18)

Asking questions is effective, Aristotle advises, whenever it allows one to expose the absurdity of the opponent's position, to show that he has conceded one's argument, to reveal that he has contradicted himself or put forth a paradox, or to force him into answering with a sophistical reply that will turn the listeners against him (1418b38-1419a17). The last point, it should be noted, shows again Aristotle's belief that the common opinions of men run contrary to sophistry. It also shows that the noble rhetorician must not resort to sophistical techniques unless it is absolutely necessary. If he uses such devices and is forced by his opponent to reveal his sophistry to the listeners, he will lose their confidence.

It is important, however, to avoid raising questions if the opponent can answer them in a way that strengthens his position. Further, one should avoid a long series of questions because of the incapacity of the listeners to follow a long train of reasoning: brevity is as necessary in asking questions as in stating enthymemes (1419a17-19). Aristotle also offers advice on the best way to answer questions (1419a20-1419b2).

He concludes this chapter by commenting briefly on jests (1419b3-9). He agrees with the recommendation of Gorgias that one should counter seriousness with humor and humor with seriousness. He also distinguishes between irony and buffoonery by saying that irony is "more gentlemanly" and is humor for one's own use, while buffoonery is cruder and is more directly for the sake of another.

The rules for interrogation and the reference to irony might have been intended to remind the reader of Socrates (on Socratic irony, see 7. 1408b17-21). In fact, one of the examples of good questioning is Socrates' examination of Meletus, which is the same example that was used previously to illustrate argument by definition (2. 23. 1398a15-18, 3. 18. 1419a8-13). The essence of Socratic rhetoric, one might infer, is to raise questions about the definitions of things.[17]

The Epilogue (19)

"The epilogue is composed of four parts: to make the listener well-disposed toward oneself and ill-disposed toward one's opponent, to amplify and depreciate, to excite the listener to passion, and to recall to mind [what has been said]" (1419b10-13). Thus the epilogue should restate the speech as a whole in a way that intertwines its ethical, emotional, and logical elements into a single presentation of the argument. Hence, Aristotle concludes by reaffirming the theme of his entire treatise—that is, the need for rhetorical discourse to combine *ethos*, *pathos*, and *logos* so as to achieve that union of rationality and desire essential for practical reasoning.

9

CONCLUSION

A Summary

The fundamental principle of Aristotle's theory of rhetoric, I have argued, is that rhetoric is a genuine form of reasoning. He distinguishes rhetoric from science and philosophy by showing that rhetorical argument lacks the exactness and certitude of philosophic and scientific demonstration. But he also distinguishes rhetoric from sophistry by showing that rhetoric aims at truth.

The logical instrument of rhetorical reasoning is the enthymeme. I have maintained that Aristotle views the enthymeme as encompassing all the major elements of rhetorical persuasion (including the presentation of the speaker's character and the control of the audience's passions). I have also contended that Aristotle regards the enthymeme as a genuine syllogism that is both materially and formally valid.

That the premises of the enthymeme are drawn from common opinions does not make it a false inference because opinions commonly accepted among men usually reflect the truth in some manner. This became apparent in the study of Book One, chapters 4 through 15, where Aristotle presented the opinions pertaining to the subjects of rhetoric as being somewhat muddled and unrefined and yet not fundamentally contradictory to his own philosophic reflections in the *Ethics* and the *Politics*. In most cases, a common opinion will contain at least a modicum of truth, upon which the rhetorician can base a valid inference.

The actions of the sophist substantiate the veracity of common opinions; for his fallacious inferences consist not of reasoning from the common opinions of men, but rather of reasoning from what only *appear* to be common opinions or of reasoning to conclusions that *appear* to follow from common opinions when in fact they do not. While the rhetorician relies upon the commonsense understanding of men, the sophist runs contrary to it.

Yet Aristotle acknowledges that in some cases—when people have

183

become unusually corrupt or when the judgment of an audience is distorted for some reason—the rhetorician might have to resort to sophistical devices. Moreover, the rhetorician must be well acquainted with sophistical fallacies if he is to defend himself against them. Therefore, Aristotle instructs his reader in the use not only of genuine enthymemes but also of "apparent enthymemes"—that is, fallacious inferences.

Thus, the art of rhetoric is an epistemologically neutral instrument insofar as it demands a knowledge of both true and false reasoning. But truth, if it is properly advanced, is generally more persuasive than falsity. Most men are justly irritated with sophistical deception.

Moreover, the enthymeme is popular because, by providing listeners with "quick learning," it satisfies their natural desire for learning. For this reason, the enthymeme should be neither too long and complex nor too superficial and obvious. It should be simple enough to be quickly grasped, but at the same time it should give the listeners the pleasure of learning something new. A rhetorician achieves the proper effect if he leaves unstated those steps in the reasoning that the listeners can easily supply themselves because in this way he draws them into helping him construct the very arguments by which they are persuaded, and thus he gives them the satisfaction of thinking through the reasoning on their own.

Aristotle thinks there are two additional dimensions to enthymematic argument. In most cases a speaker's use of enthymemes to prove or disprove something exhibits his character and moves his listeners emotionally. Rhetorical arguments are more persuasive if they are stated so as to demonstrate the trustworthiness of the speaker. However, rhetorical argumentation is *practical* reasoning, and a rhetorician must argue in such a way as to *stir* his listeners to *action;* so he must arouse those passions that favor a particular course of action and allay those that do not. The enthymeme, therefore, comprehends all the elements of rhetorical persuasion; for it includes not just logical proof but also those appeals based on the character of the speaker and those based on the passions of the audience.

That a rhetorician can control the passions of his audience with enthymemes presupposes that the passions are amenable to argument. Indeed, Aristotle describes the passions as rational to the extent that they rest upon judgments about reality. A speaker can therefore control the passions by controlling the judgments on which they depend—that is to say, by convincing the audience that certain passions are justified by the circumstances and others are not.

184

But even if the enthymeme can encompass all three *pisteis*—*logos*, *ethos*, and *pathos*—style and composition are elements of the rhetorical art that seem to be completely extraneous to enthymematic reasoning. In fact, Aristotle is clearly reluctant to take up the style and composition of speeches since he regards this as necessary only as a concession to corrupt listeners. Yet he manages to show that even these components of the art can contribute to the rationality of rhetoric. Metaphor, for example, which is the chief instrument of style, resembles the enthymeme in the way that it pleases listeners with "quick learning." And the best arrangement of a speech is essentially a statement of the case followed by arguments proving the case. Rhetorical style and arrangement assist the speaker in presenting his enthymematic reasoning, and thus they sustain the character of rhetoric as rational discourse.

Rhetoric, Political Science, and Common Sense

What would the modern political scientist say about all this? He might protest that rhetoric is surely not a valid form of reasoning since it violates even the most elementary rules of scientific rationality.[1] The fundamental problem, he might explain, is that the rhetorician's arguments can be only as reliable as the commonsense political opinions from which he draws his premises, but common opinions are at best uncertain and inexact reflections of political reality and at worst unexamined prejudices with no claim to truth. In contrast to the rhetorician's dependence on the vague and deceptive impressions of common sense, the contemporary political scientist might appeal to the epistemological criteria of a scientific methodology for precise standards of political knowledge. But does the scientific method provide a better starting point for political inquiry than does rhetoric?

This question was first clearly posed by Thomas Hobbes when, in the seventeenth century, he rejected Aristotelian political science and applied the scientific method to political study and in so doing became the founder of modern political science. Hobbes admired Aristotle's *Rhetoric* for its psychological insights, but he certainly denied Aristotle's claim, which is essential for his rhetorical theory, that common opinions can be the foundation of political reasoning. Classical political philosophers such as Aristotle could never lead us to genuine political knowledge, Hobbes argued, because "in their writings and discourse they take for principles those opinions which are vulgarly received, whether true or false; being for the most part false."[2] Instead of starting with political opinions, Hobbes's political science would start with exact

185

definitions and axioms; and from these principles one could deduce a theoretical framework that would have the certainty and precision of geometry. Thus did Hobbes initiate the method to which many political scientists today have devoted themselves.[3]

These developments lead to a necessary question: Is there anything to be said in favor of Aristotle's reliance on common political opinions as the foundation of political knowledge? On the one hand, Aristotle's theory of rhetoric as a valid form of political reasoning depends on the assumption that common opinions reflect a rational grasp of political life. But on the other hand, Aristotle presents those opinions as often offering a confused, crude, and distorted view of political reality that falls short of the rigor, refinement, and comprehensiveness required for political philosophy. It seems that political opinions are the starting point for the Aristotelian political scientist, but they are *only* the starting point: the respect that he gives to these opinions does not require an uncritical acceptance. Since the political theorist seeks to move from opinion to knowledge, he will not completely accept the answers given in political speech. Still, even in his movement beyond the common political opinions, he will be guided by the questions to which those opinions point: he will try to give an *adequate* answer to the questions that political opinions answer only *inadequately*.[4]

But if Aristotle finds these common opinions so defective that he has to transcend them, why does he not reject them from the start in order to reason from scientific principles in the manner later to be advocated by Hobbes? Aristotle might answer with two types of arguments. First, the phenomena studied by the political scientist differ from those studied by the natural scientist in ways that justify a difference in method. Second, all reasoning — even that of the natural scientist — depends ultimately upon the truth of man's commonsense understanding of things.

Because political phenomena are contingent rather than necessary, and because they are essentially cognitive rather than physical, the political scientist, Aristotle might argue, must rely on commonsense opinions in a manner that would be inappropriate for the natural scientist. Political reality is contingent because it depends upon human choices that change from time to time and from one situation to another. The nature of political life will vary, for example, depending upon the type of regime in existence: oligarchic politics differs from democratic politics. And a regime is a product of certain choices as to the organization and the goals of political rule. To understand these choices, the political scientist must study them as they are manifest in common opinions. And it would be a mistake to try to examine these things as if they were as unchangeable as the Pythagorean theorem or the motion of the planets.

Moreover, political things are not physical objects that can be studied through sense perception. A political scientist who restricted himself to sense perceptions would never see anything political, for political phenomena come into view only when the scientist pays attention to what people *think* about politics as indicated by what they *say* about it. An appeal to political opinions is again unavoidable.

In the most fundamental respect, *all* reasoning—not just that of political science—depends upon commonsense opinions. This is so because all reasoning rests upon presuppositions drawn from man's commonsense awareness of things.

The rules of logic govern the deduction from premises, but these rules cannot determine the truth or falsity of the first premises. Reasoning is grounded upon fundamental assumptions that cannot be proven because they are the source of all proofs. A conclusion is demonstrated when it is shown to follow from certain premises. The premises may themselves be shown to follow as conclusions from other premises. But eventually one must reach principles that are taken as true without proof, these being the starting points of reasoning. Indeed, are not the rules of logic themselves assumptions that cannot be proven logically?[5]

Even the most rigorous empirical science cannot avoid reliance on unprovable assumptions. Scientific induction, for example, rests on the presuppositon that one may generalize from particular cases, which depends in turn on the broader assumption that nature falls into recurrent patterns—in other words, that the universe is governed by laws, and these laws do not change arbitrarily from one moment to another.[6]

In this way scientific knowledge presupposes a prescientific knowledge of things. This is what Aristotle means when he says that to examine the first principles of any science, one must appeal to the "common opinions" (*endoxa*) that are the source of the principles (*Top.* 100a18-100b22, 101a37-101b4). Werner Heisenberg, one of the leading physicists of the twentieth century, seems to make the same point when he observes: "the concepts of natural language, vaguely defined as they are, seem to be more stable in the expansion of knowledge than the precise terms of scientific language, derived as an idealization from only limited groups of phenomena." This is so because on the one hand, "the concepts of natural language are formed by the immediate connection with reality"; but on the other hand, scientific concepts require idealization and precise definition through which "the immediate connection with reality is lost." Heisenberg concludes: "We know that any understanding must be based finally upon the natural language because it is only there that we can be certain to touch reality, and hence we must be skeptical about any skepticism with regard to this natural language and its essential concepts."[7]

Our commonsense awareness of reality is more reliable than any epistemological theory could ever be. In fact, the truth of any epistemological theory will depend upon how well it accounts for our reliance on common sense.[8] The Hobbesian political scientist may think he can acquire political knowledge through a formal method that is totally abstracted from commonsense experience; but in practice his choice of definitions, axioms, and rules of inference will always be guided, even if unintentionally, by his own commonsense grasp of political reality. How would he even be able to begin looking for political phenomena if he did not already somehow know what politics was like? As with Lewis Carroll's Alice, he must learn that if he is completely lost, he will never find his way; for if he does not know where he wants to get to, it does not matter which way he goes. The Hobbesian political scientist knows more than he will admit; for like any sensible human being, he begins with a natural awareness of political things that can direct his scientific inquiry. He is not *completely* lost after all. He knows at the start, even if only vaguely, where he wants to go; so it is not surprising that he usually finds a way to get there.

To fully understand the fundamental importance of commonsense experience for political reasoning, one must recognize the limits of Hobbes and his legacy in order to recover the Aristotelian tradition of political science, of which Aristotle's *Rhetoric* is an essential part. More clearly than any other Aristotelian text, the *Rhetoric* brings into view the common political opinions of human beings as the primary ground of political knowledge. Even though the political scientist must go beyond those opinions through a process of philosophical refinement, he must always look to them for guidance. Only by continually turning his attention to the political questions found in ordinary political speech can the student of politics understand political things as they are in themselves.

NOTES

Chapter One

1. Thucydides, *The Peloponnesian War*, trans. Thomas Hobbes, ed. David Grene (Ann Arbor: University of Michigan Press, 1959), 2. 40.

2. *Helen* 11. Unless otherwise indicated, all translations are my own.

3. See also *Rh.* 1. 1. 1355b1-2; *Int.* 16a3-13, 26-29.

4. See Laurence Berns, "Rational Animal — Political Animal: Nature and Convention in Human Speech and Politics," *Review of Politics* 38 (1976): 177-89.

5. This interpretation was advanced by Leo Strauss, *The City and Man* (Chicago: Rand McNally, 1964), p. 23. See Plato's *Apology of Socrates* at 25c-26a, where Socrates stresses persuasion and instruction rather than punishment and compulsion as foundations of law.

6. See *Eth. Nic.* 1094a27-1094b3, 1095a1-13, 1098a3-5, 1102a27-1103a10, 1103b2-25, 1104b10-14, 1113b23-30, 1146a31-1146b2; *Eth. Eud.* 1215a1-4, 1224a13-1224b3; *Pol.* 1269a20-23; *Rh.* 2. 19. 1392a27-29; and *Top.* 113a33-113b7. On the dependence of law on both force and persuasion, see Plato *Laws* 711b-c, 718a-c, 720a-24a; *Phaedo* 89d-91c, 99d-100a; *Statesman* 304c-e.

7. See *Rh.* 1. 1. 1355a22-29.

8. *An. Pr.* 70a39.

9. Claiming that Plato was unjust in condemning rhetoric as "a voluptuary art," Francis Bacon observes:

> we see that speech is much more conversant in adorning that which is good than in coloring that which is evil; for there is no man but speaketh more honestly than he can do or think: and it was excellently noted by Thucydides in Cleon, that because he used to hold on to the bad side in causes of estate, therefore he was ever inveighing against eloquence and good speech; knowing that no man can speak fair of courses sordid and base. [*The Advancement of Learning*, in *Selected Writings of Francis Bacon*, ed. Hugh G. Dick (New York: Modern Library, Random House, 1955), p. 310].

See also Thucydides *Peloponnesian War* 3. 36 48.

Chapter Two

1. Hence this opening chapter is like the proem of a speech. See *Rh.* 3. 14-15. Is the *Rhetoric* itself an example of rhetoric? That is suggested not only by the resemblance of the first chapter to a proem but also by Aristotle's concluding the book with an example of a peroration that could serve as a peroration for the book itself (3. 14. 1420b2-4). Also consider George Anastaplo, "American Constitutionalism and the Virtue of Prudence: Philadelphia, Paris, Washington, Gettysburg," *Loyola of Los Angeles Law Review* 8 (1975): 64: "Does not the conclusion of the *Rhetoric* . . . suggest that his work as a whole

is, in a sense, rhetorical (on behalf of a genuinely good-intentioned rhetoric?) and that it itself is organized according to rhetorical principles and must be examined accordingly?" See also "A Note on the Enthymeme" in Chap. 7 below.

2. See also Plato's *Ion* and his *Apology* 22a–c. On the links between the *Rhetoric* and Plato's *Gorgias* and his *Phaedrus*, see Friedrich Solmsen, "Aristotle and Cicero on the Orator's Playing upon the Feelings," *Classical Philology* 33 (1938): 402–4; William Rhys Roberts, "References to Plato in Aristotle's *Rhetoric*," *Classical Philology* 10 (1924): 342–46; and Ingemar During, *Aristoteles: Darstellung und Interpretation seines Denkens* (Heidelberg: C. Winter, 1966), p. 134. Perhaps the most extensive comparative study of Plato and Aristotle on the subject of rhetoric is Antje Hellwig, *Untersuchungen zur Theorie der Rhetorik bei Platon und Aristoteles* (Göttingen: Vandenhoeck & Ruprecht, 1973).

Plato's criticism of rhetoric as a sophistical tool for winning arguments through pleasing illusions rather than solid truth has been the traditional objection of the critics of rhetoric. John Locke, for example, in a denunciation of rhetoric in the *Essay Concerning Human Understanding*, ed. Alexander Campbell Fraser, 2 vols. (New York: Dover, 1959), 3. 10. 34, describes it as a "powerful instrument of error and deceit," which is founded on "wit and fancy" rather than "dry truth and real knowledge," and which aims "to insinuate wrong ideas, move the passions, and thereby mislead the judgment."

The common suspicion is that rhetoric presents a "subjective" rather than an "objective" view of reality. Friedrich Nietzsche (*Darstellung der antiken Rhetorik*, in *Gesamelte Werke*, vol. 5 [Munich: Musarion Verlag, 1922], p. 298), however, takes this as grounds for *praising* rhetoric:

> This power, that Aristotle's *Rhetoric* mentions, to discover and to assert about each thing, what produces and makes an impression, is at the same time the essence of speech: this refers just as little as rhetoric to the true, to the *essence* of the thing; it will not instruct but convey a subjective excitement and assumption to the other. The speech-cultured [*sprachbildende*] man conceives not things or facts but *allurements*. . . . Our sounded utterances do not all wait until our perception and experience have helped us to have a many-sided, somehow respectable recognition of things: they succeed at once if allurement is felt. Instead of things feeling takes in only a *feature*. This is the *first* point of view: *speech is rhetoric*, for it wishes to render only a *doxa* not *episteme*.

3. See, e.g., *An. Pr.* 38a3, 39a16, 28, 33; see also Hellwig, *Untersuchungen*, p. 45. Consider the comments on "correlatives" (*antistrephonta*) at *Cat.* 6b29–8b24, 14b25–33.

4. E. M. Cope, *The "Rhetoric" of Aristotle with a Commentary*, 3 vols. (Cambridge: At the University Press, 1877), 1:1.

5. It is in this respect, Giles of Rome inferred, that dialectic and rhetoric are absolutely rational whereas the sciences are not: "Nam convenit rhetorica cum dialectica quantum ad id de quo est, cum ambae sint de actibus rationis, non autem cum aliis scientiis, cum artes aliae sint de rebus." (Quoted by S. Robert, "Rhetoric and Dialectic: According to the First Latin Commentary on the 'Rhetoric' of Aristotle," *New Scholasticism* 31 [1957]: 497.)

6. Thus, in contrast to Plato, Aristotle thinks a true art of rhetoric can be achieved by abstracting a systematic set of rules from the actual practice of rhetoric. See Cicero *De Oratore* 1. 89–93, 107–9. Cf. Aristotle *Pol.* 1257b1–5.

7. See *Gorgias* 448c, 462c, 463a–b, 465a–b, 500e–501c.

8. *Metaph.* 1032a27–1032b32.

9. *Metaph.* 980a22–981b14; *Eth. Nic.* 1112b12–28; *De Motu An.* 701a6–25.

Notes

10. See W. D. Ross, *Aristotle's Metaphysics*, 2 vols. (Oxford: Clarendon Press, 1958), 1:116-17.

11. *Metaph.* 980a22-981a13; *Poet.* 1448b8-24.

12. *An. Post.* 99b26-100b18; *Eth. Nic.* 141b14-23.

13. *Metaph.* 981a30-982a2; *An. Post.* 89b23-35, 100a9; *Eth. Nic.* 1140a10-12; and *Pol.* 1331b32-38.

14. *Metaph.* 981a30-982a2.

15. *Metaph.* 982a18-20.

16. Compare Aristotle *Top.* 100a18-23, 105b30-31, with Plato *Republic* 511a-d, 532a-534b and *Philebus* 57e-58e. For comparisons of Aristotle's dialectic with Plato's, see Friedrich Solmsen, "Dialectic without the Forms," in *Aristotle on Dialectic: The Topics*, ed. G. E. L. Owen (Oxford: Oxford University Press, 1968), pp. 49-68; and Joseph Moreau, "Aristote et la dialectique platonicienne," in *Aristotle on Dialectic*, pp. 80-90.

17. *Top.* 100a18-21; *Soph. El.* 183a37-183b8.

18. See *Top.* 100a18, 105b30-31, 162a12-18; *An. Pr.* 46a3-10, 65a36-38; and *An. Post.* 78a11-13, 81b17-23. See also L. M. Regis, *L'opinion selon Aristote* (Paris: J. Vrin, 1935), pp. 133-47; J. M. Le Blond, *Logique et Méthode* (Paris: J. Vrin, 1939), pp. 9-16; Hermann Throm, *Die Thesis* (Paderborn: Ferdinand Schöning, 1932), pp. 62-71; and Harold Joachim, *The Nicomachean Ethics* (Oxford: Clarendon Press, 1951), p. 30.

19. *Top.* 100a18-100b26, 104b19-29, 105a34-105b19.

20. *Top.* 110a14-23.

21. *Soph. El.* 172a11-172b4.

22. *Top.* 104b1-13, 105b19-29.

23. Consider Artistotle's comments on the dialectical ability "to make one argument many" (*Top.* 164a3-12, 164b4-7, 16-18; *Soph. El.* 171b7-8).

24. See *An. Pr.* 46a3-28; *An. Post.* 72a14-24, 75a37-75b2, 76a31-77a35, 88a37-88b3, 88b26-29; *Metaph.* 996b26-997a25, 1005a19-1012b32; *Top.* 164a3-12, 164b4-18; and *Soph. El.* 170a20-170b11. An instructive study of the place of *koina* in dialectic and rhetoric can be found in Throm, *Die Thesis*, pp. 37-62. Consider also Heinrich Maier, *Die Syllogistik des Aristoteles*, 3 vols. (Tübingen: H. Laupp, 1900), pp. 495-98. Aristotle's comments on *koina* in practical reasoning seem to parallel the suggestions found among some political theorists as to the existence of "first principles" in moral and political reasoning comparable to those in mathematics. See, for example, John Locke, *An Essay Concerning Human Understanding*, 4. 3. 18-20; Alexander Hamilton, James Madison, and John Jay, *The Federalist*, ed. Jacob E. Cooke (Middletown, Conn.: Wesleyan University Press, 1961), nos. 31, 37; Edmund Burke, *Reflections on the Revolution in France* (Indianapolis, Ind.: Liberal Arts Press, 1955), pp. 181-82; and Morton White, *The Philosophy of the American Revolution* (New York: Oxford University Press, 1978), pp. 3-96.

25. See *Soph. El.* 165a37-165b12, 170a20-170b11, 171b1-3, 172a12-172b4; *An. Pr.* 46a11-31, 64b33-38; and *An. Post.* 71b18-72a6.

26. *Top.* 159a2-14, 25-38, 161a25-40; *An. Post.* 72a7-11, 77a29-35.

27. *Top.* 100a18-100b22, 101a37-101b4; *Top.* 101b4.

28. Eric Weil contends that in the *Topics* opinions "constitute, for serious discussion, the sum of the knowledge acquired by humanity and form then the necessary point of departure for all scientific inquiry." The *Topics*, therefore, is Aristotle's most fundamental logical treatise since it investigates the logic of human discourse in general, of which the logic of scientific discourse narrowly defined (as set forth in the *Analytics*) is one part ("La Place de la logique," pp. 312, 292-95). Cf. Solmsen, "Dialectic without the Forms," p. 54, n. 3.

29. *Republic* 511b; see also 531d-534e.

30. But compare Weil's interpretation.

31. *Top.* 105b30-31.

32. *Metaph.* 1004b17-27.

33. *Top.* 101a35-37.

34. *Soph. El.* 165a20-165b12.

35. *Top.* 108a34, 112a10, 21, 118b12, 160b18-23; cf. *Rh.* 3. 5. 1407a32-1407b7.

36. *Soph. El.* 175a32-175b3; *Top.* 108a33-37, 111b32-112a12, 112a21-23, 133b15-134a18, 134b5-8, 160b18.

37. *An. Pr.* 23a22-24b18; *Top.* 141b36-142a3, 155b3-17, 155b10-156a23, 157b34-158a3, 161a16-161b11.

38. See Throm's comments on "das Rhetorische in der Dialektik" (*Die Thesis,* pp. 62-71).

39. *Soph. El.* 175a18-20, 176a19-24.

40. *Top.* 164b8-15. See also *Soph. El.* 165a37-165b13, 174a12-16, 175a1-4. On the difference between philosophic argument to reach the truth and contentious argument to win one's case irrespective of the truth, see Plato *Phaedo* 91a-c; *Theaetetus* 167d-168c. In Plato's *Gorgias* (519d-e), Callicles' unwillingness to answer franky Socrates' questions forces Socrates to become himself a rhetorician by delivering extended speeches, in which he displays a certainty about his subject quite unlike the tentativeness of his usual philosophic discourse. See also *Protagoras* 334c-338e.

41. *Soph. El.* 180a23-37, 180b11-14, 31-38; see also *An. Pr.* 53b4-57b18; *Top.* 162a8-12.

42. One theorist of rhetorical argument has observed: "We blame Aristotle for saddling argumentation with the logical approach to the problem, but we are obliged at the same time to credit him with being the father of the first systematic psychology of persuasion. That cannot but appear to many people as anomalous" (Edward Z. Rowell, "Prolegomena to Argumentation," *Quarterly Journal of Speech* 18 [1932]: 229-30). See also Karlyn Kohrs Campbell, "The Ontological Foundations of Rhetorical Theory," *Philosophy & Rhetoric* 3 (1970): 97-100. Those who stress the affective character of rhetoric tend to be suspicious of Aristotle's theory, as the following remark by Wayne Booth illustrates:

> Aristotle is much too interested in being scientific. . . . there is a sense in which he seems to say: Oh, yes, indeed there *are* many other forms of proof besides the apodictic proof that scientific demonstration affords, and I will deign to give you a book about them; but isn't it, after all, a pity that it cannot all be done with greater rigor. [*Modern Dogma and the Rhetoric of Assent* (Chicago: University of Chicago Press, 1974), p. 144, n. 3.]

43. See Plato *Phaedrus* 266d-3; Cicero, *De Oratore* 2. 114-16, 310-12; *De Partione Oratoria* 1. 4. See also Solmsen, "Playing upon the Feelings," pp. 390-96; and George Kennedy, *The Art of Persuasion in Greece* (Princeton, N.J.: Princeton University Press, 1963), p. 94.

44. A careful study of the *Helen* and also of the *Palamedes* can be found in Charles P. Segal, "Gorgias and the Psychology of the Logos," *Harvard Studies in Classical Philology* 66 (1962): 99-155. Unlike the *Helen*, the *Palamedes* shows Gorgias eschewing irrational appeals in favor of rational argument. Indeed it has been noticed that Plato's *Apology of Socrates* manifests numerous and striking similarities to the *Palamedes*. See Guido

Calogero, "Gorgias and the Socratic Principle *Nemo Sua Sponte Peccat,*" *Journal of Hellenic Studies* 77 (1957): 12-17. Also, one should note that in Plato's *Gorgias* (448d-49a, 461a-62a, 482c-e) Socrates seems less critical of Gorgias than of his students.

45. Deliberative rhetoric is higher in its subject matter than forensic because the public interest is higher than private interests. But later in the *Rhetoric* (3. 12. 1414a7-18, 17. 1418a2-4), Aristotle notes that forensic rhetoric is superior to deliberative insofar as speech before a small audience can have a more "finished" form than speech before a large audience; he also says that the enthymeme is most suited for forensic rhetoric and the example most suited for deliberative.

46. See *Pol.* 1286a17-20.

47. The most democratic element in Solon's constitution, Aristotle says, was the right to appeal to the courts where decisions were left to the jury, because the obscurity of the laws allowed the *demos* great freedom in its verdicts (*Athenian Constitution* 9. 1-2).

48. See, for example, Cope, *Commentary*, 1:19-21; E. M. Cope, *An Introduction to Aristotle's "Rhetoric"* (London and Cambridge: Macmillan, 1867), pp. 101-5.

49. See also *Poet.* 1450a18.

50. See 1. 6. 1362b29-30, 2. 20. 1394a9-11, 21. 1394b7-11, 22. 1396a33-1396b12, 1396b24-28, 1397a3, 23. 1400b25-33, 26. 1403a25-32, 3. 17. 1418a1-7, 1418a36-1418b5; *An. Pr.* 68b8-14; and *An. Post.* 71a1-11.

51. See also Plato *Phaedrus* 261d-62c.

52. Later in the *Rhetoric* (1. 5. 1361b10-11), Aristotle speaks of the beauty of the athlete's body as due to its "natural inclination" (*pephykenai pros*) to strength and speed. In the *Nicomachean Ethics* (1109a14-16), he refers to the "natural inclination" of human beings to pleasure.

53. Paradoxically, common opinions are both the source and the product of rhetorical reasoning. That is, the premises of rhetorical argument are drawn from common opinions; but these opinions are themselves largely the result of the rhetoric practiced, more or less unsystematically, by relatives, friends, legislators, and teachers (see 1. 1. 1354a1-11, 3. 1358b8-13, 2. 23. 1398b18-1399a6). Hence one commentator concludes:

> Aristotle is at least implicitly maintaining that the exercise of the art of rhetoric establishes in a society its ethos. . . . Not that Aristotle claims that one speaker, or even one group of speakers, creates *ex nihilo* an ethos; any society already has its own. The speaker at most modifies or changes this ethos, itself the result of the efforts of other speakers whether orators or advice-giving friends, or parents, or others responsible for guiding children, all of whom have in a sense used the art of rhetoric. [Eugene E. Ryan, "Aristotle's *Rhetoric* and *Ethics* and the Ethos of Society," *Greek, Roman, and Byzantine Studies* 13 (1972): 295.]

54. See Cope, *Introduction*, pp. 144-47.

55. Aristotle's remark that it would be shameful to be unable to defend oneself with speech (1355a37-1355b2), echoes a complaint by Callicles against Socrates (Plato *Gorgias* 485e-86d, 508c-e). Sometimes Socrates himself seems to recognize his lack of rhetorical ability and his need for the friendship of rhetoricians such as Thrasymachus and Callicles (see Plato *Republic* 498c-d; *Gorgias* 473a, 485e, 486e-88b, 499c, 500b; and Alfarabi, *The Philosophy of Plato and Aristotle*, trans. Muhsin Mahdi [Ithaca, N.Y.: Cornell University Press, 1969], pp. 66-67; but cf. Plato *Phaedo* 91a-c).

56. Cf. Plato *Gorgias* 456a-57c, 460c-61b; *Phaedrus* 260d. Aristotle says in the

Topics (143a9-12) that although a "knowledge" (*episteme*) or a "power" (*dunamis*) is applicable either to the better or the worse, it seems more applicable to the best (see also *Top.* 126a30-126b13 and *Soph. El.* 175a1-18).

57. See *Top.* 163b9-17. This same intent—that good men not be naive—would explain Aristotle's comments in the *Politics* (1313a34-1316a1) on the means for preserving tyrannies.

58. Ed. Douglas Ehninger (Carbondale: Southern Illinois University Press, 1963), p. xxxix.

59. This interpretation is defended by J. Robert Olian, "The Intended Uses of Aristotle's *Rhetoric*," *Speech Monographs* 35 (1968): 137-48. See also Kennedy, *Art of Persuasion*, p. 123.

60. See 1. 1. 1354a21-26, 1355a13-17, 20-23, 11. 1371a30-33, 1371b5-11, 13. 1373b3-13; 2. 22. 1396a4-1396b19; 3. 9. 1409a35-1409b12, 10. 1410b9-35. See also *Pol.* 1253a5-18; *Top.* 160b17-23; *Poet.* 1452b30-1453a18.

61. 1. 7. 1365a37-1365b17, 12. 1372a11-13; 2. 4. 1381b17-22, 28-32, 5. 1382b2-9, 6. 1384b25-27, 23. 1399a17-33. See also *Pol.* 1253a30-38, 1319b32; *Top.* 160b17-23; *Soph. El.* 172b36-173a6.

62. See *Pol.* 1281a39-1282b14.

63. *Rh.* 2. 23. 1397b23-25, 24. 1402a23-28; *Soph. El.* 173a7-31. See *Pol.* 1253a30-38. See also Plato *Gorgias* 474b, 475d-e, 481c-83a, 486e-88b, 492d, 508b-c, 510a-13c.

64. *Athenian Constitution* 28. 3-4.

65. *Helen* 11.

66. Cf. *Top.* 160b17-23; *Soph. El.* 176b14-25.

67. *Eth. Nic.* 1112a8; see also 1139b17, 1140b27-28.

68. *An. Post.* 88b30-89b6.

69. See *An. Post.* 100b5-8; *Top.* 121a20-27; *Soph. El.* 175a32-34.

70. See Throm, *Die Thesis*, pp. 22-27.

71. *Top.* 104a2-13, 160b17-23; see Weil, "La Place de la logique," pp. 296-99.

72. *Top.* 100b22-23; see *Rh.* 1. 5. 1361a25-27, 2. 23. 1398b18-1399a6. As indicated here, *endoxos* also bears the sense of "reputed"; so *endoxa* could be well translated as "reputable opinions."

73. Obviously, *endoxa* can sometimes conflict with one another, such as when the wise disagree with the many. See *Rh.* 2. 23. 1398b18-1399a6; 25. 1402a33-35; *Soph. El.* 173a19-31.

74. See *Pol.* 1281a39-1282a24; *Eth. Nic.* 1095a29-30, 1098b26-30.

75. *Metaph.* 997a19-25.

76. "We find in the procedure of Aristotle a resonance of modern phenomenological methods in which forward progress is measured by one's success in *explicitating* the truth mediated through an unreflected, pre-philosophic experience" (J. Donald Monan, *Moral Knowledge and Its Methodology in Aristotle* [Oxford: Oxford University Press, 1968], p. 104).

77. *Metaph.* 988a18-988b22; 993a11-23. For a general study of the place of opinion in Aristotle's works, see Regis, *L'opinion selon Aristote*.

78. Learning requires advancing from what is more intelligible to us (sense-perception) to what is more intelligible in nature (the first principles [*archai*] of knowledge): "just as in conduct one starts from the things good for each and makes the things wholly good to be good for each, so starting from the things more knowable for oneself, one makes the things knowable by nature to be knowable for oneself" (*Metaph.* 1029b1-13).

79. *Eth. Nic.* 1098b26-30.

80. The following passages are especially revealing: 1094a1-24, 1095a14-1095b14, 1098b9-30, 1103a4-10, 1129a7-11, 1146b6-7, 1153b25-36, 1168b13-15, 1173a1-2. An index of Aristotle's reliance on *doxa* is his use of the word *dokei* ("it seems" or "it is thought"), of which the following passages provide a few examples: 1094a2, 1095b24, 1097b1, 8, 28, 1098a7, 1098b17, 27, 1100b15, 1101a24, 1109b35, 1112a32, 1113a16, 1131a14, 1140a25, 1145b5, 1173a1. See also *Eth. Eud.* 1217a17-21, 1220a13-18, 1235a29-31, 1235b13-18, 1236a23-33.

81. Possible translations of *proairesis* are "choice," "intention," and "moral purpose"; in general, the word suggests a morally significant choice. See *Rh.* 1. 13. 1374a11-12; *Metaph.* 1004b17-27; *Top.* 126a30-126b13; and *Eth. Nic.* 1127b14-16. The "choice" of the sophist is to appear wise without being so (*Soph. El.* 165a20-33).

82. Cope interprets Aristotle to say: "there is a sophistry in rhetoric as well as in dialectics, and the definition of both turns upon the same distinction; that is, it resides not in the faculty, but in the moral purpose: only in the one case the Sophist passes under the general name of rhetorician; in the other we distinguish name as well as thing" (*Introduction*, p. 148). Consider also the following interpretation: "In both dialectic and rhetoric, moreover, a further shift of argument is possible from the authority of widespread and well-grounded opinion to the distortion of opinion or the manipulation of consequences derived from opinion: this shift in the moral attitude toward the opinions and words used constitutes the difference between dialectic and sophistic and distinguishes one of the possible modes of rhetoric" (Richard McKeon, "Aristotle's Conception of Language and the Arts of Language," in *Critics and Criticism*, ed. R. S. Crane [Chicago: University of Chicago Press, 1952], p. 180).

83. *Top.* 136b34-137a8. Compare Aristotle's remarks on the art of moneymaking at *Pol.* 1257b1-8. On the comparision of rhetoric and medicine, see *Rh.* 1. 2. 1356b29-33; *Metaph.* 1032b1-15; *Top.* 101b5-10, 149b24-31. Aristotle seems to contradict himself by stating in the *Nicomachean Ethics* (1112b11-16) that the "end" (*telos*) of the doctor is health just as the "end" of the rhetorician is persuasion, but to view arts in reference to their "ends" does not entail that arts by definition must and therefore can always achieve their ends. One should also consider Plato's comparisons of rhetoric and medicine—*Gorgias* 456a-d, 459a-c, 464b-66a; *Phaedrus* 268a-69c, 270b-d. See also Hellwig, *Untersuchungen*, pp. 51-53.

84. Plato *Gorgias* 452e, 453a; see also *Philebus* 58a-b and *Republic* 365d.

85. For Aristotle the "power" (*dunamis*) of rhetoric is limited, but Gorgias and his students regard it as the source of an almost unlimited "power" over men. Plato *Gorgias* 452d-e, 455d-56c, 466b-67a, 492a-c, 509c-11a, 522c, 525d-26e.

86. See 1354a6-11. To define the rhetorician as one able to see the possible means of persuasion in any situation is to define "not the activity [*to pragma*], but the activity done well or perfected" (*Top.* 149b24-31). Hellwig contends that while for Plato there is a disparity between the ideal rhetoric—rhetoric that coincides with philosophy—and the rhetoric actually practiced among men, for Aristotle the disparity is between the theoretical knowledge of the means of persuasion and the successful employment of these means (*Untersuchungen*, p. 52).

87. On the importance of particulars in practical matters, see *Rh.* 2. 19. 1393a18; *Metaph.* 981a22-24; *An. Pr.* 43a25-44; *Eth. Nic.* 1141b14-23, 1143a28-35; *Pol.* 1269a11-12. But cf. *Rh.* 1. 2. 1356b29-34. Cope claims that Aristotle shifts from rhetoric as an "art" to rhetoric as a "power" (*dunamis*), a shift from emphasis on the theoretical to emphasis on the practical: "arts in their practical aspects are called *dunameis*"

(*Introduction*, pp. 14-19). For comments on the senses of *dunamis*, see *Metaph.* 1019a15-1020a7. Since "rational powers" are said by Aristotle to issue in opposite directions (*Int.* 22b37-23a7; *Eth. Nic.* 1103a14-1103b25), his definition of rhetoric as a "power" might be intended to stress the rhetorical capacity for arguing opposites (see *Rh.* 1. 2. 1356a19-20). Cf. *An. Pr.* 43a20-24.

88. Nietzche, *Darstellung*, pp. 291-92, 295-96.

89. Although *epieikeis* can be translated correctly as "good men," it could also be understood more narrowly to refer to "equitable" men — that is, men who apply laws to particulars with "equity." See *Eth. Nic.* 1137a31-1137b6; Cope, *Commentary* 1:30; and cf. *NE* 1172b9-19.

90. This distinction in the *Rhetoric* between the individual characters of men and the collective characters of regimes is noted by Eric Voegelin, who observes:

> In the restrained advice of the *Rhetoric* . . . we sense the social atmosphere of men who do not want to be lectured and demand respect for their "character" as it is, as well as the urbanity, sometimes desperately strained, of the author who will not impose his Truth on gentlemen with firm convictions. [*Plato and Aristotle*, vol. 3, *Order and History* (Baton Rouge: Louisiana State University Press, 1957), p. 366.]

91. This conclusion is sustained by the etymology of *enthymema*. In its usages before Aristotle, *enthymema* can often be translated as "thought," but the Greeks preserved a distinction between *enthymema* and *ennoema*, reflecting their differing roots — *thymos* and *nous*. Whereas *nous* is precisely identified with "thought" or "intellect," *thymos* suggests both feeling and thought and thus presents an ambiguity comparable to that conveyed by *Geist* in German, *esprit* in French, or *spirit* in English. One German commentator has claimed that to convey this combination of intellectual and affective elements, one might translate *enthymema* as *Suggestivschluss* (Throm, *Die Thesis*, p. 63). For an extensive study of the etymology of *enthymema*, see W. M. A. Grimaldi, *Studies in the Philosophy of Aristotle's "Rhetoric"* (Wiesbaden: F. Steiner, 1972), pp. 70-82. See also Kennedy, *Art of Persuasion*, p. 99.

92. Hence Cope is wrong to assume that Aristotle uses *pistis* in the *Rhetoric* to indicate the low degree of certainty characteristic of rhetoric (*Commentary*, p. 136). See *An. Pr.* 72a26-72b4; *Soph. El.* 165b3; *Top.* 100b18-22; *De An.* 428a23-24; *Pol.* 1323a34-1323b7; *Eth. Nic.* 1139b32-34, 1142a18-21; cf. Plato *Gorgias* 453d-455b.

93. Grimaldi (*Studies*, pp. 57-67) makes a detailed study of these usages, from which he concludes:

> The substance for the demonstrative presentation is the source material drawn from *pragma, ethos, pathos* (*pistis* as a methodological instrument) which creates conviction or acceptance in the mind of the auditor (*pistis* as a state of mind).

See also Grimaldi, "A Note on the *pisteis* in Aristotle's *Rhetoric*," *American Journal of Philology* 78 (1957): 188-92; G. H. Wikramanayake, "A Note on the *pisteis* in Aristotle's *Rhetoric*," *American Journal of Philology* 82 (1961): 193-96; and J. T. Lienhard, "A Note on the Meaning of *pisteis* in Aristotle's *Rhetoric*," *American Journal of Philology* 88 (1966): 446-54.

94. On the problem of defining the subject matter of rhetoric, see Plato *Gorgias* 449c-54c. Also consider these remarks by Bacon:

> Logic handleth reason exact and in truth, and Rhetoric handleth it as it is planted in popular opinions and manners. And therefore Aristotle doth wisely place Rhetoric as between Logic on the one side and moral or civil knowledge on the other, as par-

ticipating of both: for the proofs and demonstrations of Logic are toward all men indifferent and the same; but the proofs and persuasions of Rhetoric ought to differ according to the auditor. [*Advancement of Learning*, in *Selected Writings*, ed. Hugh G. Dick (New York: Modern Library, Random House, 1955), p. 311.]

Bacon is somewhat misleading, however, in identifying dialectic as "Logic" and thus being "toward all men indifferent and the same." Dialectic is like rhetoric in being founded on the *endoxa* of the interlocutors.

95. For amplification of the political subject matter of rhetoric, see *Top.* 100a18-21; *Rh.* 1. 2. 1356a25-27, 1356a24-27, 4. 1356b10-18. On the particularity of rhetoric, see *Rh.* 1. 1. 1354a26-1354b12, 2. 1355b25-26; *Top.* 104b1-18. See also Hellwig, *Untersuchungen*, pp. 46-47; and Sally Raphael, "Rhetoric, Dialectic and Syllogistic Argument: Aristotle's Position in *Rhetoric* I-II," *Phronesis* 19 (1974): 157.

96. Aristotle is very careful in reminding the reader that dialectic and rhetoric require a knowledge of both true and apparent syllogisms (1. 1. 1355b14-17, 2. 1356a19-22). As he has explained, this is necessary not for the sake of encouraging fallacious reasoning but in order that the dialectician or rhetorician may defend himself against such deception (1. 1. 1355a29-34).

97. See *An. Post.* 71a1-11.

98. According to Thomas Aquinas (*Commentarium in Posteriorum Analyticorum*, lect. 1), the difference between the enthymeme and the syllogism is a difference in matter. The enthymeme and the example concern particulars as to which there cannot be certain knowledge, but the syllogism and induction concern universals as to which certain knowledge is possible. Similarly, Giles of Rome believes that Aristotle considers dialectical and scientific reasoning to differ from rhetorical reasoning because of the connection of the former to speculative reason and of the latter to practical reason. Whereas dialectic and science are purely speculative, rhetoric is a tool for action and practical judgment; thus rhetoric appeals to the intellect as moved by the appetite. (Cited by S. Robert, "Rhetoric and Dialectic: According to the First Latin Commentary on the *Rhetoric* of Aristotle," *New Scholasticism* 31 [1957]: 491-92.)

Aristotle makes clear in the *Topics*, however, that dialectic is not purely theoretical, either in its subject matter or in its audience. Dialectical inquiries may concern "choice and avoidance" as well as "truth and knowledge," and the dialectician may speak with the "many" as well as the "few" (*Top.* 104b1-13, 105a16-19, 157a17-22, 164a13).

On comparing rhetoric and dialectic, see J. M. Le Blond, *Logique et Méthode*, pp. 47-50; and Throm, *Die Thesis*, pp. 37-62.

99. Comments on the "practical syllogism" may be found in *Eth. Nic.* 1142b23-33, 1143a35-1143b16, 1146b35-1147b9, 1149a25-1149b3; *De An.* 431a1-20, 434a16-21; and *On the Movement of Animals* 701a7-702a21. Interest in Aristotle's "practical syllogism" has been revived by G. E. M. Anscombe, *Intention* (Ithaca, N.Y.: Cornell University Press, 1957), pp. 56-69. See Mary Mothersill, "Anscombe's Account of the Practical Syllogism," *Philosophical Review* 71 (1962): 448-60; Judith Jarvis, "Practical Reasoning," *Philosophical Quarterly* 12 (1962): 316-28; Donald Davidson, "Actions, Reasons, and Causes," *Journal of Philosophy* 60 (1963): 67-79; Georg Henrik von Wright, *Explanation and Understanding* (Ithaca, N.Y.: Cornell University Press, 1971), pp. 26-27, 96-118; and Alexander Broadie, "Aristotle on Rational Action," *Phronesis* 19 (1974): 70-80.

An example of Aristotle's own use of "practical syllogisms" has been pointed out by Harry Jaffa, who says, in reference to the beginning of the *Politics:*

There is this syllogism: Every *polis* is a community; every community aims at some good; therefore every *polis* aims at some good. The minor premise is itself the conclusion of an implied syllogism: Every community is constituted by common action; every action aims at some good; therefore every community aims at some good. ["Aristotle," *History of Political Philosophy*, ed. Leo Strauss and Joseph Cropsey (Chicago: Rand McNally, 1963), p. 68.]

100. *Rh.* 2. 25. 1402b21-37; *Eth. Nic.* 1094b13-27; *Metaph.* 995a12-20.

101. *Eth. Nic.* 1139a4-1129b13; *Metaph.* 993b20-33; *De An.* 433a10-433b31; *Int.* 17a1-9.

102. In Plato's *Gorgias* this seems to be the grounds for distinguishing rhetoric from dialectic. That is, the rhetorician must win the adherence of large crowds, and therefore he must resort to crude appeals to the "many"; the dialectician, on the other hand, seeks agreement among small groups of interlocutors, and through discussion he can be truly instructive (453d-55b, 471e-72c, 473e-74b).

Hellwig (*Untersuchungen*, p. 48) argues that while the sciences attain exactness because their subject matter allows necessary inferences, rhetoric draws its inferences not from the subject itself but from the listener. He thinks that Aristotle follows a similar method at the beginning of the *Nicomachean Ethics* by setting up as his standard not the truth of certain ethical doctrines but the judgment of a certain kind of student with experience in good moral habits.

103. The traditional example of the syllogism of the first figure is: All men are mortal; Socrates is a man; therefore, Socrates is mortal. But in fact, this is not a true example of the Aristotelian syllogism; a genuine example would be: "If A is predicated [*kategoreisthai*] of all B and B of all C, A is necessarily of all C" (*An. Pr.* 25b37). The significance of the differences is explained by Jan Lukasiewicz, *Aristotle's Syllogistic* (Oxford: Oxford University Press, 1957), pp. 1-12, 20-23; and by W. D. Ross, *Aristotle's Prior and Posterior Analytics* (Oxford: Oxford University Press, 1949), p. 289.

104. In Plato's *Phaedrus* (244b-46b) Socrates claims that his speech of recantation is a "demonstration" (*apodeixis*) that erotic madness is sent by the gods for the benefit of men. He begins with a syllogistic proof of the soul's immortality. He then confesses that to describe the "form" (*idea*) of the soul would be difficult since it would require a *divine and long discourse*, but he offers to deliver a *human and short discourse* that will present a "likeness" of the soul through the image of a pair of winged horses and a charioteer.

105. On the history of the definition of the enthymeme as an incomplete syllogism, see R. C. Seaton, "The Aristotelian Enthymeme," *Classical Review* 28 (1914): 113-19. See also Thomas Aquinas, *In Posteriorum Analyticorum*, lect. 1. Arguments against interpreting the enthymeme as a truncated syllogism have been made by Ross, *Prior and Posterior Analytics*, p. 300; E. H. Madden, "The Enthymeme: Crossroads of Logic, Rhetoric, and Metaphysics," *Philosophical Review* 61 (1952): 373-76; and Kennedy, *Art of Persuasion*, pp. 97-98.

106. *An. Post.* 76b1-28.

107. Antoine Arnauld and Pierre Nicole, *La Logique ou l'Art de penser* (Paris: Presses Universitaire de France, 1965), p. 22.

108. See *An. Pr.* 68b36-37.

109. The frequent omission of the major premises of enthymemes might suggest that in political reasoning, men commonly reach conclusions in particular cases without full awareness of the general principles assumed in their inferences. Or perhaps it is because men *are* fully aware of the general principles that they do not need to hear them stated.

Notes

The advantage in omitting the major premise of a syllogism is illustrated by Descartes's *cogito* argument. Descartes concedes that his argument—"I think, therefore I am"—could be stated as a syllogism with the major premise "Everything that thinks exists." But he contends that, although this premise is *logically* prior to the conclusion, the conclusion is *experientially* prior. That is, only by drawing the conclusion in this particular case—that I exist because I think—do I become fully aware of the general proposition that whatever thinks must exist. For it is characteristic of human thought, he declares, "to form general propositions from the knowledge of particulars" (*Oeuvres de Descartes*, ed. Charles Adam and Paul Tannery, 13 vols. [Paris: Cerf, 1897 and 1913] 5:147, 7:140, 9:205).

110. According to Grimaldi (*Studies*), Aristotle seeks "to make the constraining force inherent in deductive inference as immediate for an ordinary audience as the appeal of induction" (p. 89). That Aristotle favors abbreviated enthymemes is thought by Grimaldi to be indicated by the sources and inferential forms of enthymemes:

eikota are general probabilities in which frequently the minor premise may be assumed; *semeia* permit either a major or minor premise to be omitted, e.g., I.ii.1357a19-21; and the *koinoi topoi* offer a form of inference which is usually a relation: if x then y, a form in which either a premise or a conclusion may be assumed depending upon the evidential immediacy of the topic used. (P. 87.)

111. Aristotle's modal logic, simply stated, is his attempt to work out the logical implications of his view that propositions are necessary, possible, impossible, or contingent. He assumes thereby a correspondence between logic and objective reality: since events in the world exhibit necessity, possibility, or contingency, syllogisms must have corresponding features (*An. Pr.* 25a1-3, 29b29-30a14; *Int.* 21a34-23a27). It is not surprising, therefore, that modern formal logicians have objected to this portion of Aristotle's logic. See Lukasiewicz, *Aristotle's Syllogistic*, pp. 133-208; and J. L. Ackrill, ed. and trans., *Aristotle's Categories and De Interpretation* (Oxford: Clarendon Press, 1963), pp. 132-36.

112. That an enthymeme can be constructed from necessary premises is regarded by Stephanus in his commentary as an indication of "the communion of philosophy and rhetoric" (quoted by Hugo Rabe, ed., vol. 21, *Commentaria in Aristotelem Graeca* [Berlin: George Reiner, 1896], p. 263).

113. The difficulties involved in Aristotle's distinction between "probabilities" and "signs" and in his differentiation of "signs" according to the figures of the syllogism are surveyed in an instructive manner by Heinrich Maier, *Die Syllogistik*, 3:478-91, 498-500. For some differing interpretations, see James H. McBurney, "The Place of the Enthymeme in Rhetorical Theory" (Ann Arbor, Mich.: University of Michigan Library, 1936), pp. 56-58, 62; Madden, "The Enthymeme," pp. 370-73; Kennedy, *Art of Persuasion*, pp. 96, 100; Grimaldi, *Studies*, pp. 109-13; Raphael, "Rhetoric, Dialectic, and Syllogistic Argument," pp. 160-61. E. H. Madden, "Aristotle's Treatment of Probability and Signs," *Philosophy of Science* 24 (1957): 167-79, considers Aristotle's views in comparison with modern theories of probability. McBurney interprets Aristotle's "probabilities" as *rationes essendi* and his "signs" as *rationes cognoscendi*, but Madden argues that both "probabilities" and "signs" are *rationes cognoscendi* rather than *rationes essendi*.

114. *Rh.* 1357b15-16; *An. Pr.* 70a14-16.

115. But see *Rh.* 1. 5. 1361a28-30 and 2. 19. 1392b25-33 for examples of "signs" converted into *eikoi*. "Sign"-inferences may be found at *Rh.* 1. 9. 1366b25-32, 1367b26-37, 2. 5. 1383a6-8, 6. 1383b26-1384a23, 1384b18-20, 3. 8. 1408a26-36; *Eth. Nic.*

1104b4-10, 1140a28-32, 1143b8-10, 1153a2-8, 1153b25-30; and *Pol.* 1272b30-33.

116. Madden believes, however, that enthymemes constructed from *eikoi*—e.g., "most men who envy hate; this man envies; therefore, this man probably hates"—are formally invalid because the middle term is not distributed (used universally) at least once ("The Enthymeme," p. 370). According to Ross, an *eikos* is the major premise of a syllogism in the first figure—"*B* as a rule is *A*, *C* is *B*, therefore *C* is probably *A*" (*Prior and Posterior Analytics*, p. 500).

117. *An. Pr.* 70a4-6. Cf. *Phaedrus* 272d-273c.

118. Cf. *An. Pr.* 70a14-16.

119. Cf. *An. Pr.* 70a17-37.

120. *An. Pr.* 40b30-33, 41a13-16.

121. See 1357b15-16 and *An. Pr.* 70a14-18.

122. *An. Pr.* 70a21-23, 34-37.

123. *An. Pr.* 29a19-24, 41b7-29, 70a34-36.

124. *An. Pr.* 26b34-28a9.

125. See *An. Pr.* 70a17-20, 31-34.

126. *An. Pr.* 28a10-28b4, 29a11-18.

127. Raphael, "Rhetoric, Dialectic, and Syllogistic Argument," claims that all arguments from "non-necessary signs" or from "probabilities" are arguments from examples (pp. 160-61). In a fundamental sense *all* reasoning, according to Aristotle, could be said to depend on induction (*An. Post.* 99b15-100b17).

128. An anonymous commentator suggests, however, that this example could be stated as a syllogism with a false major premise: "All bad men are thieves" (*Commentaria in Aristotelem Graeca*, p. 151).

129. Note the conformity between *endoxa* and truth. It would seem that in shaping his argumentation to accord with *endoxa*, the rhetorician must prefer enthymemes in the first figure.

130. *An. Pr.* 69a14-19.

131. Ross, *Prior and Posterior Analytics*, explains: "Induction reasons from all the particulars and does not apply the conclusion to a new particular; example does so apply it and does not reason from all the particulars." He concludes that the real interest of reasoning by example, unlike that of induction, is "not, like that of science, in generalization but in inducing a particular belief" (pp. 487-88). See also Hellwig, *Untersuchungen*, p. 46, n. 20.

132. One could judge an aggressive war by Athens against the neighboring city of Thebes to be bad if one observed that the aggressive war of the Thebans against the city of Phocis was bad and concluded from this that all such wars against neighbors are bad (*An. Pr.* 68b38-69a19).

Isocrates once declared (*To Demonicus 34*): "When you are deliberating, regard things which have happened as examples of what will happen. For the unknown may be learned most quickly from the known."

133. The syllogism is naturally prior and *more intelligible* to us, Aristotle observes, but "syllogism by induction" is *more apparent* to us (*An. Pr.* 68b15-38). That is, reasoning from general principles to conclusions about particular facts is perfectly intelligible, but it is often easier to begin with the facts, which are available to sense experience, and work up to the general principles. See also *Top.* 105a16-19, 110a36-110b8, 157a17-22, 164a13.

134. This "topic" rests on the principle that if something is not the case where it is more likely, it is not the case where it is less likely; or that if something is the case where it

is less likely, it is the case where it is more likely. Aristotle explains this "topic" at 2. 23. 1397b12-27.

135. See 2. 22. 1395b20-1396b19 and *An. Pr.* 46a11- 31.

136. The term *epideiktikon* suggests that this type of speech tends to involve a mere "display" or "show" (*epideixis*) of the oratorical abilities of the speaker. Gorgias, for example, was criticized for delivering long, "showy" speeches that prevented a true "discussion" (*dialektos*) of the subject being examined; he was said to be more concerned with praising and blaming than with defining things. See Plato *Gorgias* 447a-49c, 453c, 454c, 462b-d, 463c, 471d-72c.

137. Aristotle says later in the *Rhetoric* that while examples are best for deliberative rhetoric, because the future can be known by the past, enthymemes are best for forensic, because the past can be proved and can be analyzed according to causes (1. 9. 1368a29-34, 2. 20. 1394a6-7, 3. 17. 1418a1-5).

138. As with his tripartition of the kinds of rhetoric according to their "times," Aristotle's tripartition of regimes according to the number of rulers insures that there is no fourth possibility, but at the cost of abstracting from substantive considerations. It turns out, for example, that democracy is defined more accurately as the rule by the poor who are many than as the rule by the many simply. *Pol.* 1279a22-1280a7.

139. This same tripartition of the aims of rhetoric may be found in Plato *Gorgias* 459d, 461d; and *Phaedrus* 260a, 276c, 278a. Moreover, since Aristotle discusses pleasure in connection with epideictic rhetoric (1. 11), one might infer that the three types of rhetoric correspond to the three motives of desire—the noble, the expedient, and the pleasant. See *Eth. Nic.* 1104b30-36, 1110b9-12; *Eth. Eud.* 1214a1-8; and *Top.* 105a28, 118b28.

140. See Thucydides *Peloponnesian War* 5. 84-116. But compare the debate between Cleon and Diodotus in which the advocate of a particular act of cruelty in war appeals to the claims of justice while his opponent appeals to expediency. Ibid., 3. 36-48. See *Rh.* 2. 22. 1396a15-21.

141. See *Rh.* 1. 1. 1354b9, 3. 1359a1-7, 2. 13. 1389b36-1390a1, 3. 16. 1417a35; *Eth. Nic.* 1110b30-31, 1129b14-19, 1130a5-6, 1140a25-28, 1141b6, 1160a9-30; and *Pol.* 1276a13-14, 1276b28-31, 1278b23, 1279a17-22, 26-33, 1282b16-18.

But even when "expediency" is understood in connection with the "common good" of a regime, it can still conflict with justice in relations between regimes and in cases where certain individuals are so superior that the subordination of their private interests to the interests of the whole is unjust.

Aristotle would probably agree with the advice of Demosthenes: "It is necessary always to find and to do the things that are just, but one must take care at the same time that these are also the expedient things" (*For the People of Megapolis* 10). It has been noticed that "some form of *sumphero* occurs at the beginning or end of all but two of the first sixteen orations of Demosthenes" (Georgiana P. Palmer, "The *topoi* of Aristotle's *Rhetoric* as Exemplified in the Orators" [Ph.D. diss., University of Chicago, 1934], p. 65). Cicero claims that although *apparent* expediency may conflict with moral virtue, *true* expediency cannot (*De Officiis*, Book III).

142. Although Aristotle is not completely clear on the point, it seems that *eide* and *koina* should be understood to be not the premises of enthymemes, but the *sources* of premises, because they become premises only when they are put into statements of probability, which are either "signs" or "probabilities." Viewed in this way, Aristotle's treatment of enthymemes as founded on "topics" does not contradict his statements that "signs" and "probabilities" are the only materials for enthymemes.

Friedrich Solmsen has argued, however, that there is a contradiction in the *Rhetoric* between the account of reasoning based on "topics" and the account based on "probabilities" and "signs" and that it reflects two stages in the development of Aristotelian logic (see *Die Entwicklung der aristotelischen Logik und Rhetorik* [Berlin: Weidmannsche Buchhandlung, 1929], especially pp. 13–37.) A useful summary of Solmsen's book can be found in J. L. Stocks, "The Composition of Aristotle's Logical Works," *Classical Quarterly* 27 (1933): 115–24. For some cogent criticicms of Solmsen's thesis, see Throm, *Die Thesis*, pp. 42–45; Eric Weil, "La Place de la logique dans la pensée aristotelicienne," *Revue de Metaphysique et de Morale* 56 (1951): 283–315; and Raphael, "Rhetoric, Dialectic, and Syllogistic Argument," pp. 157–66.

143. For examples of Aristotle's use of *koinoi topoi* to organize *eide*, see 1. 5. 1360b14–18, 6. 1362b30, 2. 23. 1397a7–19, 1398a15–28.

Special care should be taken to distinguish the "common topic" of "more and less" from the "commonplace" of "greater and less." See 1. 2. 1358a11–17, 2. 19. 1393a9–18, 23. 1397b12–27, 26. 1403a16–24.

Instructive comments on Aristotle's use of "topics" may be found in McBurney, "The Place of the Enthymeme," pp. 60–62; Kennedy, *Art of Persuasion*, p. 101; Grimaldi, *Studies*, pp. 35–41; Raphael, "Rhetoric, Dialectic, and Syllogistic Argument," pp. 162–66.

144. The following are the key passages with respect to the organization of the first two books of the *Rhetoric*: 1. 2. 1358a29–36, 3. 1359a27–29, 2. 1. 1378a29–31, 3. 1380b30–33, 11. 1388b29–30, 18. 1391b22–1392a3, 20. 1393a21–24, 22. 1396b20–1397a6, 26. 1403a17–24, 3. 19. 1419b26–28. See Grimaldi, *Studies*, pp. 18–52.

145. "The *Rhetoric* of Aristotle, as some of the difficulties of its composition make clear, is undoubtedly a compilation of several different sets of notes" (John Herman Randall, Jr., *Aristotle* [New York: Columbia University Press, 1960], p. 286). See also Cope, *Introduction*, pp. 175, 245; Friedrich Solmsen, "Introduction," *The "Rhetoric" and the "Poetics" of Aristotle* (New York: Modern Library, Random House, 1954), pp. xv–xix, xxii; Kennedy, *Art of Persuasion*, pp. 82–87; and Paul D. Brandes, "The Composition and Preservation of Aristotle's *Rhetoric*," *Speech Monographs* 35 (1968): 482–91.

146. "The rhetoric of Aristotle covers three fields: a theory of argumentation that constitutes the principal axis and that furnishes at the same time the bond of its articulation with demonstrative logic and with philosophy (this theory of argumentation covers by itself two-thirds of the treatise) — a theory of elocution — and a theory of the composition of a discourse" (Paul Ricoeur, *La métaphore vive* [Paris: Editions du Seuil, 1975], p. 13).

Chapter Three

1. On ethics as a part of political science, see *Eth. Nic.* 1094a11–18, 1094a27–1094b12, 1180b23–31, 1181b12–16.

2. Some commentators assume that this comment refers to the practice of the sophists rather than to Aristotle's book. But see Antje Hellwig, *Untersuchungen zur Theorie der Rhetorik bei Platon und Aristoteles* (Gottingen: Vandenhoeck & Ruprecht, 1973), p. 107, n. 125.

3. See E. M. Cope, *An Introduction to Aristotle's "Rhetoric"* (London and Cambridge: Macmillan, 1867), p. 99.

4. Aristotle seems to have drawn this list from a passage in Xenophon's *Memorabilia*

(3. 6). Socrates rebukes a young man for eagerly seeking political influence through oratory without a detailed knowledge of the subjects of deliberation. Socrates criticizes him for being uninformed about such subjects as the city's finances, its naval and military power in comparison with that of its enemies, the condition of the city's defenses, the operation of its silver mines, and its corn crops. The most striking discrepancy between this list and Aristotle's is that Socrates does not mention legislation (but compare Plato *Gorgias* 517b-c, 519a). Presumably, Socrates thinks the eager young man should first learn about the most necessary (even if mundane) needs of the city.

Aristotle's list should also be compared with his statement in the *Politics* (1298a4-9) that the "deliberative part" of a regime decides questions "concerning war and peace and alliances and the dissolution of alliances, concerning laws, concerning death and exile and confiscation, and the calling of magistrates to account."

5. See Leo Strauss, *What Is Political Philosophy?* (New York: Free Press, 1959), p. 83. In his comments on the importance of preserving the character of the regime, Aristotle restates arguments that are elaborated in the *Politics;* indeed, both at the beginning and at the end of his remarks on deliberative rhetoric (1. 4. 1359b17-18, 8. 1366a17-23), he refers the reader to the *Politics* for a more extensive treatment of the subject. In the *Politics* (1282b9-14, 1289a10-25), Aristotle explains that the laws should reflect the nature of the regime and that the laws are therefore just or unjust according to the justice or injustice of the regime. Moreover, it is necessary for the laws to educate the citizens in a manner suitable for each regime; "for the character [*ethos*] appropriate to each regime customarily guards the regime and establishes it from the beginning—for instance, the democratic character democracy and the oligarchic character oligarchy; and the better character is always the cause of the better regime" (1337a15-19). Aristotle points out, however, that although civic education generally produces virtuous character, the education of a good man is not always the same as the education of a good citizen (*Pol.* 1276b16-1277a16, 1278b1-5; *Eth. Nic.* 1130b22-29).

It is significant that while the regime analysis of the *Politics* is carried out with reference to standards of excellence, according to which the regimes, their laws, and the characters of their citizens can be judged as better or worse, the treatment of the regimes in the *Rhetoric* contains hardly any suggestions of such standards. Aristotle's doctrine of the best regime, for example, which is essential for the regime analysis of the *Politics* receives only a passing reference in the *Rhetoric* (1. 4. 1360a24). The rhetorician is necessarily more practical and less theoretical in his view of politics than is the political philosopher. Although he must understand the differences among the regimes, the rhetorician must generally accept the claims of whatever regime he happens to live in.

6. See *Eth. Nic.* 1094al-12, 1179a33-1181b24; *Pol.* 1252al-7, 1323a14-19.

7. See *Eth. Eud.* 1214al-8; *Eth. Nic.* 1094al-3, 18-26, 1094b3-12, 1104b30-33; *Pol.* 1252al-8, 1323a14-1324a4.

8. Aristotle seems to regard happiness and goodness as interchangeable; either may be said to be the final end of human action (*Rh.* 1. 5. 1360b4-7, 6. 1362a21-25). See also *Eth. Nic.* 1095a14-21.

9. *Aristotle* (New York: Oxford University Press, 1959), p. 223.

10. See Don M. Burks, "Psychological Egoism and the Rhetorical Tradition," *Speech Monographs* 33 (1966): 400-418.

11. *Introduction,* p. 13.

12. Of the six major definitions in Book One, four are accompanied by *esto* (1. 5. 1360b3, 6. 1362a22, 7. 1363b8, 10. 1368b8). One exception is the use of *hupokeistho* ("let it be laid down") in defining pleasure (1. 11. 1369b33); the other exception is the defini-

tion of *to kalon* (9. 1366a34-35). Aristotle also employs *esto* in defining the passions in Book Two (2. 1378a32, 3. 1380a7, 4. 1380b36, 5. 1382a21, 6. 1383b14, 7. 1385a18, 8. 1385b13; cf. 9. 1387a8, 10. 1387b12, 11. 1388a30).

13. *Introduction*, p. 177.

14. See *Eth. Nic.* 1094a25-27, 1094b19-27; *Pol.* 1323b37-1324a4; *Top.* 101a18-23, 153a7-26, 154a23-155a37.

15. In regard to absolute intelligibility, see *Top.* 141a26-142a16. Godo Lieberg has argued that it would be absurd for Aristotle to provide the rhetorician a false account of happiness, because presumably the good rhetorician should not be deceived about something so fundamental for human action (*Die Lehre von der Lust in den Ethiken des Aristoteles* [Munich: Beck, 1958], pp. 24-25).

16. See the use of *esto* in the comments on happiness in the *Politics* (1323b21-24). See also *Eth. Nic.* 1139b15.

17. See, e.g., *An. Pr.* 25a14, 30b33; *An. Post.* 75a6-9, 78a31-40.

18. In Euclid's *Elements* the first premise of every demonstration begins with *esto*. (But on the contrast between rhetoric and geometry see *Rh.* 3. 1. 1404a11-12; *Eth. Nic.* 1094b23-27.) See William W. Fortenbaugh, "Aristotle's *Rhetoric* on Emotion," *Archiv für Geschichte der Philosophie* 52 (1970): 45-53. Reasoning by definition as employed in dialectic is said to be very similar to geometry (*Top.* 141b3-14, 158b24-159a2, 160b33-38).

19. Of the twenty-eight topics of enthymemes listed in Chapter 23 of Book Two, the topic of definition is the only one that Aristotle illustrates with arguments made by Socrates. Of the four examples given, the first and the last are Socratic. Argument by definition, it seems, is distinctively Socratic. See *Rh.* 3. 18. 1419a6-13 and *Metaph.* 987b3. Plato suggests in the *Phaedrus* (263d-64d), it should be noted, that a good speech should begin with a definition and that the rest of the speech should follow according to a necessary order.

20. See, e.g., 1. 5. 1360b19-20, 6. 1362a34-35, 1362b3, 1362b10, 7. 1363b16-19, 9. 1366a35-36, 11. 1369b34-1370a4, 1370a27-35, 13. 1373b32-34, 1374b1-3. Aristotle's concern throughout these chapters is to show the rhetorician how to use syllogisms in discussing the subjects examined (see 1. 6. 1362b28-30, 10. 1368b1-3).

21. The only item in the list of the parts of happiness that is not discussed later in the chapter is *arete*, which is more appropriately discussed in connection with epideictic rhetoric. Virtue is considered both an element of one of the definitions of happiness and a part of happiness (1. 5. 1360b15-1361a12, 1362a13-15, 9. 1367b35-36).

22. Some scholars, however, have seen a correspondence between these definitions of happiness and the views of the different members of Plato's Academy; so they have concluded that Aristotle's treatment is intended to reflect not common opinions, but the positions debated in the Academy. See Fortenbaugh, "Aristotle's *Rhetoric*," pp. 42-44.

23. See 1. 5. 1360b4-14, 1361a25-27, 6. 1362a21-29, 1363a8-19, 31-33, 7. 1363b14-21, 1364b8-27, 1364b37-1365a3, 9. 1366b20-22; see also *Eth. Nic.* 1098b9-29. On the disagreement between the many and the wise as to what constitutes happiness, see *Eth. Nic.* 1095a22, 1098b13-17; *Eth. Eud.* 1214b28-1215a3; and *Soph. El.* 173a26-28. See also *Rh.* 1. 9. 1366b8-9.

24. E. M. Cope, *The "Rhetoric" of Aristotle with a Commentary*, 3 vols. (Cambridge: At the University Press, 1877), 1:73-75.

25. Eugene E. Ryan, "Aristotle's *Rhetoric* and *Ethics* and the Ethos of Society," *Greek, Roman, and Byzantine Studies* 13 (1972): 298.

26. *Commentary*, 1:93-94.

27. See *Eth. Nic.* 1155b31-1156a5.
28. See *Eth. Nic.* 1155b18-27, 1157b7-1157b6, 1157b25-28.
29. See *Eth. Nic.* 1159a13-27.
30. On the influence of this chapter and other portions of the *Rhetoric* on Thomas Hobbes, see Leo Strauss, *The Political Philosophy of Hobbes,* trans. Elsa M. Sinclair (Chicago: University of Chicago Press, 1952), pp. 35-43.
31. See *Eth. Nic.* 1144b1-14.
32. See, e.g., *Eth. Nic.* 1140a24-1140b11, 1144a7-1144b33.
33. See *Eth. Nic.* 1094a1-7.
34. See *Eth. Nic.* 1153b25-1154a2, 1157b17.
35. See *Eth. Nic.* 1095b14-22, 1153b25-1154a2.
36. *Cat.* 13b36-14a7.
37. See Plato *Republic* 332a-336a, 375a-376c.
38. Cf. 1. 7. 1364b37-38. Just as the "many" may appear to be the same as "all," what happens *often* (habit) may appear to be the same as what happens *always* (nature) (1. 9. 1367b21-26, 9. 1370a3-10, 2. 9. 1387a16-17, 21. 1395a9-12.)
39. *De An.* 433a10-31.
40. Commenting on this passage, Cope says:

> *epei . . . anangke* are grammatically protasis and apodosis; but the latter is not a con-sequence of the former, nor in *necessary* connexion with it. . . . The *anangke* does not in any way depend upon this, for what has the meaning and definition of good to do with the superiority of the larger number to one or fewer? [*Introduction,* p. 178]

One possible answer to Cope's question is that although the meaning of good is not necessary for concluding that the larger number of anything is superior to the smaller or to one, it *is* necessary in some sense for concluding that the larger number of *good things* is superior to the smaller or to one. That is, in order to apply the abstract principle of the superiority of the larger over the smaller to something in particular, one must define what it is to which the principle is being applied.

41. This chapter shows how the "common topic" (*koinos topos*) of "more and less" (2. 23. 1397b12-27) may be applied to a particular subject. The chapter is also a striking ex-ample of the similarity of rhetoric and dialectic, because these topics of comparison are derived in most cases directly from Book Three of the *Topics* (116a4-119a33). For an elegant summary of these topics, see Cicero *Topica* 18. 68-70.

42. Ryan ("Aristotle's *Rhetoric* and *Ethics,*" p. 300) cites this as an example of the "technical" portions of the *Rhetoric,* as distinguished from the "substantive" portions. He claims that while the "technical" parts are "immune from questions about right and wrong or good and evil," the "substantive" parts assume the moral standards of the *Ethics.* But perhaps one need not go this far, for is it not sufficient to note that Aristotle differen-tiates arguments founded merely on what "seems" so, and thus not necessarily endorsed by him, from arguments founded on firmer ground?

43. See 2. 23. 1399a18-33; *Soph. El.* 172b36-173a31. Another possible source of sophistical arguments is the topic of comparison according to which what is good for someone in particular is a greater good than what is good absolutely (1365a36). But see 1. 15. 1375b18-19 and the comments on this passage in chap. 5, below.

44. Related remarks can be found at *Rh.* 1. 6. 1362b12-16, 1362b28, 9. 1367a15-20, 11. 1371a8-23, 15. 1375b2-5, 2. 4. 1381b20-23, 6. 1384b25-27, 11. 1388b2-7; *Top.* 118b20-27. See also Plato *Gorgias* 474b, 475d-e, 482c-483a, 486e-488b, 492d, 508b-c.

45. Insofar as the practice of rhetoric presupposes political freedom exercised through

public discussion, rhetoric would seem most in harmony with democracy. On the connection between rhetoric and "liberty" (*eleutheria*), see Plato *Gorgias* 452d, 461e, 485c-d, 492c, 502d-e, 518a; Plato *Menexenus* 239a-b, 240e, 242b-c, 244c, 245c-d; and Demosthenes *Crown Speech* 53ff. But although rhetoric is most important in regimes with political assemblies, it has a place in any regime since each must have some sort of "deliberative part." See *Pol.* 1298a4-1299a2.

46. See *Eth. Nic.* 1180b35-1181a7; *Pol.* 1289a1-6.

47. See, e.g., Cope, *Introduction,* pp. 181-83, 208-12; and Cope, *Commentary,* 1:151-57.

48. Cf. *Pol.* 1291b39-42, 1292a39-1292b10.

49. That is, the four regimes other than the "best city" (the "city in speech"), which is either a true aristocracy or a true monarchy (see Plato *Republic* 544a-545d; see also Aristotle *Pol.* 1316a2-1316b27).

50. *Pol.* 1285a23-1285b6, 1311a1-8.

51. See *Rh.* 1. 4. 1360a30-37; also *Metaph.* 994b33-995a12, 1074b1-14.

52. If the portions of the *Rhetoric* devoted to the specific topics of enthymemes are considered as a single unit, extending from the beginning of Chapter 4 of Book One to the end of Chapter 17 of Book Two, then it becomes evident that Aristotle begins by studying the characters of regimes and ends by studying the characters of individuals (2. 12-17). On the need for rhetoricians to respect the characters of their regimes, see Plato *Gorgias* 481c-482c, 484c-d, 510a-513c. See also *Rh.* 1366a9-17, 2. 18. 1391b18-22; *Pol.* 1310a12-36.

53. See *Eth. Nic.* 1094a27-1094b11, 1181a12-16.

Chapter Four

1. See *Eth. Nic.* 1103a9-11, 1105b28-1106a13, 1169a6-1169b2.

2. See 1. 5. 1360b4-7, 1360b15-18, 1360b24, 6. 1362a22-29, 1362b2-15, 9. 1366a34-1366b2, 1366b20-22, 1366b37-38, 1367b35-36.

3. E. M. Cope, *The "Rhetoric" of Aristotle with a Commentary,* 3 vols. (Cambridge: At the University Press, 1877), 1:159-60.

4. *Eth. Nic.* 1105b19-1106a13; See also *Cat.* 8b25-9a28.

5. This passage in the *Metaphysics* is cited by Eugene E. Ryan in his reply to Cope ("Aristotle's *Rhetoric* and *Ethics* and the Ethos of Society," *Greek, Roman and Byzantine Studies* 9 [1972]: 301).

6. As to Cope's claim that the doctrine of the mean is absent from the *Rhetoric,* see the commentary on 1367a34-1367b26 ("Praise and Appearance") in chap. 4 below.

7. See *Eth. Nic.* 1116a18-1116b3 (on "political courage"), 1129b26-1130a13 (on "political justice").

8. The only other virtue on the first list that is not included among the subsequent definitions is "gentleness" (*praotes*) (1366b3). But "gentleness" is defined later in the *Rhetoric* when Aristotle discusses it as the passion that is opposite to anger (2. 3. 1380a5-8). This might explain why it is not defined among the virtues.

Cope points out that the *Nicomachean Ethics* treats *praotes* as a virtue, but not as a passion. He thinks that its inclusion in the *Rhetoric* among both the virtues and the passions is a "singular mark of the unscientific character of this work" (*Introduction,* p. 97). Cope (*Commentary ,* 1:160) also indicates that some of the virtues listed in the *Ethics* are not listed in the *Rhetoric:* for example, the anonymous mean between ambition and lack of ambition, "the three social virtues of an accomplished gentleman" (truthfulness, wittiness, and friendliness), and the two virtues for restraining the passions — shame and indignation. It should be noted, however, that the two virtues for controlling the passions are discussed in the *Rhetoric* (2. 6, 9) as passions!

9. See *Rh.* 1. 11. 1371b27-29. The arrangement of the first list of nine virtues — justice first, magnanimity in the center (with related virtues on each side), and wisdom last — might be intended to suggest that the clash between justice and wisdom can be mediated through magnanimity. This same conclusion is suggested by Cicero, who puts magnanimity sometimes on the side of justice in opposition to wisdom and sometimes on the side of wisdom in opposition to justice. See *De Officiis* 1. 12-13, 16-19, 42, 153-54; *De Oratore* 2. 343-44.

For comments on the popular attitudes toward the wise, see 2. 23. 1398b10-18 and the remarks on this passage in chap. 7 below.

10. For evidence of the influence upon Hobbes of Aristotle's treatment of nobility, see Leo Strauss, *The Political Philosophy of Hobbes*, trans. Elsa M. Sinclair (Chicago: University of Chicago Press, 1952), p. 36.

11. *Rh.* 1. 9. 1367a33-1367b7; see also 1. 4. 1360a22-30, 5. 1361b7-16, 1361b21-23, 6. 1363a1-2, 2. 14, 3. 3. 1406a16-17.

12. Cf. *Rh.* 1367a33-1367b7 with *Eth. Nic.* 1108b30-33, 1109a5-12, 1109b13-18.

13. See *Top.* 115b23-35; *Metaph.* 994b33-995a12.

14. See the opening remarks in "The Kinds of Law" in chap. 5 below.

15. See "Rhetoric, Dialectic, and Sophistry" in chap. 2 above.

16. For an excellent elaboration of this interpretation of epideictic rhetoric, see Christine Oravec, " 'Observation' in Aristotle's Theory of Epideictic," *Philosophy & Rhetoric* 9 (1976): 162-74.

17. See Plato *Gorgias* 448d-449b, 462c-d, 463b-c.

Chapter Five

1. According to Max Hamburger, *Morals and Law* (New York: Biblo and Tannen, 1965), p. 65, "the *Rhetoric* contains the consummation of Aristotle's legal philosophy and theory."

2. By calling them "syllogisms," he stresses their genuinely syllogistic character. To construct an epideictic enthymeme, for example, a speaker would have to use one of Aristotle's topics of virtue or nobility as a major premise, and to this he would add a minor premise stating that the man he wished to praise had satisfied the standard of the major premise; from these premises, he would then conclude that the man was worthy of praise. Rarely, of course, would a speaker have to state verbally the entire syllogism, because he could usually leave something to be supplied by the listeners.

3. Aristotle uses this same tripartition in his analyses of the passions (see 2. 1. 1378a22-31). See Antje Hellwig, *Untersuchungen zur Theorie der Rhetorik bei Platon und Aristoteles* (Göttingen: Vandenhoeck & Ruprecht, 1973), pp. 174-75, 239.

4. See 1. 12. 1372b12-16. One of the reasons that Cope gives for believing that the account of virtue in the *Rhetoric* contradicts the *Ethics* is the absence of a discussion of continence and incontinence (*The "Rhetoric" of Aristotle with a Commentary*, 3 vols. [Cambridge: At the University Press, 1877], 1:160).

5. *Metaph.* 1026b28-1027a28; *An. Pr.* 25a1-3, 25b14-16, 32b5-23; *An. Post.* 75b24-27, 85b16-23; *Top.* 112b1-21, 134a5-8, 134b5-8.

6. See *Eth. Eud.* 1225a14-33.

7. See *Rh.* 1. 11. 1370a6-10; *Cat.* 8b25-9a14; *Eth. Nic.* 1103a14-1103b25, 1152a29-32.

8. See *Eth. Nic.* 1114a13-22.

9. *De An.* 432b5-8; *Eth. Eud.* 1223a21-28; *Metaph.* 1072a23-1072b1.

10. *Eth. Nic.* 1139a4-32; *An. Post.* 100b5-8; see Plato *Philebus* 11b-c.

11. According to the *Nicomachean Ethics* (1112a32-33), the causes of things are "nature, necessity, chance, and in addition mind [*nous*] and everything that is through the human being." Whereas *logismos* in the list of causes in the *Rhetoric* is classified as one of the causes that come from men, *nous* is listed in the *Ethics* as a cause outside human agency: *nous* is independent of men in a way that *logismos* is not.

12. *Eth. Nic.* 1139a36-1139b7; *De An.* 432b8-433b31.

13. See, e.g., *Rh.* 1. 11. 1370a19-27; *Eth. Nic.* 1149a25-1149b4; *Top.* 113a33-113b7.

14. Aristotle commonly uses the words *orge, thymos,* and *pathos* interchangeably (*Eth. Nic.* 1111a24-1111b4, 1116b23-1117a9; *Pol.* 1327b37-1328a17). In Book Two of the *Rhetoric*, anger is the archetypal passion (2. 1. 1378a20-31).

15. The use of *logismos* as a guide to action by incontinent and bad men shows that it can be employed for the sake of things that *appear* to be but are not *truly* good (*Eth. Nic.* 1142b18-22). On the aim of appetite, see *Eth. Eud.* 1235b19-24; *Top.* 146b1-147a11.

16. *Commentary,* 1:200. The influence of this study of pleasure is evident in Hobbes, *De homine,* chap. 11, art. 2.

17. *Philebus* 31d, 42d, 46c; see also *Timaeus* 64c-65a.

18. *Die Lehre von der Lust in den Ethiken des Aristoteles* (Munich: Beck, 1958), pp. 27-42.

19. Ibid., pp. 27-31, See, e.g., *An. Pr.* 29a19-26, 29b29-32; *Metaph.* 1005b19, 1028b8-9.

20. See *Eth. Nic.* 1152b13-1153b20, 1175a11-22, 1176a24-29; *De An.* 405b31-406b26, 408a29-408b32; *Top.* 121a27-38. Cf. *Top.* 111b5-12, *Rh.* 2. 23. 1399a7-8.

21. *Eth. Nic.* 1152b13-21, 1152b26-1153a17, 1154a26-1154b33.

22. See *Eth. Nic.* 1152b13-25; Plato *Philebus* 53c-55c.

23. See *Eth. Nic.* 1095b14-17, 1099a6-31, 1104b4-1105a16, 1153b24-1154a1, 1172b26-1173a6, 1175a11-21, 1175b37-1176a29, 1177a23-38; *Top.* 146b13-19, 160b17-23. On the difference between the pleasures of the many and those of the thoughtful few, see Plato *Gorgias* 492d, 497e, and *Philebus* 51a-55b.

Support for the definition of pleasure in the *Rhetoric* can be found in the *Physics* (247a16-17): "pleasures and pains are alterations of the sensitive part [*alloioseis tou aisthetikou*]." (For other similarities, cf. *Physics* 247a7-9, and *Rh.* 1370a27-35, 1376b27-28.) In *Top.* 121a27-37, Aristotle refers to the argument that pleasure is not any kind of motion because it is neither "locomotion" nor "alteration" nor any other particular kind of motion; it is unclear, however, whether he intends this to be a statement of his own views.

24. Stressing the importance of pleasure for Aristotle's account of virtue, Eric Weil says: "Pleasure is a good, because it is the natural sign of a natural good" ("L' anthropologie d'Aristote," *Revue de Metaphysique et de Morale* 51 [1946]: 14).

25. See *Eth. Nic.* 1174a1-3; Plato *Philebus* 21a-d, 33c-36c, 46b-47e, 60c-e.

26. "For that which has become habitual becomes as it were natural; for habit is something like nature, for what is often is close to what is always, and nature is of that which is always, habit of that which is often" (1370a6-10). See also Plato *Laws* 798a-d, 890d.

27. In the *Philebus* (46b-47e), Socrates speaks of the mixtures of pleasure and pain

and argues that some belong only to the body, some only to the soul, and some both to soul and body.

28. According to this view, the appetitive art of the soul is simply irrational and unresponsive to persuasion: we cannot be persuaded not to feel heat, hunger, pain, or other such things (*Eth. Nic.* 1113b27-30). The passionate part of the soul, however, "does not possess reason in itself, but it is capable of obeying it"; the passionate part listens to reason, while the appetitive can be restrained only by force. Moral virtue pertains to the passionate part of the soul; intellectual virtue pertains to that part that *possesses* reason. *Eth. Nic.* 1102a27-1103a10; *Pol.* 1332a39-1332b8, 1333a17-30; *Top.* 113a33-113b7. See also Plato *Timaeus* 70a-71d.

Aristotle employs both a threefold and a twofold distinction in analyzing the soul. In the one, he divides the soul into nutritive, sensitive, and noetic parts; in the other, he divides the noetic part into that which *possesses* reason and that which is *obedient* to reason through persuasion (*epipeithes*). The cognitive status of the emotions is indicated by their belonging to that subdivision of the noetic art that is obedient to reason (*Eth. Nic.* 1097b33-1098a5, 1102b29-1103a3). For an extensive study of the relation between the bipartite and tripartite psychologies, see William W. Fortenbaugh, *Aristotle on Emotion* (New York: Barnes & Noble, 1975), pp. 26-44.

29. See *Rh.* 1. 10. 1369a3-8, 1369b10-17, 1370a19-27, 2. 12. 1388b33, 19. 1392a24-26; *Eth. Nic.* 1105b20-23, 1149a25-1149b4; *Eth. Eud.* 1224a39-1224b2.

30. Although Godo Lieberg divides the pleasures into a list of seventeen, learning and wondering are ninth and thus still central (*Die Lehre von der Lust*, pp. 38-41).

31. See *Eth. Nic.* 1175a4-11.

32. See *Rh.* 2. 21. 1395b1-13, 23. 1400b25-33, 3. 2. 1404b1-22, 9. 1409a31-1409b8, 10. 1410b6-35, 11. 1412a9-28; *Poet.* 1448b4-23, 1459a1-7.

33. Aristotle is careful to say that learning and wondering are pleasant "for the most part" (1371a32); the statement recognizes that, to the extent that learning requires mental exertion, it is painful (see 1370a12-14). For other uses of this qualification, see 1371b13-25.

34. *Metaph.* 982b12-18.

35. Cf. *Eth. Nic.* 1177a27.

36. See, e.g., 1. 1. 1355a20-23, 1355a36-37, 2. 21. 1395b1-18, 22. 1396a32-1396b19, 23. 1400b25-33, 3. 2. 1404b1-26, 8. 1408b22-29, 9. 1409a31-1409b12, 10. 1410b6-35, 11. 1411b22-1412b32.

37. See also *Poet.* 1452a21-1452b13.

38. Note the uses of the *epei de* . . . *kai anangke* construction at 1370b35, 1371b4-6, 18-20, 22-24, 29-30, 34-36.

39. Things akin are pleasant only "for the most part," since sometimes like is not attracted to like and opposites attract. Hence, the premise that things akin are pleasant is a probability at most. Furthermore, the commonality among men as men that makes them pleasant to one another is surely balanced by the variety of types among men that makes men pleasant only to others of the same type. See *Eth. Nic.* 1155a20-23, 1167b34-1168a3. Also, cf. *Rh.* 1. 11. 1371a33-1371b4.

40. See *Eth. Nic.* 1153b25-1154a2, 1177a12-27.

41. See 1. 12. 1372a11-17, 23-24, 28-32, 1372b34-1373a5, 1373a9-20; cf. 2. 24. 1401a34-1401b3, 1402a2-28.

42. Aristotle says, for example, that friends are likely victims of injustice since they are easy to attack (1373a3). This might remind one of a passage in Xenophon's *Anabasis*.

Describing Meno's notoriously ignoble life, Xenophon says that he thought that anyone who was not corrupt was "uneducated" (2. 6. 26). Meno thought, for instance, that "he was the only one who knew that it was easiest to steal the property of friends since it was unguarded" (2. 6. 24-25). One might argue that, like Xenophon, Aristotle discusses the tricks of the base in order to instruct good men and to dispel the smug assumption of bad men that good men must be naive.

43. Sophocles *Antigone* 456.

44. *Commentaria in Aristotelem Graeca*, vol. 21, ed. Hugo Rabe (Berlin: George Reimer, 1896), p. 74.

45. On these three examples, see Rudolph Hirzel, *Agraphos Nomos* (Leipzig: B. H. Teubner, 1900), pp. 28-29, 65-68, an essential work for any serious study of the Greek notion of unwritten law.

46. See 1. 13. 1373b8-13, 15. 1375a32-1375b2, 3. 16. 1417a27-32, 17. 1418b32-33. According to Eric Voegelin, "Das Rechte von Natur," *Anamnesis* (Munich: R. Piper, 1966), p. 121, Aristotle's conception of the "just by nature" resembles thoughts expressed by Heraclitus and Sophocles, except that while they referred to the *theios nomos*, Aristotle speaks of the *physei dikaion*—that is, the criterion of *nomos* for Aristotle is not divinity but nature.

47. Later in the *Rhetoric* (3. 16. 1417a27-32), as an example of giving a reason for something that is initially implausible, Aristotle cites Antigone's argument that she cared more for her brother than for her husband and children because brothers cannot be replaced once one's parents are dead. George Anastaplo has suggested that these comments by Antigone "reflect the fact that the family (one's parents and brothers) is for a child something 'given,' perhaps even natural. One realizes, on the other hand, that one's own husband or child depends upon marriage and hence upon the city." The problem, then, according to Anastaplo, is that Antigone "challenges a new convention (Creon's decree) in the name of an older one (which some mistakenly see as either natural or divine in its origin)" (*The Constitutionalist: Notes on the First Amendment* [Dallas: Southern Methodist University Press, 1971], p. 798). On the superiority of the city to the family, see *Pol.* 1253a19-29, 1260b8-21; *Top.* 105b19-29.

48. See, for example, R. A. Gauthier and J. Y. Jolif, *L'Éthique à Nicomaque*, 4 vols. (Louvain: Publications Universitaires de Louvain, 1959), 2:391; and Hamburger, *Morals and Law*, pp. 36, 61-65.

49. This is the argument of Harry Jaffa, *Thomism and Aristotelianism* (Chicago: University of Chicago Press, 1952), pp. 168-69: "there is nowhere in Aristotle's *Ethics* or *Politics* any mention of natural *law*. There is only a single doubtful mention of natural law in the *Rhetoric*. But in the context of a discussion of the means of forensic persuasion one can draw no serious conclusion from it alone."

50. See, e.g., Hamburger, *Morals and Law*, pp. 99-100; Charles E. Butterworth, "Rhetoric and Reason: A Study of Averroes's *Commentary on Aristotle's 'Rhetoric'* " (Ph.D. diss., University of Chicago, 1966), pp. 164-65.

51. Aristotle's central example—"to do good in return to one who does good"—corresponds exactly to one of the "unwritten laws" to which Socrates refers in Xenophon's *Memorabilia* (4. 4. 24). For the traditional examples, see Cope, *Introduction*, pp. 240-41. See also Hamburger, *Morals and Law*, pp. 56-65. On Aristotle's distinction between conventional and natural justice, see *Eth. Nic.* 1134b19-1135a14, 1136b32-35, 1137a31-1138a4, 1162b21-37, 1180b1-5; *Pol.* 1253a30-38, 1287b5-10, 1319b40-1320a5; *Metaph.* 1014b17-1015a19; *Mag. Mor.* 1194b28-1195a8.

52. See the comments by two scholiasts in *Commentaria in Aristotelem Graeca,* (21:74, 79, 286-87), who both assume that Aristotle's "common law" is founded on "custom" (*ethos*). In the *Rhetorica ad Alexandrum,* 1421b37-1422a3, which was probably written by one of Aristotle's students, the "common law" is equated to the "unwritten custom" (*ethos agraphos*) of all or most men. It was common for Greek authors to identify "unwritten law" and "customary law." See Hirzel, *Agraphos Nomos,* pp. 13-26. See also *Top.* 115b23-35; *Soph. El.* 173a7-31; *Metaph.* 994b33-995a12; *Eth. Nic.* 1179b29-35, 1180a1.

The notion of a "common law" established in those customs of men which manifest men's commonsense grasp of the "just by nature" has, of course, been important in Anglo-American jurisprudence.

53. See "Anger as the Paradigmatic Passion" (the part on "anger and the moral sense of man") and "The Other Passions" (the part on "indignation and envy") in chap. 6 below; see also "Grandeur of Style" (the end of the part on "rhetoric, Socrates, and the gods of the city") in chap. 8.

Although the perfection of "natural justice" is found in the "best regime" (*Eth. Nic.*1135a3-6), Aristotle makes only one brief reference to the "best regime" in the *Rhetoric* (1. 4. 1360a22-24); this indicates the limitations of the popular conception of "natural justice" with which the rhetorician must work.

54. Cf. *Rh.* 1374b24-26 with *Eth. Nic.* 1135b20.

55. According to Hamburger, "the concept of *epieikeia* as defined by Aristotle has no antecedent in the whole of pre-Aristotelian literature" (*Morals and Law,* pp. 89-90). Hamburger compares the handling of "equity" in the *Magna Moralia,* the *Nicomachean Ethics,* and the *Rhetoric* (pp. 93-105); he concludes that the *Rhetoric* contains "the consummation of Aristotle's theory of equity."

56. See Plato *Statesman* 294a-96d and *Laws* 875a-76e.

57. See *Top.* 163b9-17.

58. *Rh.* 1375b18-19. See 1. 7. 1365a36, 9. 1366b35-38, 2. 13. 1389b36-1390a2, 23. 1399a28-31. Men necessarily choose what is good for themselves, Aristotle says in the *Nicomachean Ethics* (1113a29-1113b2, 1129b1-7), but they should pray that what is good for themselves is also good simply. See *Top.* 116b8.

Chapter Six

1. See, for example, E. M. Cope, *An Introduction to Aristotle's "Rhetoric"* (London and Cambridge: Macmillan, 1867), p. 245; Lane Cooper, ed. and trans., *The "Rhetoric" of Aristotle* (New York: Appleton-Century-Crofts, 1932), p. 90.

2. See Antje Hellwig, *Untersuchungen zur Theorie der Rhetorik bei Platon und Aristoteles* (Gottingen: Vandenhoeck & Ruprecht, 1973), pp. 252-53.

3. Cf. Plato *Gorgias* 487a, 512e-513c.

4. See *Eth. Nic.*1172b15-18.

5. The cognitive theory of the passions could be said to have originated with Plato's *Philebus.* But more recently there have been attempts within the phenomenological tradition to elaborate such a theory, of which the most noteworthy are Alexius Meinong, "Über emotionale Prasentation," in *Gesamtausgabe,* vol. 3, *Abhandlungen zur Werttheorie,* ed. Rudolf Haller and Rudolph Kindinger (Graz, Austria: Akademische Druck- und Verlagsanstalt, 1968), esp. sec. 12; and Max Scheler, *Der Formalismus in der Ethik und die materiale Wertethik* (Bern: Francke Verlag, 1966). Recently, a spirited defense of the theory has been made by Robert C. Solomon, *The Passions* (Garden City, N.Y.: Double-

day Anchor Books, 1976). See also Errol Bedford, "Emotions," in *Essays in Philosophical Psychology*, ed. Donald Gustafson (Garden City, N.Y.: Doubleday Anchor Books, 1964), pp. 77-98; George Pitcher, "Emotion," *Mind* 74 (1965): 326-46.

6. *Poet.* 1448b28, 1456a37. Aristotle often lists anger, pity, and fear as exemplifying the passions generally. Pity and fear pertain to tragedy. Does anger pertain to comedy? See Laurence Berns, "Aristotle's *Poetics*," in *Ancients and Moderns*, ed. Joseph Cropsey (New York: Basic Books, 1964), p. 84.

7. Martin Heidegger adopts Aristotle's mode of analysis in *Sein und Zeit* (Tübingen: Max Niemeyer Verlag, 1972), pp. 134-40. For example, Heidegger studies fear from three perspectives: the attitude of fearing, that about which we fear, and that before which we fear. And thus, as with Aristotle, Heidegger stresses that passions are always *about* something. Declaring that "the fundamental ontological interpretation of affectivity in general has been able to take hardly one noteworthy step forward since Aristotle," Heidegger claims that Aristotle's treatment of the passions in the *Rhetoric* must be understood to be "the first systematic hermeneutic of the everydayness of being-with-one-another [*der Alltaglichkeit des Miteinanderseins*]." Thus, Heidegger implies that Aristotle has anticipated his own view of passion as a mode of awareness of the world and of one's place in the world that shows an openness to Being.

8. For more on the deductive method, see Friedrich Solmsen, "Aristotle and Cicero on the Orator's Playing upon the Feelings," *Classical Philology* 33 (1938): 390-404.

9. See Hellwig, *Untersuchungen*, p. 243.

10. Since anger is a response to an "apparent injustice," Aristotle says (*Eth. Nic.* 1135b25-30), the "beginning" (*arche*) of the anger is not in the angry man but in the man with whom he is angry.

11. The definition of anger in Plato's *Philebus* (37e) as pain "with" (*meta*) the thought of slight leaves the precise meaning of "with" unstated. But Aristotle argues in the *Topics* (150b27-151a19, 156a32-156b3) that this "with" should be understood to mean "on account of" (*dia*): anger is pain *on account of* the thought of slight. The thought of slight is the *efficient cause* of anger. Moreover, since knowledge of something's essence and knowledge of its cause are reciprocal (*An. Post.* 90a14-15, 31-32, 93a3-4), to know that a certain thought or judgment *causes* an emotion is to know the *essence* of the emotion. Compare the following comment by Charles S. Peirce:

> If a man is angry, his anger implies, in general, no determinate and constant character in its object. But, on the other hand, it can hardly be questioned that there is some relative character in the outward thing which makes him angry. . . . any emotion is a predication concerning some object, and the chief difference between this and an objective intellectual judgment is that while the latter is relative to human nature or to mind in general, the former is relative to the particular circumstances and disposition of a particular man at a particular time. [*Selected Writings*, ed. Philip P. Wiener (New York: Dover, 1966), p. 33.]

12. Aristotle implies in the *Rhetoric* that in the formation of every passion there is a syllogism of the following form: A certain set of conditions (*A*) makes a certain passion (*B*) appropriate; a particular man finds himself to be in the situation *A*; therefore, for the man in question passion *B* is appropriate. A man adopts a passion if he believes that his situation warrants it, and he gives up the passion if he believes it does not.

13. See "Rhetoric, Dialectic, and Sophistry" in chap. 2 above.

14. See "Pleasure" in chap. 5 above; cf. 2. 2. 1378b2-9 and 1. 11. 1370a27-1370b15.

15. See 2. 1. 1377b30, 2. 1378a32, 1378b7, 9, 5. 1382a21, 1382b30, 1383a17, 6. 1383b13, 1384a23, 8. 1385b13, 9. 1387a9, 10. 1387b22, 11. 1388a30. See also Hellwig, *Untersuchungen*, p. 243.

16. See *Eth. Nic.* 1147b4-6.

17. *De An.* 403a8-10, 432a7-14.

18. *Eth. Nic.* 1114a30-1114b5; see also *De An.* 433b10-13 and *Eud. Eth.* 1235b28-30.

19. 1. 13. 1375b5-8, 1374a18-24, 2. 2. 1378a32-33, 1379b2-17, 27-31, 3. 1380b17-18. The term *to prosekon* may imply a standard of natural justice (see 2. 2. 1378a33, 1378b33-1379a8, 1379b2-4, 9-12). "I believe it has not hitherto been noticed," Cope says, "that the four terms usually employed in Greek to express the notion of duty or obligation may be distinguished as implying four different sources of obligation." The four are *prosekei, dei, chre,* and *prepei.* "The first, *to prosekon,* expresses a natural connexion or relationship, and hence a law of *nature,* the prescriptions of *physis;* as *hoi prosekontes* are our *natural relations*" (*The "Rhetoric" of Aristotle with a Commentary,* 3 vols. [Cambridge: At the University Press, 1877], 2:11). Cope goes on to associate *to deon* with a moral bond, *to chreon* with expediency, and *to prepon* with decorum.

20. A contemporary statement of this point may be found in John Rawls, *A Theory of Justice* (Cambridge, Mass.: Harvard University Press, 1971), secs. 73-74. Rawls argues that "moral emotions" cannot be explained simply as sensations or patterns of behavior, even if these exist, because these emotions rest upon moral judgments that appeal to certain principles of morality.

21. See *De An.* 403a16-17. Aristotle says in the *Ethics* (1179b11-14) that it is not the nature of the many before they have been habituated by the laws to be restrained by a sense of shame. And yet shame appears as a passion in the *Rhetoric.* See *Eth. Nic.* 1108a31-1108b2, 1128b10-36; *Top.* 126a8-12, 129a12-16, 133a31-33. (Also, on comparing the lists of the passions in the *Rhetoric* and the *Ethics,* see Cope, *Introduction,* pp. 116-18.)

22. See *An. Pr.* 70b6-38.

23. See *Top.* 156a30-33.

24. See, e.g., *Eth. Nic.* 1117a6-9, 1135b20-30, 1144b17-30, 1145b21-1146a10, 1147a10-23, 1147b9-19, 1150b20-28, 1151a20-28, 1169a4-6, 1179b29; *Pol.* 1254b7-10, 1312b29; *Mag. Mor.* 1182a15-24; *De An.* 429a7. The sophists sometimes deliberately arouse their opponents to anger by appearing willing to do injustice or to act shamelessly. They do this because they know that angry men are less on their guard against deceptive arguments (*Soph. El.* 174a20-23).

25. See Robert C. Solomon, "Emotions and Choice," *Review of Metaphysics* 27 (1973): 25-26, where this example is developed.

26. *Eth. Nic.* 1126a9-28; *Cat.* 9b10-10a10.

27. Thucydides (*History of the Peloponnesian War,* 2. 65) provides an example of how good rhetoric can do this in his praise of Pericles: "whenever he saw them out of season insolently confident, by speaking he would put them into fear; and again when they were afraid without reason, he would likewise restore them to confidence."

28. For comments elsewhere on *eros,* see 2. 6. 1384a28-31, 7. 1385a22-25, 10. 1388a12-17, 12. 1389a2-5, 19. 1392a24-26.

29. See also *De An.* 433a10-433b13; *Top.* 146b5-13.

30. See *Eth. Nic.* 1179b10-14; *Top.* 126a8-12, 129a12-16, 133a31-33.

31. See *Eth. Nic.* 1157b18-19, 1170b33-1171a5.

32. Cf. *Poet.* 1452a22-1452b13, 1452b28-1454a15, and *Rh.* 1382b14-18, 1383a7-13, 1385b35-1386a2.

33. Knowledge of our mortality arouses neither fear not pity because death is too distant. But the experience of actually being on the verge of death — especially if the death is a violent one — does give rise to both fear and pity. See 1382a24-27, 1386a5-7.

34. See also *Eth. Eud.* 1234a24-34.

35. These points are suggested in *Eth. Nic.* 1120b11-20 and 1168a22-24.

36. Cf. *Pol.* 1269a4.

37. After this definition, Aristotle discusses the dispositions of envious men (1376b25-34), the things that excite their envy (1388a1-4), and the men that they envy (1388a5-28).

The resemblances between Aristotle's account of envy and Plato's in the *Philebus* have been noticed by William W. Fortenbaugh:

> Both works agree in calling envy a pain (48b, 50a; 1386b18, 1387b23), in emphasizing the grounds (*epi*) that explain an envious response (48b, 49d-e, 50a; 1386b19, 1387b22-23, 1388a25), in pointing out that envious men are delighted at the misfortune of a neighbor or peer (48b, 50a; 1386b32-1387a3, 1388a24-27), in associating envy with bad character (49d; 1386b33-1387a2), and in dissociating envy from the fearsome (49a-c; 1386b20-24). ["Aristotle's *Rhetoric* on Emotion," *Archiv für Geschichte der Philosophie* 52 (1970): 40-70.]

38. *Eth. Nic.* 1107a9-14, 1108b1-6; see Cope, *Commentary*, 2:112-13.

39. See 2. 2. 1378b28, 5. 1382b33-1383a3, 9. 1386b9-16, 1386b32-1387a6, 10. 1388a20-22, 11. 1388a37-1388b3, 12. 1389a26-28, 13. 1389b27-33, 1390a17-22, 15. 1390b22-25, 16. 1390b31-1391a7, 13, 17. 1391a20-29, 1391b1-3. See also Hellwig, *Untersuchungen*, pp. 247-49.

Eric Voegelin sees this portion of the *Rhetoric* as foreshadowing the *Characters* of Theophrastus (*Plato and Aristotle*, vol. 3, *Order and History* [Baton Rouge: Louisiana State University Press], p. 367). One might also see here an anticipation of Bacon, *Advancement of Learning*, in *Selected Writings*, ed. Hugh G. Dick (Garden City, N.Y.: Doubleday Anchor Books), pp. 334-37.

40. It may be significant that Aristotle's description of man in his prime and of his adherence to the "mean" comes at the middle of the *Rhetoric*. Remarks on the "mean" may be found at 1. 4. 1360a22-30, 5. 1361b7-16, 21-24, 6. 1363a1-2, 9. 1367a33-1367b7, 1371a25-27, 2. 17. 1391a27-29, 3. 2. 1405b32-33, 3. 1406a16.

41. Aristotle says in the *Ethics* (1155a13-17) that while the young need friends to help them avoid error, and the old need them to care for them and to tend to their failing powers of action, those in their prime need them for noble deeds. Only those in their prime, it seems, are fitted for acting well.

42. See Plato *Republic* 503c-d, and *Laws* 671a-72d; see also *Rh.* 2. 15. 1390b28-31. In seeking *to metrion* (1390b9), the man in his prime seeks that which is said in Plato's *Philebus* (64c-66b) to be the highest end for man.

43. Aristotle's point was restated by Averell Harriman in his remark that "people have to be given big jobs when they are young, or else their minds become permanently closed. The men who work their way step by step to the top in business are no good for anything

big in government. They have acquired too many bad habits along the way" (Arthur M. Schlesinger, Jr., *A Thousand Days* [Boston: Houghton Mifflin, 1965], pp. 149-50).

44. Passages relevant to piety and divinity may be found at 1. 10. 1369a5-7, 13. 1373b8-23, 15. 1376a1-3, 1377a8-1377b13, 2. 5. 1383b2-8, 9. 1386b14-16, 23. 1397b12-13, 1398a15-28, 1398b18-1399a8, 1399a17-28, 1399b4-13, 18-30, 3. 5. 1407a32-1407b7, 10. 1411b12-14, 18. 1418b39-1419a19. It is in considering the dependence of happiness on good fortune that Aristotle in the *Nicomachean Ethics* (1099a31-1101a22) must take up the question of whether happiness is a gift of the gods. But he does not mention love of the gods as a virtue. In the *Eudemian Ethics* (1247b29-1248b8), however, after commenting on the connection between good fortune and divinity, he concludes the book by declaring that the highest end for man is "serving and contemplating god" (1249b10-25). See J. Donald Monan, *Moral Knowledge and Its Methodology in Aristotle* (Oxford: Oxford University Press, 1968), pp. 139-42. See also *Metaph.* 1074b1-14.

Chapter Seven

1. See 3. 10. 1410b9-35 and "Metaphor" in chap. 8 below.

2. The following "topic" deserves to be noted: "And those things are possible of which the beginning of genesis is in those which we would force or persuade; and these are those of which we are superiors, rulers or friends" (1392a27-29; see also 1392b29.) Cope says: "The two first classes illustrate the *anangkazein* the force of superior strength, and of authority natural (as that of a parent or master) or legal (the authority of the magistrate); the third, friends, who are amenable to persuasion, exemplify the *peithein*" (E. M. Cope, *The Rhetoric of Aristotle with a Commentary,* 3 vols. [Cambridge: At the University Press, 1877], 2:185). What is politically "possible" depends upon moving men to action either through compulsion or through persuasion. To the extent that a community is held together by agreement to communal norms, public matters can be decided by persuasion through rhetoric. But insofar as politics depends on coercion (and no community could long endure without it), political relationships are those of ruler and ruled, master and slave. Yet the more the community rests upon agreement through the persuasion of rhetoric, the closer the community approximates an association of friends.

3. See *An. Pr.* 25a1-3, 25b14-16, 32b5-23; *Top.* 134a5-18, 134b5-8.

4. The first "topic" is "if the naturally less likely has happened, then the more likely has already happened" (139b15-16).

5. See 1. 2. 1358a26-36, 3. 1359a7-29, 2. 1. 1377b15-21, 1378a27-31, 18. 1391b22-1392b7, 22. 1396b28-1397a6, 26. 1403a34-1403b2, 3. 1. 1403b6-14.

6. See 1. 2. 1356a36-1356b25, 1357b25-37, 2. 20. 1394a9-18, 23. 1398a31-1398b18, 25. 1402b13-21.

7. See *An. Post.* 99b15-100b17; *Eth. Nic.* 1139b28-31.

8. See 1. 1. 1367b7-11, 2. 23. 1398a15-23, 1398b28-31, 1399a7-8, 1399b4-13, 3. 4. 1406b32-37, 7. 1408b17-21, 14. 1415b29-31, 16. 1417a19-21, 18. 1419a6-19. See also the complaint by Callicles about Socrates' use of comparisons (Plato *Gorgias* 490d-91c).

9. Cf. Plato *Phaedrus* 269e-70a, 272d-74a.

10. See "Proofs" in chap. 8 below.

11. On what makes the uneducated more popular than the educated, see 1. 1.

1355a22-29, 2. 21. 1394a28-33, 23. 1399a9-17, 3. 1. 1404a22-28, 7. 1408a32-33, 17. 1418a8-12.

12. See chap. 2., n. 1, above.

13. This classification is made by William M. A. Grimaldi, *Studies in the Philosophy of Aristotle's "Rhetoric"* (Wiesbaden: F. Steiner, 1972), p. 131. Georgiana Paine Palmer comments on all of the "topics" in this chapter and cites examples of their use by ancient rhetoricians ("The *topoi* of Aristotle's *Rhetoric* as Exemplified in the Orators," [Ph. D. diss., University of Chicago, 1934]).

14. See 1397b12-13, 22-27, 1398a15-18, 23-26, 1398b9-18, 28-31, 1399a8-16, 21-27, 1399b4-10, 1400a22-28. "Topic" 23 is questionable, since it is only indirectly related to the trial of Socrates.

15. See 1398a23-26, 1398b28-31, 1399a8-9, 1399b8-10, "Topic" 17 is doubtful and requires further comment.

16. See Xenophon *Memorabilia* 4. 2. 13-18.

17. See Plato *Gorgias* 470c-71d.

18. See *Soph. El.* 173a19-31.

19. See also Xenophon *Apology of Socrates* 10-13.

20. In Xenophon *Memorabilia* 4. 2. 33, Socrates challenges the assumption by Euthydemus (a name meaning "straight to the *demos*") that wisdom is an indisputable good with stories of wise men who have suffered because of envy or because of the desire of other men to benefit from their wisdom. In *The Education of Cyrus* 3. 1. 38-39, Xenophon implies that the trial of Socrates was due to the envy of his accusers. See Plato *Apology of Socrates* 18c-d.

21. Plato *Apology of Socrates* 17a-18a, 30d-31b, 35c-d.

22. *Soph. El.* 172b36-73a6, 173a19-31; see also Isocrates *Panathenaicus* 241-44.

23. See *Top.* 160b17-23.

24. Perhaps the reader should be reminded of the tribute to Isocrates by Socrates in Plato's *Phaedrus* (278e-79b). Socrates is said to praise Isocrates for his philosophic mind. Aristotle's respect for Isocrates in this chapter of the *Rhetoric* has been noted by Georgiana Palmer: "however much Aristotle profited by listening to oratory, the only considerable section of Attic oratory studied in the producing of this chapter of the *Rhetoric* was the epideictic oratory of Isocrates" ("The *topoi* of Aristotle's *Rhetoric*," p. 84). Extensive references to Isocrates may be found elsewhere in the *Rhetoric*; see 3. 9. 1409b32-1410a23.

25. The parallels become evident through comparison of the following passages: 1400b17-24 and 1401a12-23, 1397a27-1397b13 and 1401a33-1401b3, 1399b4-13 and 1401b19-29, 1400a5-14 and 1402a2-27. Questionable reasoning also appears at 1399a4-6.

26. For a comparison of the "topics" in this chapter and those in *On Sophistical Refutation*, see E. M. Cope, *An Introduction to Aristotle's "Rhetoric"* (London and Cambridge: Macmillan, 1867), pp. 95-96.

27. See Plato *Symposium* 182b-c.

28. See the comment by the anonymous commentator in *Commentaria in Aristotelem Graeca*, vol. 21, ed. Hugo Rabe (Berlin: George Reimer, 1896), p. 151.

29. See Plato *Phaedrus* 272d-73c.

30. See Plato *Protagoras*, 319a, 337c-38b.

31. For further remarks on these passages, see Cope, *Introduction*, pp. 267-76; Grimaldi, *Studies*, pp. 100-103; and Heinrich Maier, *Die Syllogistik des Aristoteles*, 3 vols. (Tübingen: H. Laupp, 1900), 3:451-73.

Chapter Eight

1. See Friedrich Nietzsche, *Darstellung der antiken Rhetorik*, in *Gesammelte Werke*, 23 vols. (Munich: Masarion Verlag, 1922), 5:291-96.

2. See *Pol.* 1281a39-1282a24, 1288b23-1289a6, 1342a15-30, 1242b18-34; *Poet.* 1453a30-37.

3. See *Rh.* 3. 2. 1404b1-13, 1405a5-12, 33-37, 8. 1408b22-29, 9. 1409a23-1409b12, 1410a18-22, 10. 1410b6-35, 11. 1412a9-12, 18-28, 1412b21-32, 12. 1414a21-28, 17. 1418b2-4.

4. Carnes Riley Lord, "Poetry and the City: An Interpretation of Aristotle's *Poetics*" (Ph.D. diss., Cornell University, 1972), pp. 71-78.

5. *Rh.* 3. 2. 1405a2-9, 10. 1410b6-9; *Poet.* 1459a5-8.

6. Cf. Plato *Phaedrus* 269d-70a.

7. Consider, for example, Plato *Philebus* 23c-27b. See E. M. Cope, *The "Rhetoric" of Aristotle with a Commentary*, 3 vols. (Cambridge: At the University Press, 1877), 3:84-86.

8. *Rh.* 3. 11. 1412a9-12; *Poet.* 1459a5-7; see also *Soph. El.* 169a31-33.

9. *Rh.* 3. 2. 1405a5-12, 10. 1401b6-35, 11. 1412a9-12, 18-28, 1412b21-32.

10. *Rh.* 10. 1410b13-28; cf. *Poet.* 1458a17-34.

11. *Rh.* 1. 11. 1371a32, 3. 2. 1404b11-13, 1405a34-37, 11. 1412a9-12.

12. *Rh.* 3. 2. 1405b3-6, 11. 1412a23-25; see also *Poet.* 1458a24-30.

13. See *Soph. El.* 169a31-33.

14. See *An. Pr.* 24b19-23, 25b32-26a2, 41a3-13, 44b38-45a23.

15. See *An. Post.* 89b10-11.

16. See *Rh.* 1. 2. 1357a2-5, 11. 1371b5-11, 2. 20. 1393a25-1394a9, 23. 1400b25-33, 3. 9. 1410a22, 10. 1410b6-35, 11. 1412b22-24, 18. 1419a18-19; and *Poet.* 1448b12-18.

17. See "On Examples" and " 'Topics' of Enthymemes" in chap. 7 above for additional comments on Socratic rhetoric.

Chapter Nine

1. From the perspective of the contemporary political scientist, rhetoric may appear to be nothing more than the manipulation of irrational symbols that do not reflect empirical reality. See, for example, Murray Edelman, *The Symbolic Uses of Politics* (Urbana: University of Illinois Press, 1964), pp. 18-21, 29-35, 41-42, 96-98, 115-17, 121, 124-25, 161, 172-73, 179-81; and Edelman, *Politics as Symbolic Action* (New York: Academic Press, 1971), pp. 1-2.

2. *The Elements of Law Natural and Politic*, ed. Ferdinand Tönnies (London: Frank Cass, 1969), 1. 13.3. See John W. Danford, *Wittgenstein and Political Philosophy* (Chicago: University of Chicago Press, 1978), pp. 16-42.

3. See, for example, Harold Lasswell and Abraham Kaplan, *Power and Society: A Framework for Political Inquiry* (New Haven: Yale University Press, 1950).

4. Here and elsewhere in these concluding remarks I have drawn ideas from Leo Strauss, "An Epilogue," in *Essays on the Scientific Study of Politics*, ed. Herbert J. Storing (New York: Holt, Rinehart and Winston, 1962), pp. 307-27; Wilhelm Hennis, *Politik und praktische Philosophie* (Berlin: Luchterhand, 1963), pp. 98-115; and Eugene F. Miller, "Primary Questions in Politics," *Review of Politics* 39 (July 1977): 298-331.

5. A clever presentation of this point is Lewis Carroll's "What the Tortoise Said to Achilles," *The Complete Works of Lewis Carroll* (New York: Modern Library, Random

House, 1936), pp. 1225-30. The profound implications of this problem for modern science are worked out by Douglas R. Hofstadter, *Gödel, Escher, Bach: An Eternal Golden Braid* (New York: Basic Books, 1979).

6. On the assumptions necessary for modern science, see A. D'Abro, *The Rise of the New Physics,* 2 vols. (New York: Dover Publications, 1951), 1:14-27. See also my article, "Language and Nature in Wittgenstein's *Philosophical Investigations,*" *Journal of Thought* 10 (July 1975): 194-99.

7. *Physics and Philosophy* (New York: Harper & Row, 1958), pp. 200-202.

8. One should keep in mind here the long rhetorical tradition of speculation about the nature of "common sense." See, for example, Thomas Reid, *Essays on the Intellectual Powers of Man* (Cambridge: M.I.T. Press, 1969), pp. 556-68; and Hans Georg Gadamer, *Truth and Method* (New York: Seabury Press, 1975), pp. 19-29.

BIBLIOGRAPHY

Ackrill, J. L., ed. and trans. *Aristotle's "Categories" and "De Interpretatione."* Oxford: Clarendon Press, 1963.

Alfarabi. *The Philosophy of Plato and Aristotle.* Translated by Muhsin Mahdi. Ithaca, N.Y.: Cornell University Press, 1969.

Anastaplo, George. "American Constitutionalism and the Virtue of Prudence: Philadelphia, Paris, Washington, Gettysburg." *Loyola of Los Angeles Law Review* 8 (1974): 1-54.

_____. *The Constitutionalist: Notes on the First Amendment.* Dallas: Southern Methodist University Press, 1971.

Anscombe, G. E. M. *Intention.* Ithaca, N.Y.: Cornell University Press, 1957.

Aquinas, Thomas. *In Aristoteles Libros Peri Hermeneias et Posteriorum Analyticorum Exposito.* Edited by R. M. Spiazzi. Rome: Marietti, 1955.

Arnauld, Antoine, and Nicole, Pierre. *La Logique ou l'Art de penser.* Paris: Presses Universitaire de France, 1965.

Arnhart, Larry. "Language and Nature in Wittgenstein's *Philosophical Investigations.*" *Journal of Thought* 10 (1975): 194-99.

Bacon, Francis. *Selected Writings.* Edited by Hugh G. Dick. New York: Modern Library, Random House, 1955.

Bedford, Errol. "Emotions." In *Essays in Philosophical Psychology,* edited by Donald F. Gustafson. Garden City, N.Y.: Doubleday Anchor Books, 1964.

Berns, Laurence. "Aristotle's *Poetics.*" In *Ancients and Moderns,* edited by Joseph Cropsey. New York: Basic Books, 1964.

_____. "Rational Animal—Political Animal." *Review of Politics* 38 (1976): 177-89.

Booth, Wayne C. *Modern Dogma and the Rhetoric of Assent.* Chicago: University of Chicago Press, 1974.

Brandes, Paul D. "The Composition and Preservation of Aristotle's *Rhetoric.*" *Speech Monographs* 35 (1968): 482-91.

Broadie, Alexander. "Aristotle on Rational Action." *Phronesis* 19 (1974): 70-80.

Burke, Don M. "Psychological Egoism and the Rhetorical Tradition." *Speech Monographs* 33 (1966): 400-418.

Burke, Edmund. *Reflections on the Revolution in France.* Indianapolis, Ind.: Liberal Arts Press, 1955.

Butterworth, Charles E. "Rhetoric and Reason: A Study of Averroes's *Commentary on Aristotle's Rhetoric.*" Ph.D. dissertation, University of Chicago, 1966.

Calogero, Guido. "Gorgias and the Socratic Principle *Nemo Sua Sponte Peccat.*" *Journal of Hellenic Studies* 77 (1957): 12-17.

Campbell, Karlyn Kohrs. "The Ontological Foundations of Rhetorical Theory." *Philosophy & Rhetoric* 3 (1970): 97-108.

Cicero, Marcus Tullius. *De Officiis.*

_____. *De Oratore.*

———. *De Partione Oratoria.*

———. *Topics.*

Commentaria in Aristotelem Graeca, vol. 21. Edited by Hugo Rabe. Berlin: George Reimer, 1896.

Cooper, Lane, ed. and trans. *The "Rhetoric" of Aristotle.* New York: Appleton-Century-Crofts, 1932.

Cope, Edward M. *An Introduction to Aristotle's "Rhetoric."* London and Cambridge: Macmillan and Company, 1867.

———. *The "Rhetoric" of Aristotle with a Commentary.* Edited by John E. Sandys. 3 vols. Cambridge: At the University Press, 1877.

D'Abro, A. *The Rise of the New Physics.* 2 vols. New York: Dover Publications, 1951.

Danford, John W. *Wittgenstein and Political Philosophy.* Chicago: University of Chicago Press, 1978.

Davidson, Donald. "Actions, Reasons, and Causes." *Journal of Philosophy* 60 (1963): 67-79.

Demosthenes. *Crown Speech.*

———. *For the People of Megalopolis.*

Descartes, René. *Oeuvres.* Edited by Charles Adam and Paul Tannery. 13 vols. Paris: Cerf, 1897 and 1913.

Dodgson, Charles Lutwidge [Lewis Carroll]. "What the Tortoise Said to Achilles," *The Complete Works of Lewis Carroll.* New York: Random House, 1936.

During, Ingemar. *Aristoteles: Darstellung und Interpretation seines Denkens.* Heidelberg: C. Winter, 1966.

Edelman, Murray. *Politics as Symbolic Action.* New York: Academic Press, 1971.

———. *The Symbolic Uses of Politics.* Urbana: University of Illinois Press, 1964.

Fortenbaugh, William W. *Aristotle on Emotion.* New York: Barnes & Noble, 1975.

———. "Aristotle's *Rhetoric* on Emotion." *Archiv für Geschichte der Philosophie* 52 (1970): 40-70.

Gadamer, Hans-Georg. *Truth and Method.* New York: Seabury Press, 1975.

Gauthier, R. A., and Jolif, J. Y. *L'Éthique à Nicomaque.* 4 vols. Louvain: Publications Universitaires de Louvain, 1959.

Gorgias. *Helen.*

———. *Palamedes.*

Grimaldi, William M. A. "A Note on the *pisteis* in Aristotle's *Rhetoric.*" *American Journal of Philology* 78 (1957): 188-92.

———. *Studies in the Philosophy of Aristotle's "Rhetoric."* Wiesbaden: F. Steiner, 1972.

Hamburger, Max. *Morals and Law: The Growth of Aristotle's Legal Theory.* New York: Biblo and Tannin, 1965.

Hamilton, Alexander; Madison, James; and Jay, John. *The Federalist.* Edited by Jacob E. Cooke. Middletown, Conn.: Wesleyan University Press, 1961.

Heidegger, Martin. *Sein und Zeit.* Tübingen: Max Niemeyer Verlag, 1972.

Heisenberg, Werner. *Physics and Philosophy.* New York: Harper & Row, 1958.

Hellwig, Antje. *Untersuchungen zur Theorie der Rhetorik bei Platon und Aristoteles.* Göttingen: Vandenhoeck & Ruprecht, 1973.

Hennis, Wilhelm. *Politik und praktische Philosophie.* Berlin: Luchterhand, 1963.

Hirzel, Rudolf. *Agraphos Nomos.* Leipzig: B. G. Teubner, 1900.

Hobbes, Thomas. *De homine.* Translated by Charles T. Wood, T. S. K. Scott-Craig, and Bernard Gert. In *Man and Citizen,* edited by Bernard Gert. Garden City, N.Y.: Doubleday, 1972.

Bibliography

_____. *The Elements of Law Natural and Politic*. Edited by Ferdinand Tönnies. London: Frank Cass, 1969.

Hofstadter, Douglas R. *Gödel, Escher, Bach: An Eternal Golden Braid*. New York: Basic Books, 1979.

Hume, David. *A Treatise of Human Nature*. Edited by L. A. Selby-Bigge. Oxford: Oxford University Press, 1888.

Isocrates. *Antidosis*.

_____. *To Demonicus*.

Jaffa, Harry V. "Aristotle." In *History of Political Philosophy*, edited by Leo Strauss and Joseph Cropsey. Chicago: Rand McNally, 1963.

_____. *Thomism and Aristotelianism*. Chicago: University of Chicago Press, 1952.

Jarvis, Judith. "Practical Reasoning." *Philosophical Quarterly* 12 (1962): 316-28.

Joachim, Harold. *The Nicomachean Ethics*. Oxford: Clarendon Press, 1951.

Kennedy, George. *The Art of Persuasion in Greece*. Princeton, N.J.: Princeton University Press, 1963.

Lasswell, Harold, and Kaplan, Abraham. *Power and Society: A Framework for Political Inquiry*. New Haven: Yale University Press, 1950.

Le Blond, J. M. *Logique et Méthode chez Aristote*. Paris: J. Vrin, 1939.

Lieberg, Godo. *Die Lehre von der Lust in den Ethiken des Aristoteles*. Munich: Beck, 1958.

Lienhard, J. T. "A Note on the Meaning of *pisteis* in Aristotle's *Rhetoric*." *American Journal of Philology* 87 (1966): 446-54.

Locke, John. *Essay Concerning Human Understanding*. Edited by Alexander Campbell Fraser. 2 vols. New York: Dover Publications, 1959.

Lord, Carnes Riley. "Poetry and the City: An Interpretation of Aristotle's *Poetics*." Ph.D. dissertation, Cornell University, 1972.

Lukasiewicz, Jan. *Aristotle's Syllogistic*. Oxford: Oxford University Press, 1957.

McBurney, James H. "The Place of the Enthymeme in Rhetorical Theory." Ann Arbor, Mich.: University of Michigan Library, 1936.

McKeon, Richard. "Aristotle's Conception of Language and the Arts of Language." In *Critics and Criticism*, edited by R. S. Crane. Chicago: University of Chicago Press, 1952.

Madden, E. H. "Aristotle's Treatment of Probability and Signs." *Philosophy of Science* 24 (1957): 167-79.

_____. "The Enthymeme: Crossroads of Logic, Rhetoric, and Metaphysics." *Philosophical Review* 61 (1952): 368-76.

Maier, Heinrich. *Die Syllogistik des Aristoteles*. 3 vols. Tübingen: H. Laupp, 1900.

Meinong, Alexius. "Über emotionale Präsentation," *Abhandlungen zur Werttheorie*. Vol. 3 of *Gesamtausgabe*. Edited by Rudolph Haller and Rudolf Kindinger. Graz, Austria: Akademische Druck- und Verlagsanstalt, 1968.

Miller, Eugene F. "Primary Questions in Politics." *Review of Politics* 39 (1977): 298-331.

Monan, J. Donald. *Moral Knowledge and Its Methodology in Aristotle*. Oxford: Oxford University Press, 1968.

Moreau, Joseph. "Aristote et la dialectique platonicienne." In *Aristotle on Dialectic: The Topics*, edited by G. E. L. Owen. Oxford: Oxford University Press, 1968.

Mothersill, Mary. "Anscombe's Account of the Practical Syllogism." *Philosophical Review* 71 (1962): 448-60.

Nietzsche, Friedrich. *Darstellung der antiken Rhetorik*. In *Gesammelte Werke*, vol. 5. Munich: Musarion Verlag, 1922.

Olian, J. Robert. "The Intended Uses of Aristotle's *Rhetoric*." *Speech Monographs* 35 (1968): 137–48.

Oravec, Christine, "'Observation' in Aristotle's Theory of Epideictic." *Philosophy & Rhetoric* 9 (1976): 162–74.

Owen, G. E. L., ed. *Aristotle on Dialectic: The Topics*. Oxford: Oxford University Press, 1968.

Palmer, Georgiana. "The *topoi* of Aristotle's *Rhetoric* as Exemplified in the Orators." Ph.D. dissertation, University of Chicago, 1934.

Peirce, Charles S. *Selected Writings*. Edited by Philip P. Wiener. New York: Dover Publications, 1966.

Perelman, Chaim, and Olbrechts-Tyteca, L. *The New Rhetoric*. Translated by John Wilkinson and Purcell Weaver. Notre Dame, Ind.: University of Notre Dame Press, 1969.

Pitcher, George. "Emotion." *Mind* 74 (1965): 326-46.

Plato. *Apology of Socrates*.

_____. *Gorgias*.

_____. *Ion*.

_____. *Laws*.

_____. *Menexenus*.

_____. *Phaedo*.

_____. *Phaedrus*.

_____. *Philebus*

_____. *Protagoras*.

_____. *Republic*.

_____. *Statesman*.

_____. *Theaetetus*.

_____. *Timaeus*.

Randall, John Herman. *Aristotle*. New York: Columbia University Press, 1960.

Raphael, Sally. "Rhetoric, Dialectic, and Syllogistic Argument: Aristotle's Position in *Rhetoric* I-II." *Phronesis* 19 (1974): 153–67.

Rawls, John. *A Theory of Justice*. Cambridge, Mass.: Harvard University Press, 1971.

Regis, L. M. *L'opinion selon Aristote*. Paris: J. Vrin, 1935.

Reid, Thomas. *Essays on the Intellectual Powers of Man*. Cambridge, Mass.: M.I.T. Press, 1969.

Rhetorica ad Alexandrum. Edited and translated by Henry Rackham. Loeb Classical Library. Cambridge, Mass.: Harvard University Press, 1937.

Ricoeur, Paul. *La métaphore vive*. Paris: Editions du Seuil, 1975.

Robert, S. "Rhetoric and Dialectic: According to the First Latin Commentary on the *Rhetoric* of Aristotle." *New Scholasticism* 31 (1957): 484–98.

Roberts, W. R. "References to Plato in Aristotle's *Rhetoric*." *Classical Philology* 19 (1924): 342-46.

Ross, W. D. *Aristotle*. New York: Oxford University Press, 1959.

_____. *Aristotle's Prior and Posterior Analytics*. Oxford: Oxford University Press, 1949.

Rowell, Edward Z. "Prolegomena to Argumentation." *Quarterly Journal of Speech* 18 (1932): 224–48.

Ryan, Eugene E. "Aristotle's *Rhetoric* and *Ethics* and the Ethos of Society." *Greek, Roman, and Byzantine Studies* 13 (1972): 291-308.

Scheler, Max. *Der Formalismus in der Ethik und die materiale Wertethik*. Bern: Francke Verlag, 1966.

Bibliography

Schlesinger, Arthur M., Jr. *A Thousand Days*. Boston: Houghton Mifflin, 1965.

Seaton, R. C. "The Aristotelian Enthymeme." *Classical Review* 28 (1914): 113-19.

Segal, Charles P. "Gorgias and the Psychology of the Logos." *Harvard Studies in Classical Philology* 56 (1962): 99-155.

Solmsen, Friedrich. "Aristotle and Cicero on the Orator's Playing upon the Feelings." *Classical Philology* 33 (1938): 390-404.

———. Dialectic without the Forms." In *Aristotle on Dialectic: The Topics*, edited by G. E. L. Owen. Oxford: Oxford University Press, 1968.

———. *Die Entwicklung der aristotelischen Logik und Rhetorik*. Berlin: Weidmannsche Buchhandlung, 1929.

———. "Introduction," *The "Rhetoric" and the "Poetics" of Aristotle*, edited by Friedrich Solmsen. New York: Modern Library, Random House, 1954.

Solomon, Robert C. "Emotions and Choice." *Review of Metaphysics* 27 (1973): 20-41.

———. *The Passions*. Garden City, N.Y.: Doubleday Anchor Books, 1976.

Stocks, J. L. "The Composition of Aristotle's Logical Works." *Classical Quarterly* 27 (1933): 115-24.

Strauss, Leo. *The City and Man*. Chicago: Rand McNally, 1964.

———. "An Epilogue." In *Essays on the Scientific Study of Politics*, edited by Herbert J. Storing. New York: Holt, Rinehart and Winston, 1962.

———. *The Political Philosophy of Hobbes*. Translated by Elsa M. Sinclair. Chicago: University of Chicago Press, 1952.

———. *What Is Political Philosophy?* New York: Free Press, 1959.

Throm, Hermann. *Die Thesis: Ein Beitrag zu ihrer Entstehung und Geschichte*. Paderborn: Ferdinand Schöningh, 1932.

Thucydides. *The Peloponnesian War*. Translated by Thomas Hobbes. Edited by David Grene. Ann Arbor: University of Michigan Press, 1959.

Voegelin, Eric. "Das Rechte von Natur," *Anamnesis*. Munich: R. Piper, 1966.

———. *Plato and Aristotle. Order and History*, vol. 3. Baton Rouge: Louisiana State University Press, 1957.

von Wright, Georg Henrik. *Explanation and Understanding*. Ithaca, N.Y.: Cornell University Press, 1971.

Weil, Eric. "L'anthropologie d'Aristote." *Revue de Metaphysique et de Morale* 51 (1946): 7-36.

———. "La Place de la logique dans la pensée aristotelicienne." *Revue de Metaphysique et de Morale* 56 (1951): 283-315.

Whately, Richard. *Elements of Rhetoric*. Edited by Douglas Ehninger. Carbondale: Southern Illinois University Press, 1963.

White, Morton. *The Philosophy of the American Revolution*. New York: Oxford University Press, 1978.

Wikramanayake, G. H. "A Note on the *pisteis* in Aristotle's *Rhetoric*." *American Journal of Philology* 82 (1961): 193-96.

Xenophon. *Anabasis*.

———. *The Education of Cyrus*.

———. *Memorabilia*.

INDEX

Achilles, 157, 167
Aesop, 144
Alcidamus, 102, 150, 167
Alfarabi, 193 n.55
Anastaplo, George, 189 n.1, 210 n.47
Anaxagoras, 150
Anger, 89-91, 114-26, 212 n.11
Antigone, 102-4, 121, 210 n.47
"Appetite" (*epithumia*), 89-90, 94-95, 106, 117, 127-28, 209 n.28. *See also* "Desire"
Aquinas, Thomas, 197 n.98
Aristippus, 150
Aristophanes, 152
Aristotle: *De Anima*, 118-19, 123-24; *Eudemian Ethics*, 31; *Metaphysics*, 30, 78, 149; *Nicomachean Ethics*, 5, 15, 30-31, 56, 60-63, 72, 78-80, 82, 85, 88, 92-93, 95-97, 99, 101, 103, 105-6, 116, 118, 121-23, 129, 132, 134, 140, 183; *On Sophistical Refutations*, 17, 33, 155-56; *Physics*, 30; *Poetics*, 35, 129, 131-32, 163, 171-73; *Politics*, 5, 7, 32, 56, 65, 72-74, 102, 113, 132, 183; *Posterior Analytics*, 24-25, 39, 172, 174; *Prior Analytics*, 24-25, 39, 43-45, 159; *Topics*, 17, 39, 155, 172
"Arrangement" (*taxis*), 11-12, 53, 177-82
"Art" (*techne*): and instinct, 164-65; and rhetoric, 13-15; and the definition of rhetoric, 34-35; nature of, 15-16

Bacon, Francis, 27, 189 n.9, 196 n.94, 214 n.39
Booth, Wayne C., 192 n.42

Callicles, 152, 192 n.40, 193 n.55, 215 n.8
"Calmness" (*praotes*), 78, 80, 116-17, 121-23
Carroll, Lewis, 188, 217 n.5
"Character" (*ethos*): and age, 135-37; and arrangement of speeches, 177, 179-81; and fortune, 137-40; and maxims, 146; and style, 169-70; and the moral ends of rhetoric, 36-37; as a cause of action, 89; as entering rhetoric in various ways, 36-37; as individual and collective, 196 n.90; of individuals, 135-40; of regimes, 57, 203 n.5; of regimes and of individuals, 74-75, 206 n.52; of the speaker, 10, 77, 111-13. *See also* "Habit"
Cicero, Marcus Tullius, 80, 201 n.141, 207 n.9
"Commonplaces" (*koina*), 18, 141-43; and the other "topics," 50-51; in dialectic and rhetoric, 191 n.24; of amplification, 81, 85-86; of possibility, 100
"Common proofs" (*koinoi pisteis*), 143-44
"Common topics" (*koinoi topoi*), 147-55; and the other "topics," 51, 141; of more and less, 82
Common sense: and natural justice, 211 n.52; and rhetoric, 218 n.8; as prephilosophic experience, 194 n.76; as the natural starting point of reasoning, 183, 185-88; as the prescientific basis of science, 187-88, 191 n.28; in the opinions of men, 28-30; rationality of, 147. *See also* Learning; "Opinions"

225

Index

"Comparisons" (parabole), 144, 167
Cope, Edward M.: on *antistrophos*, 14;
on Aristotle's definitions, 58-59; on
natural justice, 213 n.19; on *pistis*, 196
n.2; on rhetoric as a "power," 195
n.87; on sophistry and rhetoric, 195
n.82; on the account of happiness,
60-63; on the definition of goodness,
205 n.40; on the definition of pleasure,
92; on the definition of the virtues,
78-79; on the doctrine of the "mean,"
82, 206 n.6; on the "topic" of possibility, 215 n.2; on the virtues and the passions, 206 n.8; on virtue, 207 n.4

Definitions: and geometrical reasoning,
204 n.19; and Socratic rhetoric, 182,
204 n.19; as a source of reasoning,
154; as enthymematic "topics," 59-60;
in the analysis of the passions, 115; of
goodness, 64-66; of happiness, 57-61
Deliberative rhetoric, 55-75; and arrangement of speeches, 178-80; and
historical examples, 145; and passion,
22-23; and politics, 55-57; and the
"commonplaces," 142; and the tension
between justice and expediency,
49-50; as architectonic, 58; as concerned with the possible and the
future, 142; as dependent on the
regime, 75; as one of the three kinds of
rhetoric, 49-50; the style of, 176-77
Demosthenes, 158, 201 n.141
Descartes, Rene, 199 n.109
"Desire" *(orexis)*, 40-41, 89-91. *See also*
"Appetite"
Dialectic: and science, 18-19; and
sophistical fallacies, 155, 159-60; and
sophistry, 19-21; Aristotle's theory of,
17-21; as a universal art, 14, 17-18; as
concerned with "common topics,"
47-48; as concerned with the cognitive
side of the passions, 123-24; as
directed to small audiences, 40; as
more important for rhetoric than is
sophistry, 16; compared with rhetoric,
38-43; resemblance to rhetoric of,
13-15

Eikota. See "Probabilities"
Emotion. *See* "Passion"
Empedocles, 102, 168
Endoxa. See "Opinions"
Enthymeme: and a maxim, 145; and
syllogistic form, 141; and the logical
movement from the known to the
unknown, 142; and the organization of
the *Rhetoric*, 51-53, 143, 161; apparent and true forms of, 10-11,
46-47, 154-60; as a "practical
syllogism," 40; as a true syllogism, 9,
145; as an abbreviated syllogism,
41-43; as based on opinion, 6-7; as
combining reason and passion, 9-10,
22-23, 129, 196 n.91; as constructed
from "probabilities" and "signs,"
43-47; as differing from a demonstration or a fallacious argument, 5, 8; as
essential to rhetorical theory, 4; as in-
corporating all three "proofs," 37-38,
111-12, 183; as metaphorical in its
structure, 175; as most suited for
forensic rhetoric, 86; as showing the
resemblance of rhetoric and dialectic,
21; as "some sort of syllogism," 24-25;
as the "body of proof," 37-38; compared with an example, 39-40, 42, 46,
144; derived from definitions, 59-60;
rules of, 146-47
Epideictic rhetoric, 77-86; and the arrangement of speeches, 178-79; as
concerned with the importance of
things, 142; as dependent on laws, 57,
75; as one of the three kinds of
rhetoric, 49-50
Epithumia. See "Appetite"
Ethos. See "Character"; "Habit"
Euclid, 203 n.8
Examples, 143-45; as most suited for
deliberative rhetoric, 86; compared
with enthymemes, 39-40, 42, 47;
transformed into enthymemes, 46
Expediency: and goodness, 64; and
human action, 90-91; and justice,
49-50, 152, 201 nn.140-41; and the
regime, 71-72; as the end of
deliberative rhetoric, 57

226

Index

"Mind" *(nous)*, 65-66, 90, 120, 208 n.11. *See also* Philosophy; "Prudence"; "Wisdom"

Monan, J. Donald, 194 n.76

"Moral choice" *(proairesis)*, 74, 78, 82-83, 88, 105-6, 168, 195 nn.81-82

"Nature" *(physis)*, 88-90, 94; and conventional morality, 152-54; and habit, 132-33, 205 n.38; and justice, 132-34, 210 n.46; and law, 102-8, 120-21, 210 n.49; and pleasure, 97-99; and the capacity for rhetoric, 164-65; and the "commonplaces," 142; and the family, 210 n.47. *See also* "Habit"

"Necessary signs" *(tekmeria)*, 43-47. *See also* "Probabilities"; "Signs"

Nietzsche, Friedrich, 35, 163, 190 n.2

Nobility, 77-81, 83, 135-36, 137-40

Nous. See "Mind"

"Opinions" *(endoxa):* about pleasure, 93, 99; and apparent enthymemes, 155; and shame, 128-29; and maxims, 146; and the collective wisdom of people, 25-28, 30, 152-54; and the logic of deduction from definitions, 64-65; as between absolute truth and absolute falsehood, 4, 6-7; as both the source and the product of rhetoric, 193 n.53; as concerned with contingency rather than necessity, 29; as contrary to sophistry, 149, 152-53, 155, 159-60, 181-82; as corrupted in bad regimes, 164, 184-85; as shaped by the variety of human characters, 41-42; as the basis of dialectic, 17-19; as the foundation of philosophy, 30-32, 147; as the foundation of political knowledge, 185-88; as the source of rhetorical premises, 6-7, 183; as the source of definitions, 60; defined, 29-30; distorted by physical pleasures, 67; distorted by self-interest, 32; the partial truth of, 6-7, 25, 28-32. *See also* Common sense

Orexis. See "Desire"

Palmer, Georgiana Paine, 215 n.13, 216 n.24

"Passion" *(pathos)*, 111-12, 114-34; and defective judgments, 124-27; and Heidegger, 212 n.7; and imagination, 119-20; and judgment, 37; and pleasure, 118-19; and style, 169-70; and the arrangement of speeches, 177, 180-81; and the body, 123-24; and the moral sense, 120-21, 132; as an integral part of the enthymeme, 9-10, 22-23; as mistakenly used in the rhetorical handbooks, 22; as rational, 114-20, 123-27, 209 n.28, 211 n.5; as syllogistic, 212 n.12; in the *De Anima*, 123-24; in the *Nicomachean Ethics*, 121-23; most men live by, 5-6

Peirce, Charles S., 212 n.11

Pericles, 3, 173, 213 n.27

Periodic style, 171-72

Philosophy: and age, 137; and metaphor, 172, 174-76; and rhetoric, 16, 183, 203 n.5; and standards of praise, 82-83; and the ability for creating examples, 145; and the theoretical character of Aristotle's study of rhetoric, 147, 189 n.1; and wealth, 138; complex reasoning of, 147; the rhetoric of, 148-54, 180. *See also* "Mind"; "Prudence"; "Socrates"; "Wisdom"

Phronesis. See "Prudence"

Pistis. See "Proof"

Plato, 170, 189 n.9, 191 n.16; and dialectic, 17, 19; and happiness, 204 n.22; and metaphor, 172; and the list of regimes, 73; *Apology of Socrates*, 149-50, 182, 189 n.5, 192 n.44; *Gorgias*, 13-15, 33-34, 152, 190 n.2, 192 n.40, 192 n.44, 193 n.55, 198 n.102; *Meno*, 174; *Phaedrus*, 152, 190 n.2, 198 n.104, 204 n.19, 216 n.24; *Philebus*, 92, 209 n.27, 211 n.5, 212 n.11, 214 n.42; *Republic*, 90. *See also* Socrates

Pleasure, 91-99; and style, 172; and the passions, 116, 118-19; and virtue, 208

228

DATE DUE

DEMCO 38-297